+ THE COMPLETE +
NEEDLEPOINT
+ COURSE +

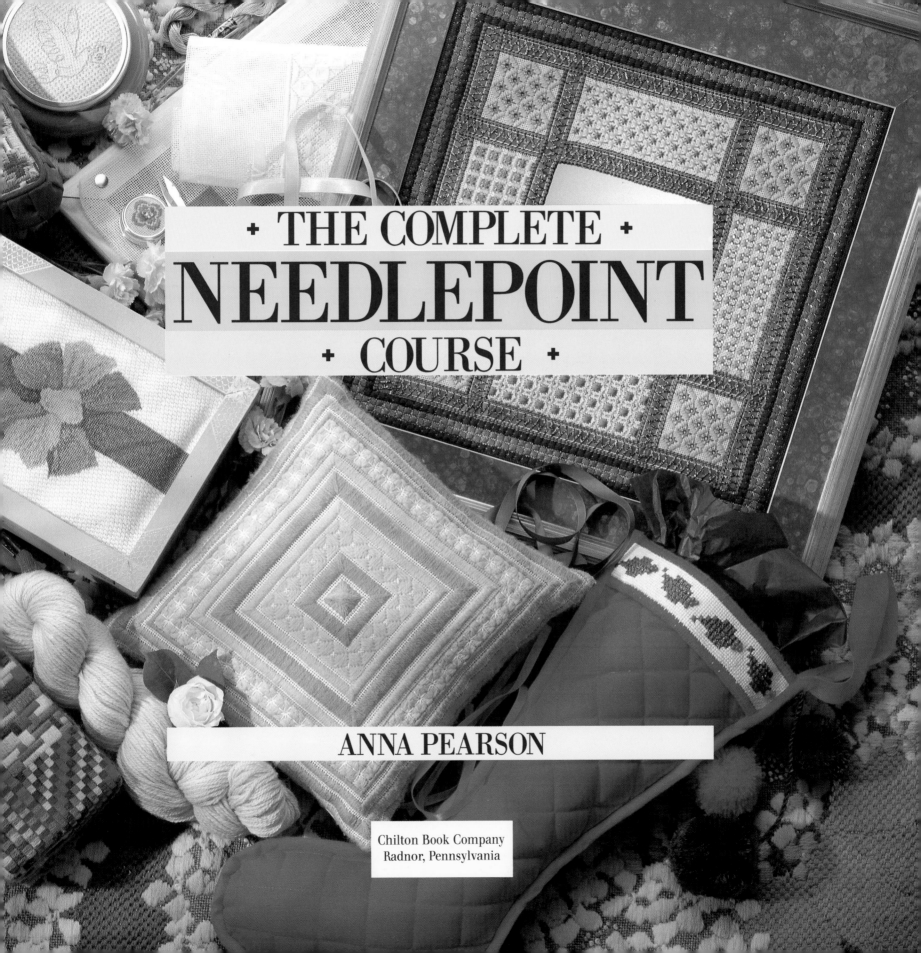

THE COMPLETE + NEEDLEPOINT + COURSE +

ANNA PEARSON

Chilton Book Company
Radnor, Pennsylvania

A QUARTO BOOK

Copyright © 1991 Quarto Publishing plc

ISBN 0–8019–8227–8

This book was designed and produced by
Quarto Publishing plc
6 Blundell Street
London N7 9BH

Senior Editor Caroline Beattie
Editor Michelle Clark
Design Debbie Sumner

Photography Paul Forrester
Illustrations Patrick Pearson, Rob Shone, Dave Kemp

Art Director Moira Clinch
Assistant Art Director Chloë Alexander
Publishing Director Janet Slingsby

Typeset by Bookworm Typesetting, Manchester
Manufactured in Hong Kong by
Excel Graphic Arts Limited
Printed in Singapore by Star Standard Industries Pte. Ltd.

CONTENTS

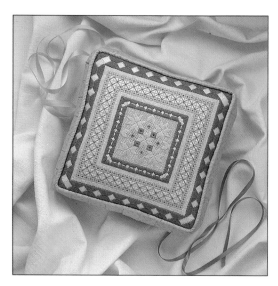

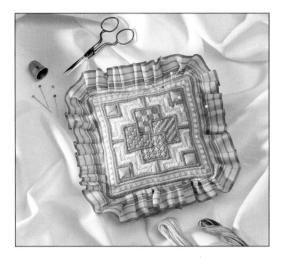

ℐNTRODUCTION

Today needlepoint encompasses a wide range of styles and techniques, both traditional and experimental. There is a growing trend toward combining different types of needlework previously worked separately in one project, to review the techniques of earlier times and update them to suit present-day tastes, and to have fun with threads not previously available.

This book is a factual and inspirational guide, with extensive information on materials and good working techniques. The combination of progressive projects and ideas for design variations provides a complete practical understanding of needlepoint covering all aspects of good design and stitch work. Over 20 exciting projects are provided to be copied or adapted. These pieces demonstrate all the stitches and designs traditionally associated with needlepoint, and added to them are techniques not usually associated with canvas, such as free embroidery, stitching with metallic threads, couching, and appliqué.

The first part begins by introducing the reader to the basic components of needlework – thread, fabrics, and equipment – and particularly how to select the best and most appropriate materials for the work to be done. It takes the reader step-by-step through reading charts, transferring designs to canvas, and starting to stitch, and encourages good working habits.

The second part is divided into 10 chapters, each dealing with a particular type of work and with at least one easy and one more advanced project within each chapter. These cover tent stitch, Bargello, samplers, embroidery (making the most of geometric, textured stitches), using canvas in the design, free embroidery, metallic and other glitter threads for festive Christmas decorations and glamorous accessories, surface work, pulled thread, converting your own designs and ideas into needlepoint, and a section on backgrounds and borders that will help you adapt existing designs and enhance your own.

Throughout each chapter, there are practical tips relevant to the projects, which help you practice a particular technique (equally useful to both beginners and stitchers who have had experience on other ground fabrics, for example). Within each chapter, there are at least two projects with full instructions for copying the original exactly, with information to enable you to change colors, mesh of canvas, or even scale if you wish.

The third part includes a section on how to finish a piece of work professionally, mounting and framing it, and how to keep your piece of needlepoint in good condition.

The Stitch Glossary is a mine of information. Each of the stitches has been illustrated and photographed. In many cases, variations of the stitches, as used in the projects or simply to inspire you to adapt them further, are also shown. This section alone will become a frequent source of reference and inspiration for future projects.

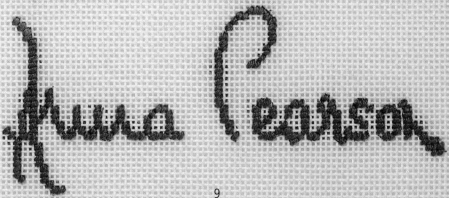

GETTING
STARTED

+ + +   + + +

The materials available for needlepoint
range from the basics such as yarn and
canvas, to extras such as floor frames
and magnifier lamps. This section gives
guidance on what to choose for the
projects, as well as all the techniques
relevant to them. It is worth reading
carefully; being well prepared for
stitching makes it more pleasureable
and the end results more satisfying.

MATERIALS

All the time more innovations in materials and equipment become available. The aim of this chapter is to help you make the best choices from all of these for each particular project. Always remember that the most precious thing you put into your work is your time so it will always be wise to buy the best possible materials to make this time well spent.

For each project, a list of materials is given to make up the projects as photographed, but I have also included notes on other colour schemes, different canvas meshes and different yarns.

CANVAS

Most good-quality canvas is 100 per cent cotton, but linen, plastic and even perforated paper are available and each are suitable for certain projects.

The two main types of canvas are double-thread (Penelope) canvas and mono (single-thread) canvas. The mono canvas is available as either an evenweave or interlocked thread.

MONO EVENWEAVE, OR REGULAR, CANVAS

This is used in all the projects in the book except for the Wedding sampler in Chapter 3. The threads weave over and under each other at regular intervals, but are not bound to each other, which is why it is essential to use this canvas for cushions, seats or any items where 'give' is needed. Because of its structure, however, evenweave canvas does need to be bound with masking tape, bias binding or overstitching along all cut edges before starting work.

MONO INTERLOCK CANVAS

Mono interlock canvas appears to be similar to evenweave canvas, but closer inspection shows that the threads pass through each other when they intersect. This means that this type of canvas does not unravel and so can be trimmed extremely close to the worked area, which makes it a good choice for small items like napkin rings.

Do not be tempted to use interlock canvas for cushions or chairs as it does not give and so a thread could easily snap with wear, leaving a hole in the canvas.

EVENWEAVE OR INTERLOCK

An easy way to tell whether unlabelled canvas is evenweave or interlock is to run your finger nail over the canvas: with evenweave you will feel ridges, with interlock there are none.

If the piece goes out of shape while you are working (particularly as a result of your warm hands pressing on the canvas) it is impossible to block and regain the original shape.

DOUBLE-THREAD, OR PENELOPE, CANVAS

This is the canvas to choose if you want to combine a wealth of detail in certain areas and a larger stitch for other areas. The two areas are stitched in *petit point* (over single threads) and *gros point* (over pairs of threads) respectively. In 19th-century canvas work, flowers or human figures were worked in *petit point*, while the background was worked in *gros point*.

PLASTIC CANVAS

The rigid construction of plastic canvas makes it perfect for such items as boxes, tissue-box covers, luggage labels and key tags. Some of the designs in this book, for example, any of the small motifs worked in beads in Chapter 8 would all make nice box tops or coasters worked on plastic canvas.

Children enjoy working with plastic canvas as it does not distort and therefore does not need to be mounted in a frame or blocked when finished.

CONGRESS CLOTH OR LINEN

Congress cloth is a fine cotton canvas made in Denmark, available in white, pastels and Christmas colours. It is a good alternative to evenweave linen for working samplers, where the background is left unworked.

▶ *Some of the most popular canvases with appropriate threads. Anticlockwise: from centre back: 12-mesh antique evenweave with 4-ply crewel and 3-ply Persian in size 20 needles; 14-mesh white evenweave with 3-ply crewel, 1-ply pearl cotton no. 3 and 1.5-mm double-faced satin ribbon in size 20 needles; 16-mesh gold-sprayed evenweave with 1-ply Goldfingering in size 20 needles (larger than usual to accommodate the metallic thread) and 1-strand gold braid and frisette for couching; 18-mesh antique evenweave with 6-ply stranded cotton, 3-ply Medici wool and 1-ply pearl cotton no. 5 in size 22 needles; 24-mesh congress cloth with 4-ply Au ver à soie silk and 2-ply Medici wool in size 24 needles.*

CANVAS MESH

The canvas mesh is the number of threads per inch and is specified for each project. If you want to copy the original exactly, use the mesh given, but you will also find details of other meshes for a different effect on occasions.

When you are planning your own design, remember that the more detail you require in the area, the finer the canvas mesh will have to be.

You can use the mesh of the canvas to change the scale of a design: a motif worked on fine canvas would fit a pillow cover, for example, and the same motif worked on a coarser canvas would fit a large fire screen.

USING CANVAS COLORS

The color of the canvas can also become an integral part of the design if you leave areas showing or use cream thread in skip stitch variations on antique canvas – it is very attractive, and I thoroughly recommend experimenting with this combination.

Also, try spraying or painting canvas for decorative items. This works very well for the Christmas Tree Card in Chapter 7 and looks delicate for the Photograph Frame in Chapter 6.

Canvas is generally available in brown (called antique) and white, with other colors being available only occasionally and then mostly in the finer meshes. Except when working projects from Chapter 5, "Using Canvas as Part of the Design," when the color of the exposed canvas is important to the finished effect, it is wise to use white canvas when you are painting a pictorial design or working with pale colors and antique when you are working dark color schemes. An exception is the Tulip Rug in Chapter 6, which has a dark background but pale flowers, so special notes accompany this project.

Canvas is also available in a variety of widths, so consider which would be most economical before buying. Some canvas, only available in 27-in (68-cm) width, can be used for chair seats or pictures, while the 39-in (1-m) wide canvas can accommodate two pillows or even, if the pattern is turned 180° and planned carefully, two chair seats across the width. Occasionally, 55-in (1.40m) wide canvas can be found, which is perfect for large projects like rugs or wallhangings, avoiding the need to join two or more narrower pieces of canvas together.

THREADS

Throughout the book, the word "ply" means the individual strands of yarn which can be easily pulled apart. I specify the number of ply for each stitch. For example, the Appleton's crewel and Medici yarn come in single ply, whereas Paterna Persian yarn is made up from three ply loosely twisted together; embroidery floss is 6-ply, and pearl cotton is single ply as it is tightly twisted.

When you use a particular yarn for the first time, read about each one to make

sure that you get the best results. There are details of all the threads used in the book, plus a few more that you may enjoy using for your own projects.

YARN

There are three kinds of yarn that are suitable for canvas: Appleton's crewel, DMC Medici, and Paterna Persian. Appleton's crewel and Paterna yarn both have reference names and numbers; Medici yarn have only reference numbers, so please note that the naives given are not official.

If you decide to work a piece in a different brand from the one given or move to a finer or coarser canvas, use the same number of ply of Medici as Appleton's crewel wool, but when substituting Persian wool for either of these, use one ply less than that given. Sometimes you find that you will need an extra ply to cover the canvas completely if you are using a dark color.

The yarn that is specifically made for working needlepoint will result in the most durable finished pieces, and so it is recommended for all upholstery pieces, although, of course, you can use almost anything for decorative pieces.

Appleton's crewel yarn This yarn is available in seven to nine shades in each color family, making it particularly good for working detailed shading and subtle Bargello patterns. The individual ply come ready separated in the hanks and are usually available in two weights – 1-oz (25-g) hanks or a very small skein, useful if only a few stitches of a shade are needed.

When working on 14-mesh or coarser canvas, open out the hank, then cut it at each end to get two equal working lengths. When you work on finer canvas, cut the wool into three equal lengths. This is wise because the yarn is subject to more friction as it passes through the holes of the finer canvas and so a long length would give uneven stitches and therefore an uneven finish.

◄ *Hanks, cut and uncut, of Appleton's crewel wool (LEFT), with Paterna Persian wool (TOP RIGHT) and Medici wool in small and large skeins (LOWER RIGHT).*

FINDING THE NAP

Some people check the direction by running a ply or strand lightly across their upper lip, but I find it easier to rub the two cut ends firmly against the back of my hand; the end where the fibers hang together more closely is the one to thread. If I am using more than one ply in a strand, I find that, if I run my fingers down the length of each ply before I thread the needle, the yarn lies better on the canvas and is easier to work.

Paterna Persian yarn Each strand is 3-ply, but they are easily separated. It is generally available in ½-oz (15-g) and 4-oz (100-g) hanks, although some suppliers will sell it by the strand. Cut the opened-out hank at each end, unless you are working on canvas finer than 14-mesh, when you will need to cut the lengths in half again for reasons of wear.

Persian yarn has a distinctive nap: stroking it one way it feels smooth; stroking it the other way it feels rough. Always thread your needle so that the yarn is passing through the canvas with the direction that felt smooth. Remember, too, that when you are putting together several ply, they should all feel smooth in the same direction.

PLAN AHEAD

Do not buy lots of small skeins of yarn to work large areas, as they are more fiddly to handle in bulk and prove much more expensive. It is better to order large hanks.

Medici yarn The color range is not as extensive as that of the previous two yarns, but the natural earth and deep shades are particularly good, and the variety is being added to all the time. Medici yarn is generally available in 2-oz (50-g) hanks and small skeins, which are useful if you only want to work a small area or if you wish to experiment with colors first. The Flower and Trellis rug in Chapter 10 is worked in Medici yarn.

COTTON THREADS

The two cotton threads used extensively in the book are embroidery floss and pearl cotton. Shades from the DMC range have been used and the reference numbers are theirs: colors are my interpretation and purely for your guidance.

Embroidery floss DMC floss has been used in all the relevant projects in this book. In addition to the reference numbers, I have given a description of the color (which is not given by DMC).

All the brands are 6-ply and come in 9-yard (8-m) skeins. To cut a good working length – about 20 in (51 cm) – look closely at the wrappers (which you must leave on). You will probably see a pair of hands, one pulling a thread from the opposite end of the skein. Move the other wrapper in slightly, give the skein a firm shake and out will fall the end of the skein. Pull it gently and cut your length, threading your needle with the end you have just cut: embroidery floss, like Persian yarn, has a definite nap.

The floss needs "stripping" before you use it in order to make it lie smoothly on the canvas and cover it better. The easiest way I find is to knot the end of the thread (that is, the end you pulled from the skein) and lay it over your left-hand index finger (if you are right-handed), holding it in place firmly with your middle finger. Then, with the tip of the needle held in your right hand, simply pick up and pull out each ply individually. Be sure to knot the strands at the end you pulled from the skein: trying to pull the ply from the wrong end (against the nap) produces terrible tangles. If you think this must be a lot of work for nothing, compare one length of stripped floss to one taken straight from the skein – the difference is amazing. Another method you might have come across is to separate the ply and lay them side by side. The first method, though, is considerably easier.

If more or fewer ply are needed for a particular stitch, cut a number of lengths, or split a strand to give you the right multiple. For example, when you want 4-ply strands, cut two lengths, separate 2 ply from each strand, put these two lots of 2-ply together, and you will have three working lengths. Similarly, when 9-ply strands are needed, cut three lengths, separate one of the strands into two lengths of 3-ply, and add each of these to the complete strands. Remember to knot your adjusted strands at the end you pulled from the skein as soon as you have made them up.

Pearl cotton Again I have used DMC in the book, and the color names I have given with the reference numbers are purely for guidance. You will need the reference numbers when shopping.

Pearl cotton is softly twisted, single-ply thread that comes in four thicknesses, though not all the colors are available in all the thicknesses. No. 3 is the thickest and covers 12-mesh canvas well. No. 5 works well on 14-mesh (although sometimes 2-ply strands will be needed), as well as 16- and 18-mesh. No. 8 is suitable for 22- and 24-mesh canvas, while No. 12 is the finest.

The thread is used just as it is; to prepare a new skein for use, remove the two wrappers, untwist the skein and cut through it twice – once at the knot holding it together and once at the opposite end. This will give you two lengths of thread approximately 19 in (48 cm) long.

RAYON

This is not the easiest fiber to use, but it does give a wonderful sheen to decorative items or things that will not be subjected to much wear. The two I suggest you try are Lystwist, which is particularly pretty in the vanilla shade for backgrounds, and

ESTIMATING QUANTITIES

When you are using pearl cotton, thread the wrapper with the color number back over half the prepared strands. When you finish the first half of the cotton, have you done half the work? If you have not, you will need to buy some more.

▶ *A selection of threads that are good for needlepoint: included are pearl cotton in both twisted skeins and balls, embroidery floss, Marlitt, Au ver à soie silk with the wide white wrapper, and shades of metallic yarn. The canvases in the background are the finer mesh (16-, 18- and 24-mesh) which are particularly good for these threads.*

COUCHING RIBBON

Some tips for couching ribbon around a square:

- start stitching along one of the sides rather than in a corner; leave a tail to the left, working toward the right, and couch the ribbon down with a cross or other stitch every few threads; make sure that there is a stitch holding the corner in place, and, when all four sides have been completed, simply overlap about 1 in (3 cm) of the ribbon over the original tail and stitch as one.

Marlitt. Cutting both these into short working lengths makes handling much easier, as does lightly dampening the length before using it and stripping the same way as given for embroidery floss, though not for the Lystwist.

SILK

Silk threads are expensive, but they keep their lustrous sheen far better than embroidery floss, and so the expense is worthwhile if this is an essential element of your design. Soie d' Alger (Au Ver à Soie) is a 7-ply silk that has a low sheen and comes in a fabulous choice of colors. It is available in both small and large skeins. Use it in short lengths of 15-18 in (38-46 cm). Prepare the skein in the same way as pearl cotton, and strip the lengths before use.

METALLIC THREADS

There are three types of metallic thread: thick ones that are designed to be couched into place on the surface of the canvas, being either too thick to go through the canvas holes or too expensive to be wasted on the back of the work; others that are more flexible and so can be stitched, but still need to be used with care; and a third that can be blended with cotton or silk.

STITCHING RIBBON

Some tips for stitching with the ½0-in (1.5-mm) wide double-sided ribbon:

- use a size 20 tapestry needle
- work areas to be stitched with ribbon before areas to be worked in other materials
- start to stitch, leaving a tail of ribbon – a knot is not needed and the tail is easier to weave in later for a flatter finish
- use a laying tool (see page 19) to get each stitch absolutely flat – I find that the rounded end of the two-ended type gives me even more control than the more pointed end, which I use for other threads
- finish ribbons into the back of completed ribbon stitches immediately, as miscellaneous threads lurking behind the work will make smooth working impossible.

▶ *Clockwise, from top center: small pointed embroidery scissors, a double-ended laying tool (the pointed end is best for silks and floss, and the curved end is best for ribbons), tapestry needles, tweezers (useful for unpicking stitches), wire-ended needle threader (for fine threads and fine beading needles), scissors with a hooked end (for cutting threads out), double-ended needle threader strong enough for wool and metallics.*

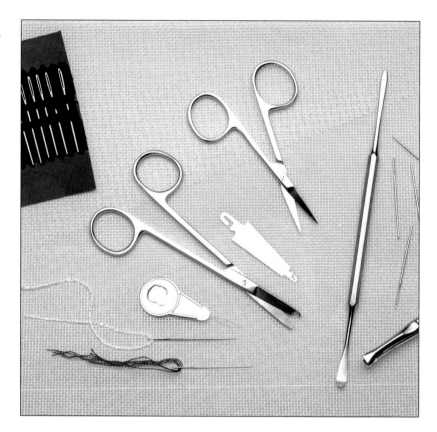

WORKING WITH METALLIC THREADS

As all metallic threads are prone to unraveling, use a needle threader so that the end of the thread is disturbed less and so unravels less.

Balger, a synthetic metallic thread, comes in gold, silver, and many basic and blended colors, and is available in four thicknesses.

Blending filament is wonderful for mixing with other thread such as stranded cotton and No. 8 is suitable for 22- or 25-mesh canvas, while No. 16 is suitable for 14-, 16-, and 18-mesh canvas, and No. 32 is suitable for couching.

Twilley's Goldfingering (used in some of the projects in the book) comes in a good range of colors, including gold and silver, and is washable. Use short lengths at a time as it does unravel easily. Their Multifingering range is also worth looking at.

Madeira is a metallic-effect yarn and is available in easy-to-handle pull-packs.

RIBBON

Offray make ribbon suitable for embroidery in three different widths, all of which have been used for projects in the book: the very narrow ¹⁄₂₀-in (1.5-mm) width, which can be stitched on 14- and 18-mesh canvas; the ¹⁄₁₀-in (3-mm), and the ³⁄₈-in (9-mm) widths, which have been couched onto the surface of the canvas. If you are stitching with ribbon, both sides of it will show, so you will need double-sided satin ribbon, whereas if it is to be couched, single-sided will be fine.

NEEDLES

Tapestry (blunt-tipped) needles range in size from 14, the biggest, to 26, the finest. Choose the size to suit the canvas mesh and the yarn. Using too large a needle will distort the canvas and too small a needle will fray and wear the yarn.

The following list of recommended sizes of needle for meshes of canvas should cover almost all the needlepoint projects you are likely to work:
● size 20 for 14-mesh canvas
● size 22 for 16- and 18-mesh canvas
● size 24 for 22- and 24-mesh canvas.

Remember, though, to use one size larger for pulled thread and one size smaller for embroidery.

Tapestry needles are available either in packets of one size or mixed sizes. I find that packets of one size are more convenient as I tend to use the same size of mesh for a lot of my projects.

SCISSORS

Two pairs of scissors are essential – a small embroidery pair with sharp points, and a larger pair for cutting the hanks of yarn and the canvas.

A seam-ripper is also useful for cutting any mistakes out. It is frequently easier and neater to do this from the back of the work and then to use a pair of tweezers to pull the cut threads out.

FRAMES

Some of the projects in this book would be physically impossible to work without a frame and, certainly, you will find that you enjoy working a piece much more and the end results will always be considerably better when you use a frame. This is because the correct stitch tension is far easier to achieve on flat, stretched canvas; it is simpler to see where you are in the design; it is easier to count threads; and the work does not distort. Working pulled- or drawn-thread pieces or couching threads is simply impossible without a frame.

There are various types of frame. The two most suitable for needlepoint are scroll frames, which have tapes top and bottom for the canvas to be sewn to, and either adjustable sides or provision to lace the canvas onto the side bars; and artist's stretcher bars, which, for ease and speed, I prefer. Stretcher bars are available in pairs of varying lengths that slot together simply and can be purchased from art and craft stores. Each project gives the most suitable size of frame to use, but this need not involve buying new sets of bars each time. For example, if you have a 16-in (41-cm) square [that is, two 16-in (41-cm) pairs] and for your next project you need a rectangle 12 by 16 in (30 by 41cm), you will only need to buy a pair of 12-in (30-cm) bars and reassemble the frame accordingly.

When you have assembled the frame, attach the canvas to it, stretching it as tautly as possible (see page 26), using flat-headed thumbtacks.

In the case of a scroll frame, center the canvas on the tapes, and sew along top and bottom with strong thread and a sharp needle. Then adjust or lace the sides.

ADDITIONAL EQUIPMENT

It is more a case of deciding what *not* to buy, as extras can be expensive. However, if you get better results by using a particular tool or are more comfortable stitching if you have a good floor stand or lamp, you will judge these extras to be worth it. I suggest you look carefully at the options open to you when you are considering a big purchase. See if it is possible to try a floor frame before committing yourself and check that there is the minimum to go wrong with a particular item and, if a friend has one, see how long that person has been using it, if they are pleased with it, and if you can try it out.

The following, working upward in size, are just a few pieces of equipment that I enjoy using and that have proved their worth to me.

NEEDLE THREADERS

Almost an essential for those of us who find threading needles an irritatingly fiddly task. The wire ones commonly available are not strong enough for yarn, so search for the more sturdy version or the ones that have two holes rather than wires.

Needle threaders are particularly helpful when you are working with metallic threads.

LAYING TOOL

Held in the left (or right) hand on the surface of the work, the stitching thread is laid over it smoothly and the implement is only pulled out as the stitch goes down onto the canvas.

There are many variations of these tools. You can use curved rug needles, plastic shirt-collar stiffeners, or whatever, but my personal favorite is quite long and feels well balanced in the hand.

PALETTES AND THREAD ORGANIZERS

Look at the thread organizers available and decide which of them you think will work best for you. You may just need to keep all the threads for one project together, or you may like to mount them on something in a color sequence so as not to make a shade error in artificial light.

Refer to Chapter 1 to see how to make a stitching card for blended yarn.

STANDS FOR FRAMES

These hold the frame you have chosen, leaving both your hands free to stitch. There are both floor-standing models and ones that slip under your knees or clamp to a table. Some of the floor stands can be angled easily to allow you to sit on either a high or low chair or even in bed, which, according to the friends I have with bad backs, is a very great help to them when they are engrossed in their stitching. They are available in wood and stainless steel.

When choosing, select one that stands firmly and will take the size of frame you usually work on. Some have a large, flat foot that tucks under the leg of a chair, making them really solid. Look for solid wood of a reasonable thickness, as narrow struts might snap. Find out, too, how easy it is to turn the work over to finish off the threads on the back. Also, see how easy it is to change frames over; if, like me, you switch from project to project, you want to be able to do this simply. If you travel a great deal or want to be able to pack your needlepoint away when you are not working on it, check how small it is once it has been collapsed.

LIGHTING

Good light while you are stitching is essential. You can choose from a small lamp that can be angled onto the work, either free-standing or clamped to a nearby table, and anything in between these and lamps that have built-in magnification, which are really helpful if you wish to do fine work without straining your eyes. Again, choice is personal and depends on space, whether or not you always stitch in the same chair, and how much you can spend.

◄ *The base of the floor frame slides under the leg of any chair the stitcher is sitting on to give it stability. Both the upright and the angle of the frame can be adjusted. The light can be used with the heavy base shown here or clamped to a sturdy table or shelf.*

GENERAL TECHNIQUES

Good working techniques make all the difference to your work: you will enjoy stitching much more and achieve a finished piece that you can be proud of. In this chapter the techniques for each part of the process are described, from the planning stages, which include estimating the right quantities for the materials you need, and marking out a pattern, to the working stages, including starting and finishing a thread.

Here are a few factors to bear in mind when planning projects, so that you enjoy the work and your finished object all the more.

Choosing color is such a personal means of expression that I have given alternative color schemes for most of the projects in this book. Color can alter the effect and look of a design completely, making one version look soft and pretty and another dramatic, or highlight different areas of the design.

The eventual setting of the finished piece of needlepoint should be taken into account when you are selecting a color scheme for a particular piece. For example, eyecatching combinations can be used in a small entrance hall, while dark, dramatic schemes are good for a dining room used mainly in the evening (especially for chair seat covers where people are likely to wear dark clothes), and soft pastels look good, in a traditional bedroom or living room.

Keep a scrapbook of color schemes of all kinds from magazines, catalogues, and so on. Pick out those things where the color combination pleases you – interiors, advertisements, editorials. If it stimulates and inspires you, keep it.

One rule I always stick to is never even to start an unusual project without either knowing how to finish it myself or have an expert lined up to do it who will do so for a reasonable price. A further cautionary note I would add regarding one-person operations is that, if you know it will take you a long time to complete

a project, check that your tried and trusted craftworker will not have retired, leaving you to search for someone else.

It is important to know the rudiments of how various items should be finished so that you can make the right decisions at the planning and stitching stages. You might then want to finish something yourself because you will have all the necessary information.

Even if you do give your finishing work to someone else, it helps enormously to know the best way and to have ideas about what finishes you want. You need to know these things at the design stage to work out the canvas allowance around the design and decide which backing fabric you will use – particularly important if the fabric is to surround the design (see mounted or ruffled pillows on page 134). When it is finished, too, you will be better able to select a craftworker by being able to ask the "right" questions, and discuss finishing techniques.

Whatever you make, always prepare and work on a square or rectangular piece of canvas stretched in a square or rectangular frame, even for a round design. These shapes are easier to mount in the frame and to block when the work has been completed.

Some finishers prefer stitched pieces to have an extra two rows of continental tent stitch worked around the edge. This does not show but provides a reinforced

IMPORTANT POINTS TO REMEMBER

- Remember that silk must only be dry cleaned – never wet it. Label any work that has silk in it to alert the finisher.
- Congress cloth will watermark if it is not completely covered with stitches.
- Test any bought painted canvas to satisfy yourself that it is waterproof before using it.

- Test permanent markers on each piece of canvas you intend to use them on to check that they remain waterproof; the sizing used in the manufacture of canvas can cause even "waterproof" pens to run when wet, a problem in blocking.
- Most important of all, it is always better to be safe than sorry.

▶ *A kaleidescope of color and shapes gives some idea of the many sources that can be tapped for embroidery. Look for patterns, texture, and colors, and ways of reinterpreting them in needlepoint. Arranging objects in this way can be a good starting point for your own inspiration. You can start with a random collection of natural, historical, and artificial objects and then move on to grouping objects in themes, textures, and colors.*

border that they can machine-stitch along. It is wise, therefore, to ask your finisher if they would like you to do this.

Now to some specific things to bear in mind for particular types of project.

PILLOW COVER

Remember two points when you are planning to work pillow covers in needlepoint as opposed to other stitches:
• use a larger than usual interior pad so the pillow is firm; this will hold the corners out well. Or work a box cushion, which displays the worked top very well.
• the canvas will tend to be firmer than any backing fabric you choose, so select a medium-weight, firmly woven fabric – good curtain fabric, such as moiré, works much better than heavy velvet or loosely woven textured fabrics or, at the other end of the scale, fine silks.

CHAIR SEATS

Choose the design and therefore stitches for any upholstered piece with care for, unless it is strictly decorative, it will need to be hardwearing. Tent and Bargello stitches are both popular in this context because they do wear so well.

There are two main types of chair seat: the upholstered sort and the drop-in variety. With any upholstered piece, it is wise to make a template in fabric: by making a reliable template, it is easier to buy just the right amount of canvas without cutting it too fine.

Upholstered chairs and stools are often shaped, so areas of canvas will be turned in, making it unnecessary to stitch that area. Some chairs have a central back post, which means that your template will need to include two flaps to go on each side of the post and down to the back rail. Since needlepoint will also need to extend to these flaps, patterns that can be repeated work best on this type of chair. Never be tempted to cut the canvas away on areas like this until the work is complete; always work on the square or rectangle, which is essential for blocking.

When you are making your template, take into account the condition of the upholstery. If the seat needs stuffing or the webbing is in a very poor state, add an extra inch or two all around to allow for this. Better still, if you can wait, get your chair stuffed or otherwise repaired as necessary and *then* make your template. Then you can be sure of a perfect fit.

◄ A chair seat ready to be upholstered. Compensation stitches have been worked around the edge to give straight sides, and no threads have been trailed across the corners that will be trimmed off by the upholsterer when the chair is covered.

Your working template can be the old piece of fabric that you take off the chair. This has the advantages of not only avoiding using fabric purely for a template, but that it is easy to see any areas that were turned in, as the colors will still be fresh.

When making a template for a drop-in seat, use strong brown paper, an old sheet, or lining fabric.
1 Lay the paper or fabric over the seat and mark where the wooden part of the seat begins all around.
2 Add ½ in (1 cm) extra all around, and make a second mark.
3 Cut out the pattern you have marked on the paper or fabric, lay it on the canvas, and mark the outline of the template, leaving 2 in (5 cm) all around.
4 Prepare the necessary square or rectangle of canvas, not cutting off any corners.

To make a template for a stuffed chair, I would recommend enlisting the help of the upholsterer who will eventually mount the work for you, especially if the chair needs new webbing, padding, or springs. However, if you wish to prepare a template yourself for such a chair:
1 Spread a square or rectangle of lining over the seat area.
2 Pin it along the front edge with upholsterers' pins, if you have them (they are longer than dressmakers' pins, which is very useful).
3 Smooth the fabric over the seat toward the back edge, keeping the straight grain at 90° to the front rail, and pin it along the back, taking it through any decorative posts or rail at the back.
4 Smooth the fabric out to the sides and mark where it meets the side rails with pins.
5 Tuck any excess fabric in at the corners and indicate the shaping needed with lines of pins.

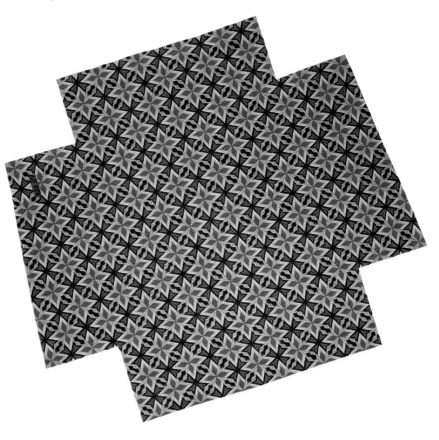

6 Mark the main top area of the seat so that you can place the motif centrally. You can even check this visually by having a tracing of your motif ready and laying it over the fabric, adjusting its position until it is exactly right. Then tape it in place so that you can transfer this positioning accurately to the canvas. This is also advisable when you are repeating a design for, say, four dining chairs, as you can then be sure they will all be the same.

FRAMING PICTURES

For needlepoint pictures, there is a vast choice of frames – modern, traditional, antique, and even fabric-covered, like the one given for the Christmas tree project in Chapter 7 – to choose from, so consult a professional framer for suggestions for your particular project. However, if your framer has not handled needlepoint before, you would be wise to mount the piece ready for framing following the lacing procedure top to bottom and side to side. Depending on the frame you select, the framer may need a margin of unworked canvas on all sides in order to fit the piece neatly into the frame, so discuss this in advance of preparing the board and attaching the work.

THREE-DIMENSIONAL OBJECTS

Bear in mind that, although the brick doorstop in Chapter 2 is the only three-dimensional piece in this book, other patterns here could be adapted to this end. For example, the Ribbon Bow design in Chapter 1 would make a pretty bedroom doorstop.

RUGS

Needlepoint rugs are both beautiful and practical. Because of their size, they do take time to stitch, so it is wise to plan carefully right from the start so that the best results can be achieved. It is best not to incorporate too many difficult stitches or techniques, as evidenced by the beautiful Kelim Rug in Chapter 2 that makes use of only three Bargello stitch patterns and two variations of straight gobelin stitch for the border.

The size of the finished rug is important. Do not be seduced into making one that is too small purely because it will be less to stitch, as you will be disappointed when it is finished. It is a good idea to take a piece of fabric or, indeed, another rug, fold it to your proposed rug size, lay it out where you want to put the finished rug, and see how it looks. Even live with it there for a few days: view it from all angles. Ask yourself, "Does that size balance the fireplace it is lying in front of?," "Do the surrounding chairs stand on it (or not) as I want?," "Does it match the scale of the room?" and so on.

▶ *Details from three rugs. Both the Hydrangea and Tulip rugs were stitched on one piece of canvas, whereas the tent stitch rug was stitched as a number of panels which were then joined together. An interesting border has been stitched around each of the squares to detract from the seams. Because of the random design of the first and the continuous garland on the second, these had to be stitched on a single piece of canvas.*

Whether or not you want to work it in one piece or as a series of squares to be joined together at the end is your next decision. Working rugs as a series of squares (often 18 in/46 cm square) and then joining them together has the advantage that each square is a manageable size, whereas the whole piece could be a little unwieldy. The disadvantages of this, however, are that it is difficult to join the finished squares so that the seams do not catch the eye and, because they are slightly raised, these areas will show signs of wear before the flat areas. Some designs, such as the Tulip Rug in Chapter 6, are impossible to make up from squares. You therefore need to give all these factors careful consideration before you decide to work a particular design in this way. If you do decide to work your rug in squares, remember to:

- buy all your canvas for the entire rug from the same roll
- keep the selvage at the side for each square, mark the top and keep to it as the thread count is quite different across and along the canvas
- work a decorative pattern or contrast line of stitching around each square to take the eye away from the final seams.

For extra-wide canvas that is 54 in (137 cm) wide, which will accommodate even large rugs in one piece, I find it easiest to use an 18- to 20-in (46- or 51-cm) frame, moving it from area to area as I work, than a large one that will take the whole piece at one time.

If you have to add canvas somewhere, it is better to work a central design and add borders on each side of it than have a seam running through the middle. This has the added advantage that the fact that there is a change in pattern between the central area and the border pattern anyway means that the seams are virtually invisible.

Although there are no wallhangings among the projects in this book, there are a number of designs here that you could work as wallhangings, particularly the Kelim Rug in Chapter 2 and the Tulip Rug design in Chapter 6.

ESTIMATING YARN QUANTITIES

It is most important to buy enough yarn, ool, all with the same dye lot number, to complete your project. If you do not, a different dye lot may be a fractionally different shade. As a rough guide, 1 oz (25 g) of crewel yarn should cover 36sq in (6 in × 6in)/2.25m² (15 cm × 15 cm) on 14-mesh canvas, using 3-ply for tent stitch. The same amount of wool and same mesh canvas, but using 4-ply for, say, Bargello stitch, should cover 25sq in (5 in × 5 in)/1.69m² (13 cm × 13 cm).

However, the only truly accurate way to determine the right quantities for any stitch in a large area is to test-stitch a 1-in (2.5-cm) square in the yarn and stitch on the mesh canvas you plan to use. If you want to use a dark color on a light-colored canvas, you are likely to need an extra ply to cover the canvas completely, which will automatically increase your yarn requirement. Approximate the number of 1-in (2.5-cm) squares there are in each color throughout the design and, for each color, multiply the length of yarn used for the test area by the number of squares there are of that color. Then, add 10 percent just to be on the safe side.

For floss and pearl cotton, allow about 1 yd/1 m of yarn per 1 square inch (2.5 cm). The skeins are 8 yd (9 m) and 27 yd (27 m) long respectively.

If you are working a set of dining chair seat covers, there is an easy way to check quantities. Purchase the yarn you have calculated by the above method and divide it by the number of covers. When you have worked the first seat cover, you will then be able to assess whether or not more yarn is needed to finish the set. If you do need more yarn, work a complete seat cover in one dye lot, as very slight variations in color are unlikely to show when you compare chairs, but inevitably show when you use the two to stitch an area of the design.

PREPARING THE CANVAS

Time and trouble put in now makes for easier stitching and better results, so it really is worth centering, marking, painting, and taping the canvas properly before you start to stitch.

ENLARGING DESIGNS
The simplest way of enlarging – or reducing – a design is on a photocopier. It need not cost very much to get one or two different enlargements done at a stationery store if you do not have ready access to a photocopier.

In the case of a large design, the final size will have to be on sheets of paper stuck together with tape.

If it should be inconvenient for you to use the above method, you can use the traditional grid method of enlargement. Draw a grid of, say, ½-in (1.5-cm) squares over a tracing of the design, then, on a larger piece of paper, draw a larger grid with the same number of squares. A grid of 1-in (2.5-cm) squares will double the size, 2-in (5-cm) squares will make it four times as big and so on. Then, simply copy the lines in each original small square in its equivalent square on the larger grid.

MARKING THE CANVAS
This can be done in several ways, depending on the type of design used:
- use a sharp, hard pencil for copying the project chart that is to be worked in dark colors, keeping the lead in the channel between two canvas threads to mark the straight lines first and drawing diagonals with the aid of a small ruler, joining

MERGING DIFFERENT DYE LOTS

If the worst happens and you are in the middle of a project when you realize that you do not have enough yarn to finish it, there is a technique that helps minimize any variation between dye lots. Buy the extra yarn immediately, checking it against the remaining hank to be matched rather than the yarn already stitched. Introduce the new yarn in stages by keeping to the total number of ply for the rest of the piece, but replacing one of the ply with one ply from the new and the remainder from the old. Then, after a few rows, substitute two of the ply with two ply of the new yarn and so on until all the ply are in the new yarn. Gauge how much of each mix you work to how much of the old yarn you have left – the more you have, the more gradual the transition can be.

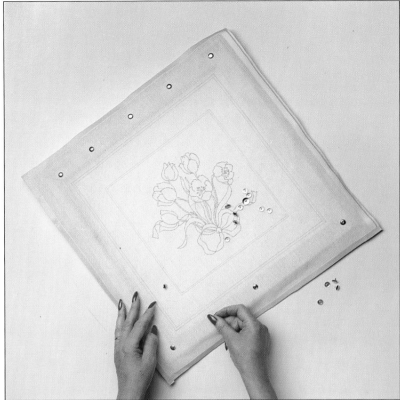

◄ *Having made a drawing of the design to the right size, trace it onto the canvas. Make sure the canvas and drawing do not shift while you are working.*

▲ *Mounting the canvas on the frame is an important stage in the preparation. Pin out each edge, keeping the canvas absolutely taut.*

ESTIMATING CANVAS

Be more generous in the border allowance you allow when you are not completely certain of the final design. Nothing is more annoying than not having room to do a fabulous border that you decide will finish off your design perfectly only once you have stitched the central panel.

The templates used for outlining chair seat covers look vast, but, be warned, trust the template. Chair seats *are* large when you allow for the upholstering and, anyway, is it not better to have the option of trimming away any excess when the work is complete rather than finding that your completed canvas is too small?

◄ *The canvas, pinned out on each side, is now ready for stitching.*

the straight lines
- when working lighter color schemes, make only tiny guide marks, or you may prefer especially when designing your own geometric piece (when you do not know what thread count will suit the stitches best), to outline the proposed areas of stitching in a contrast basting thread, as this leaves no marks and can be moved if necessary (I used this method when designing the Bokhara project in Chapter 4 and would strongly advise using it for a pristine result with the all-white Samarkand tiles in Chapter 4.)
- when drawing or tracing a picture or curved design, like the Ribbon Bow Box in Chapter 1, use either artist's oil paint thinned with turpentine or a permanent, waterproof marker pen, checking the color fastness of any marker pen first on a spare piece of the canvas you plan to use as the layer of sizing put on during the manufacturing of some canvas can affect the fastness of even those pens claiming to be waterproof.

The most common method is to put the enlarged design beneath the canvas in the correct place, checking that the design is easily visible through the canvas (if it is on tracing paper, put a sheet of white paper under the tracing). Tape them into position, making sure it is still in the right place and at the right angle. Draw over the lines you can see through the canvas as accurately as possible, using either artist's oil paint thinned with turpentine or a permanent waterproof marker pen

STARTING AND FINISHING TENT STITCH

Note that tent stitch requires different treatment of both starting and finishing threads, which is fully explained in Chapter 1.

you have tested for fastness as described above.

If it is a more complicated design where certain elements need to align exactly to the thread, further preparation is needed. Mark the center of the design on the paper drawing and the center of the canvas, and draw straight horizontal and vertical lines through the centers on both the paper and the canvas. Put the canvas on top of the drawing as before, but this time put a thumbtack through the center marked on the canvas; then push this pin through the center marked on the drawing, and finally push the thumbtack into a board. Pin in the same way through the vertical and horizontal lines at the edge and about 2 in (5 cm) apart all around the edge, pulling the canvas straight and taut. Then trace the design carefully as before.

MOUNTING THE CANVAS IN A FRAME

Allow at least a 2-in (5-cm) border of unworked canvas on all sides of the design. This will be needed, first, to attach the canvas to the frame and, second, for assembling the finished work, trimmed as necessary.

Always remember to bind any cut edges with masking tape or machine stitch bias binding over them before mounting the canvas in the frame. Plastic canvas and interlock canvas are the exceptions to this rule and need no binding.

When you are working, keep the selvage (the woven edge that needs no binding) to the side as this will help you to work all your stitches in the same direction. Remember selvages at the sides, and mark one of the other sides top.

When you are mounting a canvas on artist's stretcher bars, tack the mid-point of one side first, then the corners on each side of this point, then the opposite side in the same way, and finally the two other sides, stretching the canvas as tightly as you can at each stage. Add more thumbtacks between these until the canvas is evenly stretched. Use flat-headed thumbtacks as pins will catch your stitching thread.

For scroll frames, center the canvas on the tapes that are attached to each rounded bar and stitch firmly in place with a sharp needle and button thread. Lace to the sides tautly.

STARTING A NEW THREAD

There are three different ways of doing this, each method being suitable for specific circumstances.

THE WASTE KNOT

Make a small knot at the end of the thread and place it on the right side of the work in the path of where you are going to stitch, about 2 in (5 cm) away from where the first stitch will be made. When you have worked up to the knot, snip it off carefully, close to the canvas with sharp scissors. It will not unravel, as the rest of the thread will be firmly caught by the back of the stitches just worked.

AN AWAY KNOT

This is used when you work any isolated motif, for the Wedding Sampler project in Chapter 3, for example, or when the stitches will be surrounded by exposed canvas or pulled thread work, whose beauty depends on there being no stray threads visible behind the work. Make a small knot as before, but place it much farther away (about 4 in/10 cm) from the first stitch; once the motif or stitches have been worked, the knot can be snipped off, and this long thread can be securely woven into the back of its own stitches.

WEAVING INTO EXISTING STITCHES

This is useful when you come to work the second stage of a stitch, possibly in a contrasting color, such as crossed corners stitch. Simply weave the tail of the thread (it is not necessary to knot it) back and forth into the back of previous

▼ *A waste knot is placed on the surface of the work in the direction of the stitching to be done. The knitting stitch (worked in vertical rows) has the knot above, and the 2-4-6-8 stitch (worked in horizontal rows) has the knot out to the left. The Rhodes stitch in blue has a knot above and was started in the lower left corner so as to cover the tail as much as possible: when the stitch is* complete, *the thread will be finished off in the back of the stitches. The knot for basketweave tent stitch is placed out to the side, not on a diagonal.*

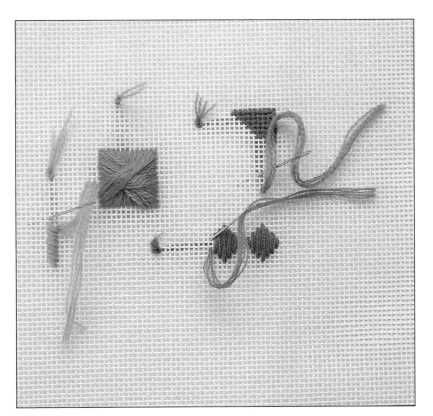

stitches. How much you can weave depends largely on the density of the existing stitches.

FINISHING A THREAD

Simply run the tail end through the back of several stitches. If, however, there are not very many stitches on the reverse side of the canvas, or if they are widely spaced and/or the fiber is slippery (particularly true of rayon threads), work a Bargello knot by running the thread through the back of eight or ten stitches, going over a few stitches and then back under the first group of stitches in the opposite direction.

If you happen to be working on a frame that does not turn over easily, bring the end up to the right side of the work, in the path of your new thread and snip it off when you reach the last bit of it. Personally, I do not favor this method, as it quickly makes the canvas look like a jungle, and it is difficult to make design decisions with all the additional clutter – much easier to make sure your frame turns over easily before you start!

'CLEAN' AND 'DIRTY' HOLES

This is a memorable phrase to help you remember always to come up in an empty, or "clean," hole, that is one that has no previous stitch in it, and to go down into a shared, or "dirty," hole. This will mean that any wisps of fluff are taken to the back of the work and is a particularly important practice when you are working a pale color beside a dark one. If there are "dirty" holes at each end of the stitch, come up in the hole occupied by a thread the same color as you are using and go down into the hole occupied by the contrasting color.

If working in one color, it is still a good idea to come up in the least busy hole and go down in a busier one.

THE
PROJECTS

+ + + + + +

Within each chapter, ranging from tent
stitch to pulled thread work, there are
at least two projects, of which the first
is the easier one and therefore the best
one to start with. Each project gives
full instructions to copy it, with
additional notes to help you vary the
piece to your taste. In addition, tips
throughout the book give you the best
method for working that technique.

CHAPTER 1

TENT STITCH

From the very earliest beginnings of needlepoint, tent stitch has been extremely popular with needleworkers (men were – and still are – very proficient with the needle). Most surviving early pieces were worked in tent stitch, because it is much more durable than any other stitch and because detail and shading can be reproduced exceptionally clearly.

The difference between tent stitch done well and done less well is immense. Even if you have worked it before, do read through this section – I hope you will pick up some useful tips. There are three different tent stitches, and it is important to know the difference to be able to use them correctly.

Basketweave, or diagonal, tent stitch

This is the stitch to use in all instances except when you want to work a single line of stitches. It is so named because on the reverse side of the work the stitches form a basketweave or interlocking texture that does not distort the canvas and wears well.

Draw yourself a corner at the top right-hand side of a scrap of canvas and practice following the diagrams. Practicing this is important as the short rows and constant need to change direction frequently confuse people and result in stitches at the edges being missed. It is better to become familiar with the method on a

piece of scrap canvas where mistakes don't matter than in a piece of needlepoint.

1 The diagram shows the stitch sequence for going up a diagonal: bring the needle up at 1, down at 2 (over one intersection of threads), pass the needle horizontally under two threads of canvas and up at 3.

2 After working a dozen or so stitches, change direction by coming up through the hole to the *side* of the last stitch, as shown in the diagram.

3 Then work diagonally down with the needle passing vertically behind two threads, as shown.

4 At the bottom of the row, you will need to work a stitch immediately below the first stitch in the first row in order to achieve a straight edge before another upward diagonal is started.

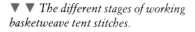

▼ ▼ *The different stages of working basketweave tent stitches.*

▲ *The suitability of tent stitch for depicting realistic detail is illustrated in*

the traditional design of this floral-motif rug.

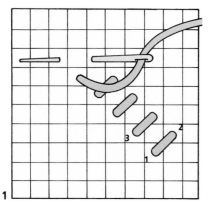
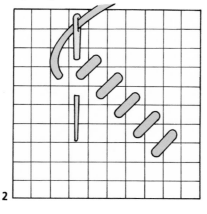
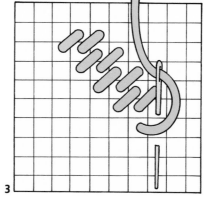
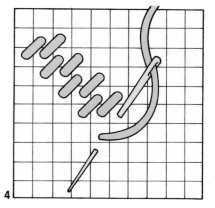

When you reach the top of a row and the next stitch would be over the outline, rotate the needle one hole towards the centre of the design. Similarly, when you reach the bottom of a row and the next stitch would be over the outline, rotate the needle one hole towards the centre of the design.

You will find that once you understand changing direction, you can work even very small areas in this stitch.

▲ ▶ *These three 19th-century Berlin wool work charts (named for the city where this printing technique originated) are typical of the lush blooms favoured by Victorian taste. Tent stitch was the obvious choice for this kind of work, but cross stitch was also used. Beads were sometimes added to heighten the opulent effect.*

READING THE GRAIN OF THE CANVAS

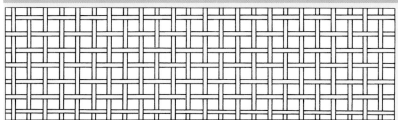

For evenweave, or plain, canvas there is a method of achieving even better results with basketweave tent stitch, using the weave of the canvas threads.

Take a close look at a piece of evenweave canvas: the threads weave over and under each other in turn. At one intersection, the *vertical* thread is on top and at the next the *horizontal* thread is on top. On any one diagonal line of intersections, they will *all* be vertical *or* horizontal, alternating on each diagonal.

Always work the row down (when the needle is in the vertical position in the diagrams) over *vertical* threads and work the row up (when the needle is in the horizontal position) over *horizontal* intersections.

There are many advantages to reading the grain: when you pick up a partly worked piece, you can tell immediately whether the next row should be up or down; you can work areas that do not touch first (for example, flowers in different places on the canvas), then when you come to work the background, you will not have the problem of diagonal ridges formed by two rows side by side being worked in the same direction; you can avoid the problem of basketweave tent stitches worked on very fine canvas disappearing between the threads of the canvas when they are worked in the wrong direction, that is, not using the grain; but, best of all you will get a really smooth, hard-wearing result!

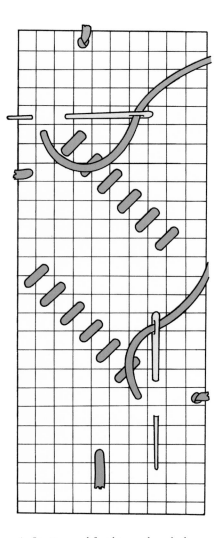

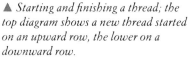

▲ *Starting and finishing a thread; the top diagram shows a new thread started on an upward row, the lower on a downward row.*

When you wish either to start or finish a thread, always do it either horizontally or vertically, never up the last diagonal row, in the following ways:

● when working up a row, take the thread to be finished out horizontally to the left (behind unworked canvas); bring the new thread in vertically from above (using the back of stitches if necessary but not digging too deeply into them);

● when working down a row, take the thread to be finished out vertically down and bring the new thread in horizontally from the right (using the back of stitches if necessary).

In "Getting Started," I stressed the importance of placing the waste knot in the direct path of the next few stitches – this is the one exception.

Interestingly, continental and basketweave tent stitches both use approximately the same amount of yarn or thread.

For details on working basketweave tent stitch as a background area around a large motif, see "Backgrounds & Borders."

Continental tent stitch

Use this version of tent stitch only when there is a single line of stitches to be worked either vertically, horizontally or diagonally from the upper right to lower left.

If you can, look at finished pieces

worked solely in this stitch. You **will** see that the overall effect frequently resembles corduroy. If you are able to examine the back, you will find that rows of continental tent stitch are worked alternately with half-cross stitches. Besides looking uneven, the piece will not wear very well, and the varying pull of the stitches will probably have distorted the canvas.

When used just once or twice in a piece or in combination with more hard-wearing stitches, it can be very useful. If you work the stitch with a long stitch on the back side of the work, it will wear well and not pull the canvas out of shape. If you need to turn a corner, continue to work a long stitch behind the canvas; otherwise, it will be a half-cross stitch and not wear well.

▲ *The ivy leaf motif used for these handsome slippers might be adapted to a larger-scale design for a pillow, as shown in the sample.*

The diagram on the right shows how to work continental tent stitch.

1 A row worked from right to left.
2 A row worked from left to right.
3 Working continental tent stitch vertically down.
4 Working continental tent stitch vertically up.
5 Continental tent stitch being worked diagonally from upper right to lower left.
6 When a diagonal row from lower right to upper left is worked, the stitches do not touch each other; to

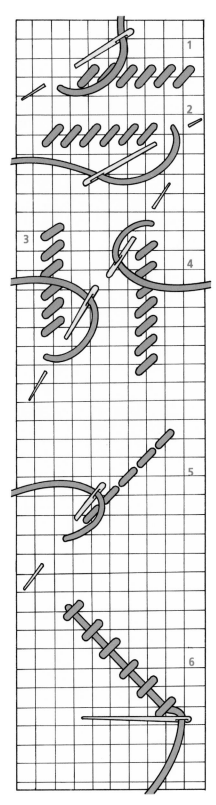

▲ *How to work continental tent stitch.*

HOW MUCH YARN?

As half-cross stitch uses less yarn to cover the same area than either of the other two stitches, always check what stitch a kit recommends before buying it. If it only comes with enough yarn to work the design in half-cross stitch, it is wise, particularly with the background color, to buy additional yarn at the same time you buy the kit, so you can work these areas in basketweave tent stitch instead. If you are unable to match the color supplied with the kit, buy enough to work these areas in basketweave tent stitch in another harmonizing color. This is more expensive than working the design in half-cross stitch, but the extra expense will more than pay for itself, because you will have a far more durable and attractive finished piece of work. The most valuable item will always be your time, and working a piece in half-cross stitch is a poor investment of it.

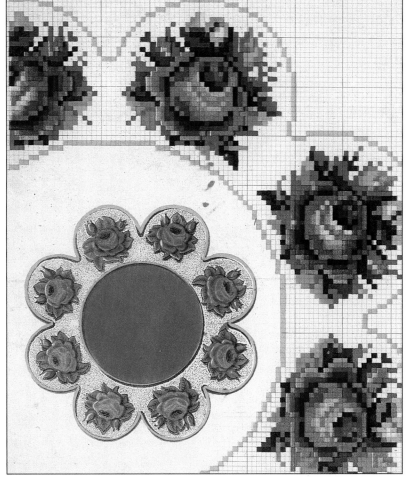

▲ *The rose motif for this little box has been adapted from an original Berlin woolwork chart for a scalloped-edge mat (below left).*

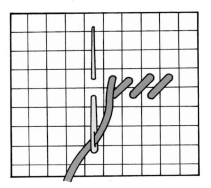

▲ *How to work half-cross stitch. It looks almost identical to tent stitch, but is much less durable and distorts the canvas.*

connect them for a better finish, run a thread of the same color under the completed row of stitches as shown. (You will find you are most likely to need this technique if you work letters, such as the second stroke of a capital A or the first stroke of a capital W.)

Half-cross stitch

If you turn a corner in half-cross stitch (see Stitch Glossary page 144) while stitching basketweave or continental tent stitch, or use it incorrectly to fill an area, you produce a piece that is not very durable and likely to be distorted.

In this chapter, the first project, the Doll's House Rug, is worked following a chart, with each color denoted by a different symbol and each square on the graph representing one stitch, while the second, the Ribbon Bow, is a shaded piece, and shows you how to work out your own shading. The simple method demonstrated for this second project will enable you to work any representational design, even in stitches other than tent stitch.

+ + + + + **TENT STITCH · PROJECT 1** + + + + +

DOLLS' HOUSE RUG

The design for this rug was inspired by an inlaid floor. Because this rug was worked for a miniature room, tent stitch was chosen for its even finish and small scale, as other textured stitches are often larger and can result in an uneven surface, causing the furniture to topple over. Also, bearing in mind the proportion of the size of the stitch to the size of the rug, it is difficult to get most stitch designs down to the right scale.

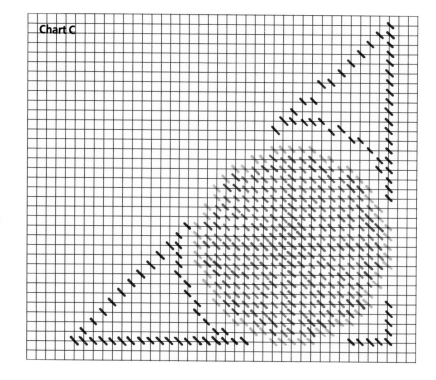

Chart C

▲ *Chart C: the corner motif.*

1 Start in the center of the canvas, working the star shape shown in detail in Chart A and by the / symbol in Chart B.
2 Thicken the points of the star where the ● symbol appears in chart B.
3 Work the single row of stitches forming a circle following the + symbol in the chart.
4 Work the background area, indicated by the × symbol.

MATERIALS

DMC embroidery floss in the following quantities and colors:
  2 skeins 926, gray blue
  2 skeins 825, cornflower blue
  2 skeins 828, light blue
  7 skeins 309, deep raspberry pink
  1 skein 3326, light pink
  2 skeins 680, bronze
  10 skeins 7399, beige
  1 skein 744, soft yellow
Size 24 tapestry needles
35.5-cm (14-in) square frame
35.5-cm (14-in) square piece of 24-mesh plain mono canvas

Working the design

On Chart B, each color is denoted by a different symbol and each square represents one stitch. The chart shows a quarter of the completed rug so, when you are working the other quarters, it may help to turn the chart to match the area you are working, but be careful not to confuse the symbols for cornflower blue and soft yellow when they are turned on their sides.

Use 3-ply embroidery floss and work in tent stitch throughout. You will find it helpful to refer to the comments on handling floss in "Getting Started" on page 16 before you start working this piece.

Chart B

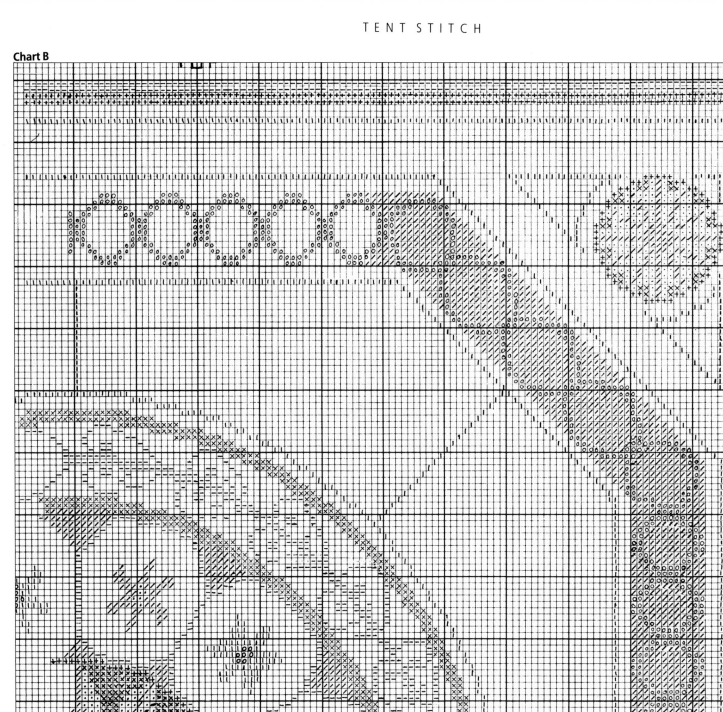
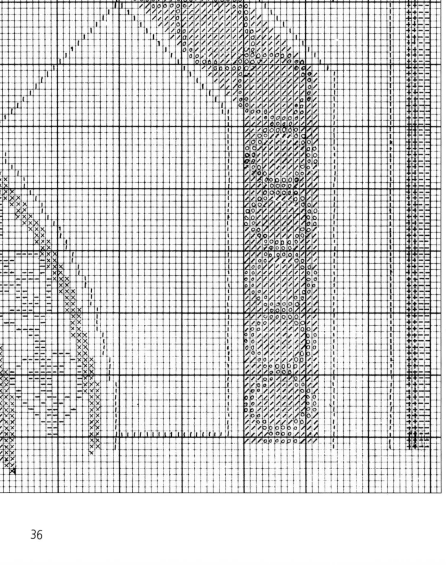

◄ Chart B shows one-quarter of the design. Each square represents one mesh of the canvas (a single intersection of threads). Colors are represented by symbols:

/ = 309, deep raspberry pink
✕ = 926, gray blue
| = 825, cornflower blue
○ = 828, pale blue
+ = 680, bronze
● = 3326, pale pink
− = 744, soft yellow
□ = 7399, beige

The chart must be turned for the remaining quarters of the rug; be careful not to confuse the symbols | and − when you have turned the chart.

5 Then work the outlines of the 12 lozenge shapes marked in Chart B with the − symbol.

6 Work the next large circle, working 2 rows, as indicated by the ✕ symbol.

7 Fill in the points marked with the / symbol in Chart B.

8 Work the "flowers" alternately, noting the color changes: one has / petals and ● centers, and the other has | petals and ○ centers.

9 Work the background behind the flowers in the beige floss.

10 Work the second large circle indicated by the ✕ symbol in the chart.

11 Then work the heart-shaped garland between the second and third circles you have already worked, indicated in chart B by the − symbol.

12 Work the background behind the previous motif in − as shown in the chart.

13 Following the chart, work the circle, two octagons, linking rays, corner triangle shapes, and large square.

14 Work the oval motifs between the two octagon frames in ○, then work the background (only shown behind part of the design in the chart) in /.

15 Work the corner roundels following the colors marked in Charts B and C.

16 Work 2 rows in + around the outer edge and a further 2 rows in − outside that shown in Chart B.

17 Finally, work all the remaining background areas (left blank in Chart B) in the beige floss.

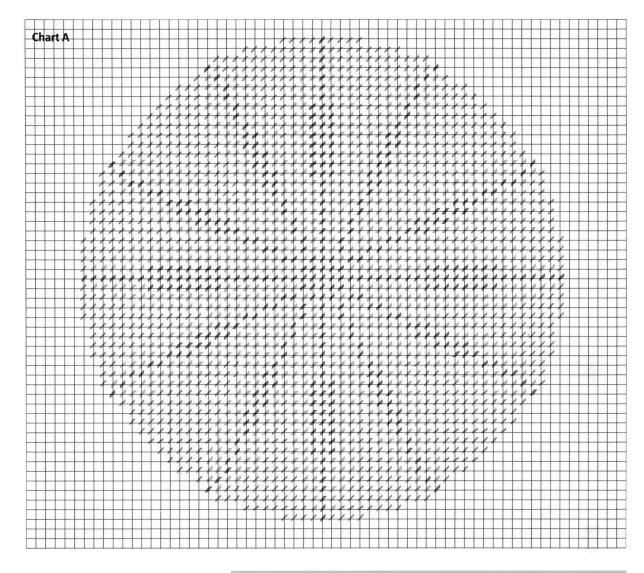

Chart A

▲ Chart A shows the central motif of the rug. As in chart C, the lines of the chart represent the canvas threads.

Finishing

In order for the rug to have neat, flat edges, block the canvas as usual (see "Finishing"). Unravel the canvas on all 4 sides back to the stitching to have an approximately 2-in (5-cm) deep fringe on each side. Thread one or two strands of the fringe through the eye of the needle and run the needle through the back of a few stitches for approximately ½ in (1.25) cm at right angles to the edge. Cut the ends off close to the work.

OTHER USES FOR THE RUG CHART

In addition to being used to make a delightful rug for a doll's house, this chart can be worked to produce a piece of needlepoint just the right size to suit your own particular purpose. The design worked on 24-mesh canvas will be approximately 10½ in (26.5cm) square; worked on 18-mesh canvas, it would be 14 in (35.5 cm) square (a good size for a pillow) and on 14-mesh, it would be 18 in (46 cm) square (a large pillow, fire screen, or even a top for a coffee table).

The complete circular motif in the center worked on its own would make a marvelous cover for a round footstool (if you carefully choose the right mesh canvas to give the correct finished size and good durability).

TENT STITCH · PROJECT 2

RIBBON BOW BOX

Tent stitch excels all others in the realistic depiction of shading. Because the individual stitches are small, it is possible to work either very gradual shading or sharp definitions of areas of color, which means light, shade, and depth can all be portrayed very accurately. You can use very small areas of color or even just the odd stitch or two to create the right effect.

Compare block-printed fabric and a photograph. In the first, each area of color is clearly defined, but in the photograph, it is impossible to see where one color finishes and the next begins: there are no harsh edges. This is the effect we shall achieve in the project.

Blending the colors

As the terms "strand" and "ply" are crucial to this project, refer to "Getting Started" for an explanation of them.

As we have seen, it is the gradual transition from one shade to another that makes shading successful. To obtain this gradual transition, a mixture of any divisible thread is used. The principle is to put one ply with another of a close shade of that color to give even more steps between the standard shades and hence even more gradual shading. Obviously only close, "next door" colors should be used together. If the shades are not close, the effect can be of a speckled area and just look messy.

Preparing your design for shading

There are two ways to record the subject of your design: photography, and hand-coloring an outline drawing. Both work well and often I use them together to even greater benefit.

If your subject is a bunch of flowers, a piece of fruit, or a landscape, a series of photographs is invaluable. Besides making a permanent record of something that may die, go bad, or that you will not see again, I find that looking through the viewfinder of the camera helps me to find the most interesting angle on the subject — what background, if any, to include and so on. A pear, for example, may have a ripe, golden bloom on one side, but look very unripe on another; the Chinese vase holding the flowers is sure to add greater excitement to the overall design. Photographs of buildings are particularly useful as you can make

▼ *Chart A shows the order of working the loops of the bow.*

sure you have all the details in proportion while you are drawing the elevation onto the canvas.

Colored drawings are helpful because, while you are doing them, you find where the shadows fall and colors

Chart A

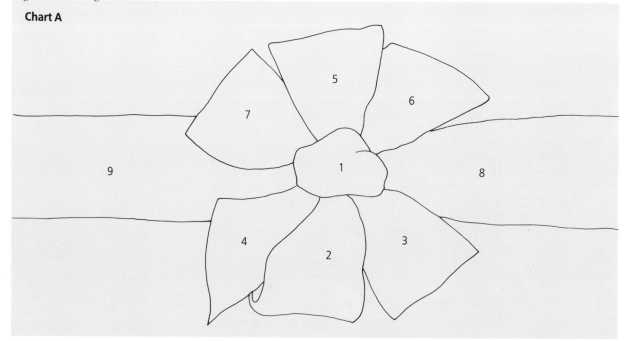

STITCHING CARD

Making a stitching card with all the blends of yarn on it before you start to stitch makes working the design much easier (see also the Hydrangea Rug in Chapter 10 and the Tulip Pillow and Rug in Chapter 6).

1 Take a strong piece of paper or thin cardboard big enough for the colored ribbon drawing to fit on one half. Fold the paper in half and mount the colored drawing on the bottom half. On the top half, make 7 horizontal divisions and label them as the diagram shows.

2 Then "park" the strands themselves. Simply make up a few of the strands you need, of the right ply and single or mixed shades, and knot each one at the end. With a size 20 tapestry needle, take it through the card, leaving the knot on the right side to hold it in place. For this project I made four strands of each color combination and tied each mix together loosely, only untying them when I was using that blend — only having one combination untied means you know exactly which one you are using at any one time — even in artificial light.

3 If you are working a design with a number of different flowers, each with their own color families, you may want to make a card for each flower type.

4 Finally, it can be very useful to keep an accurate record of the exact quantities of yarn used — you might plan to make a pair of the same design, say — so make a column on the stitching card headed "amount used," mark down the four strands you started with, and each time you "park" more strands, add them to the total in this column.

	PLY	MIXED STRANDS	AMOUNT USED
A	2 x Br China 3		
B	1 Br China 3 + 1 Br China 4		
C	2 x Br China 4		
D	1 x Br China 4 + 1 x Br China 5		
E	2 x Br China 5		
F	1 x Br China 5 + 1 x Br China 7		
G	2 x Br China 7		

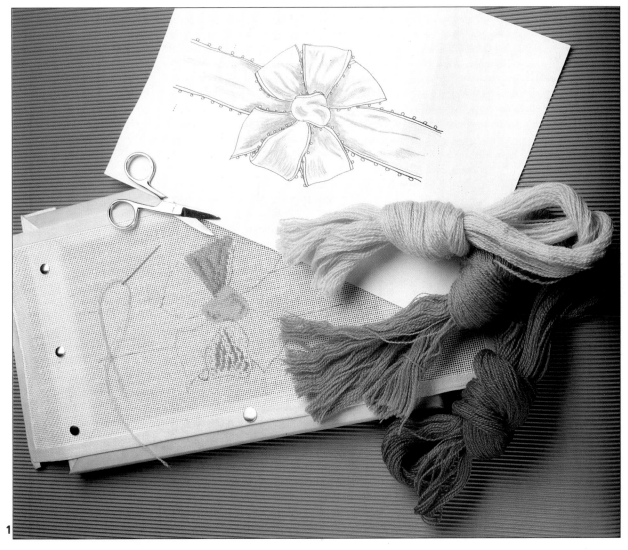

enlarge or reduce it to the size you want (see page 24).

Working the design

Refer to the diagram of the Ribbon Bow and you will see the order in which the various areas should be worked. The rule is always to work the area that lies on top first, then continue to work down in layers. Thus, area 2 is on top of area 3, so it is worked before 3; 8 and 9 are under all the rest and so are worked last.

1 Start with area 1 — the knot of the bow. Bearing in mind that you should reserve the darker colors for the lower areas, confine yourself to stitching with the paler combinations, A and B with possibly a few stitches of C.

2 Areas 2 and 5 can include A, B, C, and D.

3 Areas 3, 4, 6, and 7 can be worked in B, C, D, E, and just a few stitches of A to highlight, and some F deep down in the knot area to create a good impression of depth.

4 Areas 8 and 9 have deep shadows under the bow, created by using G, and possibly no A at all.

5 To make any particular area look curvy, don't do too many stitches of one color in a straight line. In this piece, it is best not to work an edge more than 3 stitches long; although on a larger piece, you can set the limit at 5 in a line.

Background

Obviously, tent stitch in a pale color would be very suitable as a background to this motif, but I chose to work it in continuous cashmere stitch (see Stitch Glossary, page 144) in 3-ply off-white crewel yarn. You may also like to explore Chapter 10 for some alternative ideas. When making your selection, choose a fairly small-scale stitch; otherwise, it will overpower the tent stitch.

To add a touch of the unusual, you could give the ribbon a picot edging by working a strand of white pearl cotton, couched down with 1-ply white background yarn. This should be worked last of all.

▲ *Step 1 shows the knot completed and the method of working the shading.*

▼ *More shades of blue are added for steps 2 and 3 (below).*

merge, or where there is a bright patch of color. In the case of the Ribbon Bow Box, I planned to use four colors (plus the interim shades), so I selected four colored pencils – all shades of blue – and colored in a drawing of the bow. As I colored, I remembered that anything that lies on top tends to be lighter, that colors tend to get darker as they go deeper down an object because the overlying parts, especially where they have any height, cast shadows onto the lower parts. Also, where one ribbon lies on top of another, there has to be quite a color change; otherwise, the ribbon edge will not read against the one below.

Trace the drawing of the bow and

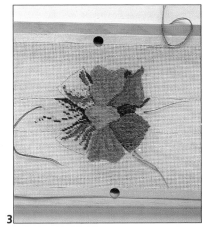

2

BARGELLO STITCH

The term Bargello stitch, which is also known as Florentine, covers a vast array of patterns, created from basic straight stitches covering four or more canvas threads, grouped in one to six stitches stepped up or down to form flame-like shapes. More interesting patterns vary the length or number of stitches in each group, reverse pattern lines, create a three-dimensional effect, or work motifs in four – or even eight – directions, radiating out from a central point.
An advantage of Bargello stitch is that it "grows" quite quickly and is very satisfying to stitch.

+ + + + + **BARGELLO STITCH · PROJECT 1** + + + + +

$\mathcal{D}$OOR STOP

Like so many designs, this doorstop was inspired by another design, a pillow cover. It can be a great way of using up left-over yarn, supplemented with new, co-ordinating yarn if necessary. When choosing colors, it is important to remember to match or coordinate them with the rug or carpet and door against which the doorstop is to be put, or the shades of the furnishings in that room.

Preparation
Read the notes overleaf about brick size before marking your canvas. Only mark the individual areas shown in the layout diagram if your brick is the size given. *It is absolutely essential to mark the "edges" of your brick onto your canvas and alter all the instructions accordingly.* The top as given here is 158 by 76 threads and each flap is 50 threads deep. Also, mark the 4-thread channel along the bottom edges of each flap, making the flaps 46 plus 4 threads. Mark the outline dimensions of the brick on the canvas using a hard pencil, a waterproof marker pen, or basting thread. Mount the canvas on the frame as described in "Getting Started."

Working the design
1 Referring to Chart H, start working in Area A 18 threads in from the top left corner, marked by a spot. Refer to Chart A for the pattern and for the spot. Work each stitch over 6 threads of canvas. The two scallops shown in Chart A will take you to the division for Area SG.

Using 3-ply, the color sequence is olive green 5, olive green 3, olive green 1, heraldic gold 2, rose pink 8, scarlet 1, rose pink 6, and bright rose pink 5. Fill the gaps left by the scallops to obtain a straight edge by working parts of the pattern row in the same sequence, that is, olive green 5 and olive

---

MATERIALS

Appleton's crewel yarn in the following quantities and colors:
- 2 small skeins olive green 1, 3 and 5
- 2 small skeins bright rose pink 3 and 5
- 2 small skeins rose pink 6 and 8
- 2 small skeins dull china blue 4
- 2 small skeins bright china blue 7
- 2 small skeins chocolate 1
- 2 small skeins heraldic gold 2

1 small skein scarlet 1
1 extra skein of one of the darkest of these colors that goes with your carpet, such as olive green 5, rose pink 8, or bright china blue 7
14- by 18-in (35.5- by 46-cm) piece of brown 18-mesh plain mono canvas
14- by 18-in (35.5- by 46-cm) frame
Size 22 tapestry needles

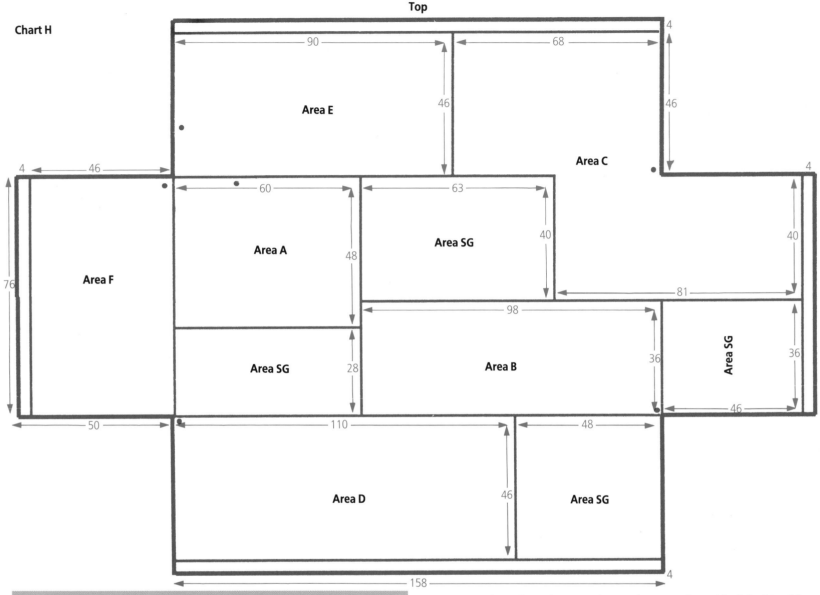

Top

Chart H

Area E

90

68

4

46

46

Area C

4

46

Area A

60

63

Area SG

40

Area F

76

48

40

Area SG

81

98

Area SG

Area B

36

Area SG

36

28

50

110

48

46

Area D

Area SG

46

158

4

FITTING A BRICK

Always choose a brick before you start to make a doorstop, as they do vary in size. It is essential that the canvas "top" fits the top face of the covered brick exactly; otherwise, the sides will never fit.

Allow for the brick to be wrapped with interlining to give smooth edges

and fill out the holes and hollows. Vary the size of the top panel of the design as necessary; try varying the thread count and altering the side panels accordingly.

Measurements are given for a brick approximately 8 ¾ by 4 ¼ by 2 ¾ in (22 by 11 by 7 cm).

green 3 to the right and rose pink 6 and bright rose pink 5 to the left. This fills Area A.

2 Start the pattern for Area B in the bottom right corner, indicated by the spot on Charts H and B. See Chart B for the pattern and spot.

Each stitch is worked over 6 threads of canvas, with 3 stitches in each group, and there are 8 "spires" in all. Use 3-ply yarn. Work the first row in bright china blue 7, the second in olive green 3, the third in olive green 1, and the fourth in rose pink 8. This completes the full rows. Then fill in the top edge with bright rose pink 5 and the

bottom edge with dull china blue 4 and chocolate 1.

3 Refer to Chart H for Area C and start stitching at the point marked with a spot. This point is also marked in Chart C. The dotted lines indicate the outline of the flaps you have marked on your canvas, which will have moved if your brick is a different size. It is important to have these marked in.

Each stitch is worked over 4 threads, and the stitches are worked in groups of 4. Start with 3-ply scarlet 1, and work a row diagonally both up and down from the starting point. At the top, there will be a group of

◀ *Chart H shows the arrangement of stitch patterns for the doorstop. The numbers represent the number of canvas threads in each direction. Work areas A-F then SG (which stands for straight Gobelin – essentially the same stitch, but worked in horizontal rows).*

▶ *Chart B shows the basic pattern for the zigzags in area B. Begin stitching at the dot and again complete a whole row, then work the following rows.*

▶ *Chart C shows the basic pattern for area C. Note the dotted line, which represents the edges of the flaps; this will be in a different position if your brick is a different size.*

WORKING BARGELLO

- Remember that you can either work up through the shades of a color, starting with the lightest, then start again with the lightest or work up and then back down through the shades of a color, which immediately gives a softer look to a piece.

- Start any but the smallest pattern in the center of the canvas – this way, it is simple to balance patterns.

- Watch the back of the work carefully as you can easily fall into the trap of having long stitches behind certain areas and hardly any yarn behind others, which is not the best way to achieve good wearing qualities (working the mountain and valley flame point designs very easily results in this error as stitching up the mountain can mean having very short stitches behind, while stitching down often produces long stitches). The easiest way to avoid this is to start each row at alternate ends, so going up becomes coming down on the next row; this automatically gives a more even distribution of yarn on the back.

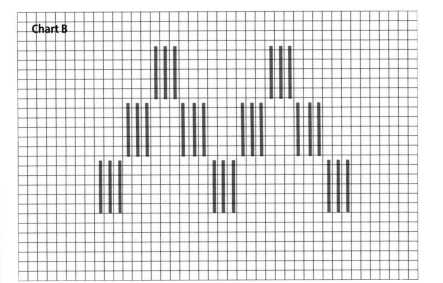

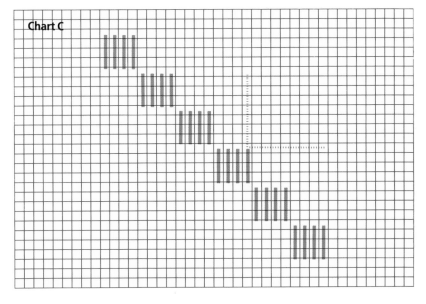

▲ *Chart A shows the basic pattern for the scallops in area A. Begin stitching at the dot and complete a whole row in this color before beginning the next row in the next color.*

stitches over 2 threads to the 4-thread line, and the bottom group will finish exactly in line with the top edge of Area B. Work successive rows in this pattern to the left – also in 3-ply – in the color sequence rose pink 6, rose pink 8, chocolate 1, and dull china blue 7. Then work 4 rows in bright china blue 7, heraldic gold 2, olive green 3, olive green 5, scarlet 1, rose pink 6, rose pink 8, chocolate 1, dull china blue 4, bright china blue 7, and heraldic gold 2 – the last full diagonal. In the lower area, work the last 2 rows to fill the bottom left corner and adjoining Area B and above Area SG

in 3-ply olive green 3 and olive green 5. Now work this pattern toward the right in 3-ply in the right color sequence up to the outline. It is important not to trail the yarn across the back; finish off each row and start afresh with a new length, because this part will be cut away when you are finishing.

4 Area D does not simply repeat a master line, so the whole scallop is charted in Chart D.

Start stitching the scallops in 3-ply rose pink 8 in the top left corner of Area D at the point marked with a spot in the layout diagram, which is

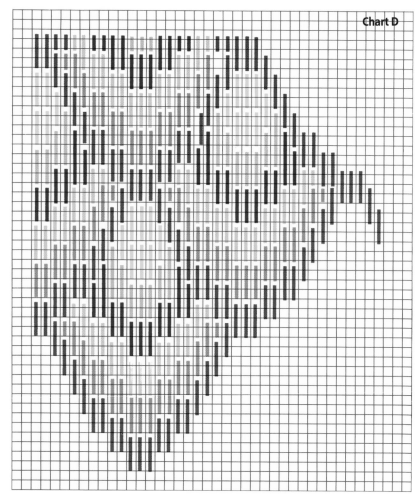

Chart D

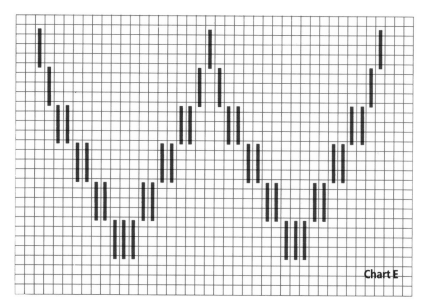

Chart E

▲ *Chart E shows the basic pattern for the flame stitch area E. (This stitch can be made quite dramatic by using colors shaded from dark to light.)*

◀ *Chart D shows the complete patterns for area D. Note that although most stitches are worked over 4 threads, some are worked over 2 or 6.*

the same point marked with a spot in Chart D. Fill in from the curve of the scallop up in rose pink 6, bright rose pink 5, olive green 3, olive green 1, and finish with heraldic gold 2. Most of the stitches are over 4 threads, but a few are over 2 or 6.

Repeat the design as charted up to the line indicating Area SG (this gives you 5 half scallops along the top edge of Area D).

5 Next, work Area E, starting at the dot on Chart H on the left-hand end, 20 threads up from the top edge of Area A. This point is indicated by the spot in Chart E.

All the stitches are worked in 3-ply

over 4 threads, and they are grouped in the order 1, 1, 2, 2, 2, 3, 2, 2, 2, 1. This sequence is then repeated. The color sequence begins with olive green 3, then, working upward from the master line, work 1 full row each in olive green 1, bright rose pink 3, bright rose pink 5, olive green 3, and olive green 1. Fill in up to the edges in this same sequence of colors.

6 For Area F, start stitching at the top right corner, marked with a spot, which is also marked on Chart F.

Work in 3-ply diagonally down and to the left as shown, working stitches over 4 threads in groups of 3. As in Area C, the stitches will be over 2 threads where they meet the line for the 4-thread channel. Work the first row in bright china blue 7, then work rows downward in the color sequence heraldic gold 2, dull china blue 4, chocolate 1, bright rose pink 5, chocolate 1, olive green 5, and olive green 1. Continue in this sequence until the area is completed. Keeping the same sequence of colors, fill the area above the master line.

7 There are now 4 areas left unworked on the canvas corresponding to those labeled SG on Chart H. SG stands for straight Gobelin stitch (see Stitch Glossary, page 145). Work straight Gobelin stitch in these areas, giving the canvas and frame a quarter

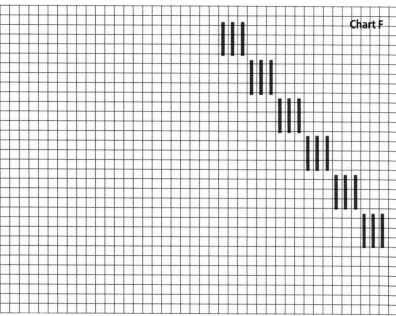

Chart F

◀ *Chart F shows the basic pattern for the stepped blocks in Area F.*

◄ More dazzling Bargello patterns are used for this exuberant pillow, which is trimmed with tassels using some of the stitching yarn. The doorstop is a slight variation on the main project; its random straight Gobelin is worked widthwise to the brick.

turn when working the 2 areas that are labeled sideways in the layout diagram. Work rows of straight Gobelin stitch in 3-ply randomly over 2, 3, 4, 6, and 8 threads, working a random number of stitches in any one color. If you have kept the ends of threads left over when rows were finished elsewhere in the design, use them at this point.

8 Finally, work crossed-corners stitch (see Stitch Glossary, page 145) in the 4-thread channels along the edges of each of the flaps in the color that you have chosen to edge the door stop.

Using 2-ply, work 19 complete stitches along the short end flaps and 39½ stitches along the long sides. To work a half crossed-corners stitch, simply cover half the diagram in the Stitch Glossary and copy what you see.

Finishing

This is demonstrated in "Finishing."

Variation

If you decide to work this project in your own color scheme, put the colors in families as the colors used in the

project instructions have been. Use a palette (filled in during the day in proper daylight, not under artificial light, to avoid confusing close shades) and label each hole.

Try out your color combinations before you start by laying the colors side by side in various orders for standard flame patterns, then try stitching lozenge shapes (you will be surprised at the different effects that can be achieved by placing accent colors or by adding or removing various shades of colors at different

points in the pattern).

You will need approximately ¼ oz each of ten shades of divisible yarn such as Appleton's crewel, Paterna Persian, or DMC Medici and ½ oz of the deep shade used along the edges of the flaps.

If you use crewel yarn, use it 3-ply; if you use Persian, use it 2-ply; and if you use Medici yarn, use it 3- or 4-ply (depending on your personal tension and the color you are using) for the Bargello stitches, and 1 less ply for the crossed-corners stitches.

BARGELLO STITCH · PROJECT 2

+ + + + +   + + + +

CHAIR SEAT COVER

This traditional Bargello design is particularly good for upholstered pieces, as none of the stitches cover more than four canvas threads and the background is worked in basketweave tent stitch which guarantees good wear.

If you work more than one chair seat, the colors can be reversed, making the design far more fun to work and also to look at and use when finished.

There are two types of four-way Bargello designs: one that starts in the center of the canvas with four stitches sharing the same hole and gradually grows to fill the whole design area (the star in the middle of the Bokhara pillow in Chapter 4 is an example of a design that could grow further), and another with individual four-way motifs repeated to form the pattern.

Working the design

All the Bargello stitches in this pattern are worked in 4-ply yarn over 4 canvas threads, with 2-thread jumps.

1 Following Chart A, start in the center of the canvas and work the rows in deep scarlet to make the circle and diamond shapes.

2 Inside each circle and diamond work a row in black.

3 Next work the flower in the center of each circle in bright scarlet. The petals are worked over 3, 5, 6, 4, 6, 5, 3 threads.

4 Work the first frill around the flower in black over 2 threads, except the corner stitches, worked over 3

5 Work the second frill in deep scarlet in the same way.

6 To fill the diamond shapes, work one row in bright scarlet, one row in elephant gray, one row in black, and the final stitch in bright scarlet.

7 Work the background in the circles in 3-ply elephant gray in basketweave tent stitch (see Stitch Glossary, page 144) and the flower centers in double cross stitch (see Stitch Glossary, 147).

As every stitcher's tension is different, check the canvas against the seat before working the final compensation flowers or outlines. If the area worked is too small (because your tension has taken it up), continue to work the pattern as needed and then work compensation stitches to give a straight outline to your chair seat.

Finishing

This is explained on page 137.

Other patterns

If you don't intend to copy the color illustrated, experiment first with your selection of shades, as you will be amazed at the different effects that can be achieved. Spending a little time playing with your colors will mean that you have the most satisfying combination or the best one to suit your décor. Care should be taken, though, if you use strong contrasts. It would be wise to finish the dark threads after working each motif rather than trail these threads from area to area, as they might show when the piece is finished and make a pale color look dirty.

If the décor you want to match is fairly plain, pairs of chairs can be done in different Bargello patterns, though

MATERIALS

It is obviously impossible to give quantities for your particular chair, so refer to page 24 for how to estimate quantities and for the tip regarding working chair seat covers to check your estimations.
Appleton's crewel yarn in the following colors:
   scarlet 1A
   scarlet 4
   black
   elephant gray 5
14-mesh plain mono canvas frame
Size 20 tapestry needles

TIPS FOR UPHOLSTERED PIECES

- Make, or have made, a good pattern.

- Be generous with the canvas size you start with – nothing is more aggravating than a finished piece which is too small.

- Whatever the shape of the area to be stitched, work and block a complete square or rectangle of canvas and let the upholsterer do any trimming when fitting the work onto the chair.

- Start the pattern in the center of the canvas to make sure that the pattern balances on all sides.

- Make sure the yarn is distributed evenly at the back, so that the finished piece lies flat and wears evenly.

- Since the finished canvas will be much thicker than any fabric, in the case of drop-in seats, take the whole chair to the upholsterer so that the drop-in frame can be eased if necessary to accommodate the extra thickness of the needlepoint.

- On a drop-in seat, work an extra ½ in (1.25 cm) of the design on all sides around the area that will be seen.

contrast. A more subtle and larger-scale design can be created with the same pattern and colors by working dark to light and then reversing light to dark.

For a busy décor, Bargello patterns can be worked in very close shades of a single color. To avoid confusing shades for lozenge patterns, complete each area in any one shade before moving on to the next; for flame patterns, complete each adjacent horizontal row in turn. When finishing for the day, either complete the row or leave a threaded needle to indicate where to start again.

The patterns with stitches of varying lengths and directions can be particularly attractive worked in one color, as the light will catch the threads in different ways. (Since dark colors tend to absorb light, medium and pale shades are best for monochrome Bargello).

With all upholstery, choose colors with care, since your work will remain on view a long time, and you need to make sure that it will give you lasting pleasure.

Choosing the scale of your design is as important as choosing the colors. Match the scale of the pattern to the size of furniture to be covered to give the right proportions. A really large pattern on a small item would be overwhelming, and a small pattern on a large piece would look too "busy." In the Kelim Rug, for example, the central pomegranate pattern was increased to give a very bold motif for a large item.

Bargello patterns can be endlessly adapted, by shortening or lengthening stitches or by working a different number of stitches in each group of stitches. In flame patterns, the peaks and troughs can be regular and matching or they can be varied in height, depth, and width to add interest, so that, for example, peaks and curves can be alternated in one row (by working single stitches for the peaks and groups of stitches to form the curves).

▲ *Center the first lozenge outline on the canvas in deep scarlet; continue to work all the circular lozenges and diamonds in the same color for the whole area.*

It is easy to check the work by running a needle from the base of one diamond or circle to adjoining ones – if they are on the same canvas channel, they are correct.

Fill in all the shapes, following the order given in the text.

patterns of a similar scale work best together. With lozenge patterns, random color infill can be most attractive, creating variety within the one unifying design. It is important to work the frame first (in this design, the lozenges and circles would be worked in deep scarlet). The spaces created by doing so can then be filled in at random with colors from the palette you have selected. In this pattern, for example, each flower looks very effective in three shades of one color.

With the frame being one color, it is amazing how many colors can be introduced satisfactorily; however, it is best to keep to either a bright or a muted palette, as they seldom look good together.

Flame patterns can be varied by stitching the sequence of colors in the chosen order and then either repeating it or reversing it. Thus shades of a family could progress from dark to light and repeat, with the palest against the darkest creating a strong

KELIM RUG

Traditionally, all the threads used to weave kelim rugs were dyed from natural materials, so the shades chosen for the rug – deep flames, wine, olive, marine blue, and biscuit brown – echo the shades that would have been used by the original weavers.

TOP LEFT *Antique brown canvas (14-mesh) was a natural choice for deep colors. The pomegranate motif, being the central and most dominant pattern, was worked first, and an attractive cut-off point was worked out before starting the border.*

TOP CENTER *A monogram was planned for the central pomegranate, and by working it in the way shown, it also enabled the pomegranate infill to be reversed from the middle one. At this stage, small areas of a wave pattern (to the left) and a double tooth pattern (to the right) were stitched as an experiment, to see which went best next to the pomegranate column.*

TOP RIGHT *The placement shown here is very attractive with the narrower column of double tooth pattern between the two wider ones. The border between each pattern is echoed in the final border, a simple pattern in bold colors which holds the different elements together.*

LEFT *Each pattern is reversed the other side of the central pomegranate pattern.*

BELOW *A completed corner of the rug showing the main border turning the corner and a double row of sloping Gobelin stitch to complete it.*

BARGELLO STITCH

VARIATIONS

The exciting patterns of Bargello and their relative simplicity to work can probably be thanked for the reawakening of interest in during the last few years. The patterns can be simple or sophisticated; smal patterns can be used for small objects such as glasses cases, needlecases, and large patterns should be reserved for large areas on furnishings, for example.

LEFT *A sampler pillow with eight Bargello designs that can be used individually for numerous other projects.*

BELOW *Bargello is often worked in close colors; mount the shades of yarn, in daylight, on a palette in the desired sequence; the correct shading can then be followed when the light is not so good.*

ABOVE LEFT AND RIGHT *When designing the piano stool, a similar process to the working of the Kelim was followed. The central panel was chosen first and the borders and side panels on each side were balanced carefully both in scale and color.*

LEFT *These pillow were designed and used as wedding kneelers. The Bargello pattern was carefully planned to work in eight directions and to meet in the same way at the eight joins.*

BELOW *The chair and the completed canvas on the left show a dramatic four-way Bargello pattern with the color schemes reversed. Altering the balance of color in this way makes for a more interesting set of chairs and also makes the pattern much more fun to work.*

BELOW *The work has been completed on a square canvas, leaving the corner: unworked so that they can be cut and tucked in when the chair is being upholstered.*

CHAPTER 3

SAMPLERS

E ven before schools as we know them existed, children were taught to stitch alphabet samplers and a whole range of motifs, as a way of learning their letters. They were made for future personal reference, or as a sort of resumé, and were never meant to be displayed. The most common samplers seem to be pictorial, but strip samplers also survive – long strips of evenweave fabric on which patterns, motifs, and repeating designs were stitched. Nowadays, samplers are usually worked to mark a wedding, birth, or other major event.

SAMPLERS · PROJECT 1

*W*EDDING SAMPLER

When stitching, never run the thread behind the canvas from one motif to another. Always use the back of stitches to get from place to place as nothing is more annoying than seeing a thread through the work from the front.

Plan out your lettering carefully on graph paper, as some lettering, particularly script letters, need to be placed carefully. For example, a small "a" will tuck *under* a capital "P."

Allow enough space between lines so that any decenders, such as the tail of a small "y," do not collide with a capital letter or any ascenders, such as the top of an "h."

Preparation

Mark the canvas or linen by running basting threads centrally both vertically and horizontally. (Find the center by folding gently both ways). No further marks should be made, as much of the ground fabric is left unworked and so any permanent marks could show.

MATERIALS

DMC embroidery floss in the following quantities and colors:	1 skein 3046, medium beige
3 skeins 3347, dark olive green	1 skein 3047, light beige
	1 skein 352, medium coral
	1 skein 353, light coral
3 skeins 3348, light olive green	17 by 19-in (40 by 48-cm) piece of natural 29-mesh plain mono linen
1 skein 350, terra cotta	
1 skein 813, light blue	17 by 19-in (40 by 48-cm) frame
1 skein 826, medium blue	Size 24 tapestry needles
1 skein 414, dark gray	
1 skein 415, light gray	

Working the design

The piece is worked in 2-ply embroidery floss throughout.

1 Start with the border, which is worked in cross stitch. Following Chart A, use the darker olive for the garland, the paler olive for the flowers and terra cotta for the four central stitches of each flower.

2 Work the house in cross stitch, centered in the bottom area: work the door in terra cotta, the baseline of the house, the upstands of the entrance steps, the wrought iron railings, and the central areas of the pillar in dark gray. Work the entrance steps and the outlines of the pillars in light gray.

3 Work the window frames and the outline of the house in cross stitch in medium beige.

4 Work the pediments, gutters and door frame in cross stitch in pale beige.

5 Work the roof in cross stitch in terra cotta.

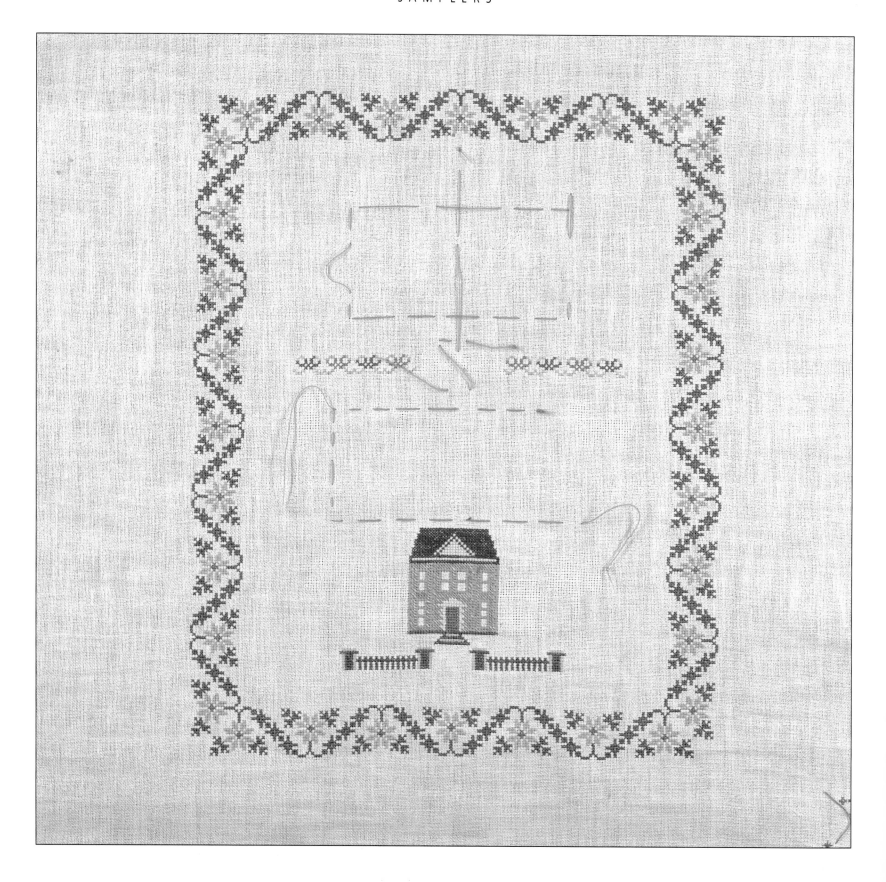

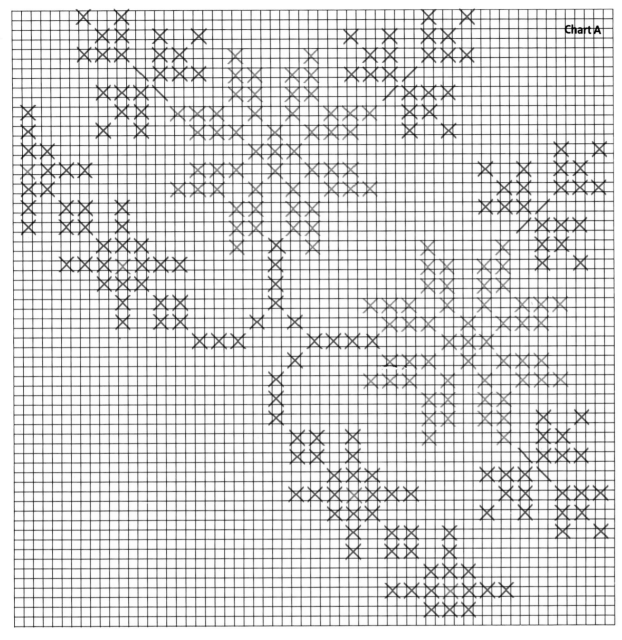

Chart A

◀ *Chart A, a detail of the border,
showing how to turn the corner.*

6 Work the bricks on the house in medium coral in half-cross stitch.

7 Chart the names you want using the alphabet on page 58 (or any other) and work them in cross stitch in terra cotta. If one name is much longer than the other, it is permissible to increase the spacing between the letters of the shorter name. Work the date in tent stitch (see Stitch Glossary, page 144), which automatically gives a smaller scale.

8 Plan and work two family trees, to stand on each side of the house. These trees are worked in chain stitch, in brown, with the leaves in braid stitch in the the two shades of olive, the circles around the initials in whipped back stitch and the initials themselves in tent stitch, both in terra cotta, (see Stitch Glossary, page 146). Vary the family trees as you wish.

9 If you want to reproduce this sampler exactly, work the bows following Chart B, each one in two shades of blue, green, and coral.

10 If you want to personalize the sampler, choose other suitable motifs or colors, and plan and stitch them in. Plan motifs on graph paper, and then transfer the overall dimensions of each one using sewing thread.

If you prefer to work the piece on canvas, 18-mesh plain mono would be a good choice, worked in tent stitch.

Finishing

Check the back for trailing threads before having your piece framed (see "Finishing").

◀ *An interim stage: both the names were counted out and marked on the linen with a basting thread; when the lower name was stitched, it was moved a few threads up the canvas as it looked too close to the roof of the house.*

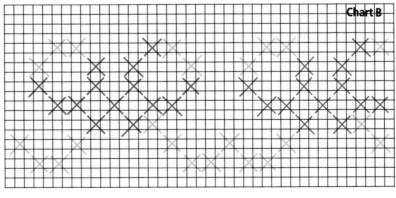

Chart B

◀ *Chart B, a detail of the bow border;
two shades of each color were used for
each bow.*

SAMPLERS

ALPHABETS

Words and letters are a good way of signing or personalizing your own projects. Choose a style to suit your design. You will need small letters for an added detail and larger ones for the focal point of a design. Use graph paper to experiment with variations and colors.

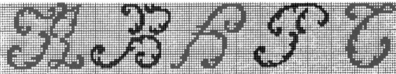

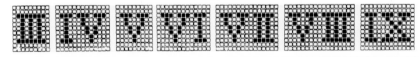

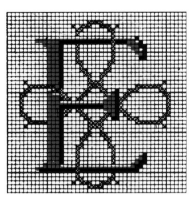

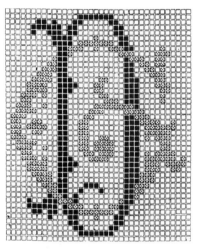

Monograms can combine someone's initials or a message and are a very personal way of decorating a piece of needlepoint. Adaptations can be plotted on graph paper. Monograms can also be enhanced with decorative devices.

SAMPLERS · PROJECT 2

$\mathscr{G}$ARDEN SAMPLER

You can either copy this piece exactly as given in the directions or, if you prefer, work the border, but substitute a view of your own yard or a landscape that you particularly like.

When choosing a different scene to work, remember that, as with all needlepoint projects, a straight-on view works best, and simple elements are the most successful. A pair of wrought iron gates with bushes on each side, variations on arches, with paving stones leading to a flight of steps, or a patio door framed with climbing plants are some ideas you could consider.

Preparation

Count out and mark the border; then sketch out the central scene.

Working the design

It is best to complete the border before starting on the central area where some delicate embroidery stitches are used. The designs are listed clockwise around the border,

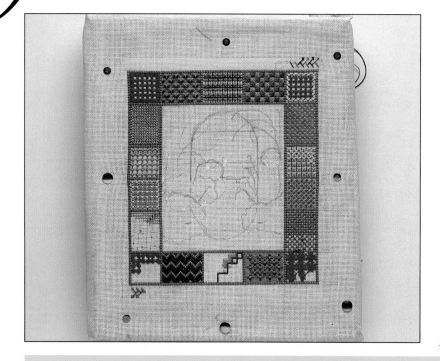

starting at the top left corner, but they can be worked in any order.

Start by working the cross stitch (see Stitch Glossary, page 146) outline to the border "flower beds" first, using 1 strand of medium green pearl cotton.
1 Work the top left corner "flower bed." Work the petals in satin stitch (see Stitch Glossary, page 146), using 9-ply scarlet embroidery floss. Work the base cross of the double cross stitch (see Stitch Glossary, page 147) in 4-ply dark green floss and the top diagonal cross in 4-ply soft green floss. Then work the small-scale Smyrna stitch (see Stitch Glossary, page 147) in 4-ply yellow floss. Note how half

◄ *The border is almost complete, but the upper right corner is not quite right, so it was altered before the piece was finished.*

MATERIALS

For the border: DMC pearl cotton No. 5 in green in the following quantities and shades:
- 1 skein 471
- 1 skein 988
- 1 skein 503
- 1 skein 3345
- 2 skeins 367
- 2 skeins 890
- 2 skeins 320

DMC embroidery floss in the following quantities and colors:
- 1 skein 369, soft green
- 1 skein 986, dark green
- 1 skein 727, yellow
- 1 skein 349, scarlet

- 1 skein 353, light coral
- 1 skein 352, dark coral

For the central scene, in addition to materials left over from the border: DMC Medici yarn in the following quantities and colors:
- 1 small skein each 8507 and 8508, all grays
- 1 small skein each 8307, 8503 and 8504, brown and beiges

DMC embroidery floss in the following quantities and colors:
- 1 skein 743, yellow
- 1 skein 828, sky blue

- 1 skein 841, medium beige
- 1 skein 898, dark brown
- 1 skein 368, medium green

DMC pearl cotton No. 5 in the following quantities and colors:
- 1 skein 842, light beige

12 by 14-in (30.5 by 35.5-cm) piece of white plain mono canvas

12 by 14-in (30.5 by 35.5-cm) frame

Several size 22 tapestry needles (a needle for each color)

stitches have to be worked to get 3 full rows of flowers into the flowerbed.

2 For the second flowerbed, use 1 strand of 503 green pearl cotton for all the groups of stitches worked first in making up the broad cross stitches (see Stitch Glossary, page 147) and 1 strand of 988 green pearl cotton for those worked over the top.

3 For the third flowerbed, work the upright base cross of the double cross stitch (see Stitch Glossary, page 148) with 6-ply dark coral floss and the diagonal cross in 6-ply light coral floss. For the vertical and horizontal stitches, use 6-ply dark green floss.

4 For the fourth flowerbed, work cushion stitch (see Stitch Glossary, page 148) over 1, 2, 3, 2 and 1 threads, using 1 strand each of 503 green and 988 green pearl cotton.

5 Next, work the fifth flowerbed in fans and double cross stitches (see Stitch Glossary, pages 148, second variation, and 147), using 9-ply scarlet floss for the fans and 6-ply dark green, soft green, yellow, and scarlet stranded cotton for the other stitches. Work 3 rows of connected fans in scarlet. For all the other double cross stitches, work the base cross in dark green and the diagonal cross in yellow.

6 For the sixth flowerbed, use 1 strand of 471 green pearl cotton to work the small boxes of mosaic stitch (see Stitch Glossary, page 149) and 1 strand of 367 green pearl cotton for the tent stitch (see Stitch Glossary, page 144). (See Stitch Glossary, page 149, for composite stitch.)

7 Next, work the seventh flowerbed: work the base crosses of the double cross stitches (see Stitch Glossary, page 147) in 6-ply darker coral floss and the diagonal crosses in 6-ply light coral floss. Work vertical and horizontal stitches over 4 threads using 1 strand of 3345 green pearl cotton and, finally, work the French knots (see Stitch Glossary, page 149) in 6-ply yellow floss. (See Stitch Glossary, page 149, for the composite stitch.)

8 The eighth flowerbed: use 6-ply dark coral floss to work the large cross stitches and 1 strand of 3345 green pearl cotton to work the straight cross

stitches (see Stitch Glossary, page 150).

9 Next, for the ninth flowerbed work the Smyrna stitches (see Stitch Glossary, page 147) using 1 strand of medium green pearl cotton and the cross stitches (see Stitch Glossary, page 146) using 1 strand of 471 green pearl cotton. (See Stitch Glossary,

page 150, for the composite stitch.)

10 The 10th flowerbed: work the lazy daisy stitches (see Stitch Glossary, page 150) in 9-ply scarlet floss. Work the base of the double cross stitches (see Stitch Glossary, page 147) in 6-ply dark green floss and the diagonal cross stitches in 6-ply yellow floss. Work half double cross stitches on all four

▲ *Chart A shows the complete design: the embroidered border (1-18) is worked first, then the central scene, and finally the open-work lopsided cross stitch on all four sides with a pinwheel stitch in each corner.*

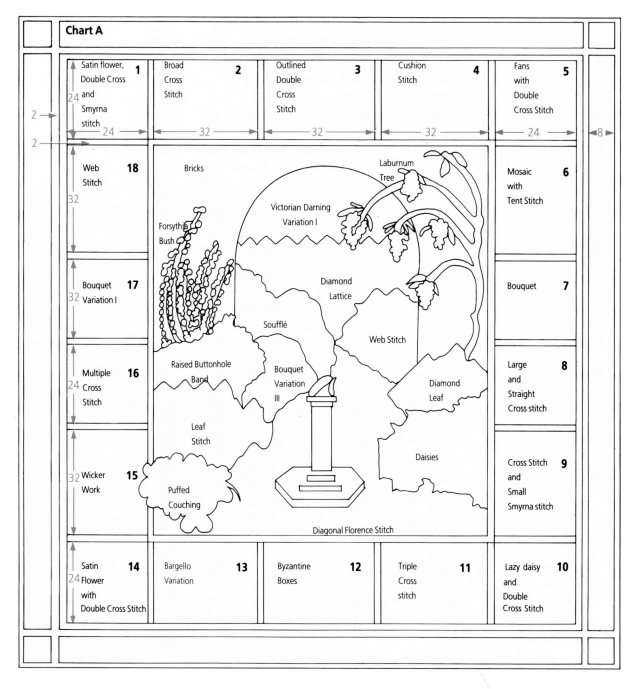

Chart A

Satin flower, Double Cross and Smyrna stitch **1**	Broad Cross Stitch **2**	Outlined Double Cross Stitch **3**	Cushion Stitch **4**	Fans with Double Cross Stitch **5**

Web Stitch **18**

Bouquet Variation I **17**

Multiple Cross Stitch **16**

Wicker Work **15**

Satin Flower with Double Cross Stitch **14**

Bricks

Forsythia Bush

Laburnum Tree

Victorian Darning Variation I

Diamond Lattice

Soufflé

Web Stitch

Raised Buttonhole Band

Bouquet Variation III

Leaf Stitch

Puffed Couching

Diamond Leaf

Daisies

Diagonal Florence Stitch

Mosaic with Tent Stitch **6**

Bouquet **7**

Large and Straight Cross stitch **8**

Cross Stitch and Small Smyrna stitch **9**

Lazy daisy and Double Cross Stitch **10**

Bargello Variation **13**

Byzantine Boxes **12**

Triple Cross stitch **11**

sides as compensation stitches (see Stitch Glossary, page 150, for the composite stitch.)

11 The 11th flowerbed: work the first 6 stitches of the triple cross stitches (see Stitch Glossary, page 151) using 1 strand of 988 green pearl cotton and the small diagonal cross using 1 strand of soft green pearl cotton. Fill in the surrounding area – not working any compensation stitches – in tent stitch (see Stitch Glossary, page 144) using 1 strand of soft green pearl cotton.

12 For the Byzantine boxes which fill the 12th flowerbed, use 9-ply light coral floss for the ladder pattern, 6-ply dark green floss for the tent stitches (see Stitch Glossary, page 144) and 6-ply dark coral floss for the boxes. (See Stitch Glossary, page 151, for the composite stitch.)

13 Work the variation of Florentine in the 13th flowerbed, shown in the Stitch Glossary on page 151, using 2 strands of 988 green pearl cotton for all the rows where the stitches are worked over 2 and 4 threads, and use 1 strand of soft green pearl cotton for the rows where the stitches are worked over 2 threads. Work this pattern in horizontal rows to avoid confusion.

14 Next, work the 14th flowerbed in satin stitch flowers (see Stitch Glossary, page 146) and double cross stitches (see Stitch Glossary, page 147). Balance the colors with the first square worked, for example, use 9-ply scarlet floss for the flowers, 4-ply dark green floss and 4-ply soft green for all the double cross stitches (see Stitch Glossary, page 147) except those in the center of the flowers – work these in 6-ply yellow floss. The use of two different ply for the same stitch makes the center of the flowers more important. Work half double cross stitches on all 4 sides as compensation stitches. (See Stitch Glossary, page 152, for the composite stitch.)

15 For the 15th flowerbed, to achieve the effect of wickerwork, first work upright cross stitches (see Stitch Glossary, page 169) using 1 strand of 471 green pearl cotton, then the vertical and horizontal stitches using 1 strand of medium green pearl cotton. (See

Stitch Glossary, page 152, for the composite stitch.)

16 For the 16th flowerbed, work the double cross stitches (see Stitch Glossary, page 147) first, working the base cross using 1 strand of 3345 green pearl cotton and the diagonal cross in 6-ply yellow floss. Next, work the cross stitches (see Stitch Glossary, page 146) in 6-ply dark coral floss and finally the upright cross stitches (see Stitch Glossary, page 169) in 6-ply dark coral floss. (See also page 152).

17 For the 17th flowerbed, work a variation of the seventh: work double cross stitch (see Stitch Glossary, page 147) in 986 green for the base stitches and the diagonal cross in 471 green, both pearl cotton. Work 4 stitches over 2 canvas threads, all going down into the center, in 4-ply dark coral.

18 In the 18th flowerbed, work the web stitch (see Stitch Glossary, page 152) using 1 strand 471 green and 1 strand 367 green pearl cotton for alternate rows.

Working the center

Referring to the outline drawing, work the scene in the center of the canvas in the following order:

1 The archway in satin stitch blocks with tent stitch (see Stitch Glossary, page 144) centered, in 6-ply medium beige and 1-ply 8504 and 8503 yarn, plus 2-ply dark brown floss for the bricks, worked in a fan pattern to outline the arch.

2 Work random bricks in satin stitch (keeping to a brick wall pattern and leaving some out) down to a midway point of the central panel (see Stitch Glossary, page 146).

3 Work the bush in leaf stitch (see Stitch Glossary, page 153) in 1-ply 988 green pearl cotton. Work whole stitches only.

4 Work the bush in raised buttonhole band in 1-ply 367 green. Start at the border edge and work each row down to fit in with the leaf stitches below. (See Stitch Glossary, page 153).

5 Work the daisies in 367 Green pearl cotton for the double cross stitches and 4-ply floss in 727 yellow, light coral, and light and dark coral mixed

for the flower heads. (See Stitch Glossary, page 153).

6 Work the diamond leaf bush in 6-ply 368 green floss. Start at the top of the area with full stitches, and work compensation stitches at the bottom to fit in with the daisies. (See Stitch Glossary, page 154).

7 Work bouquet variation III (see Stitch Glossary, page 154). Work double crosses in 4-ply 986 green floss. Work vertical and horizontal stitches over 2 threads in 4-ply scarlet floss, and the small diagonal stitches in 4-ply 369 green floss. Tuck these stitches into the leaf stitch and raised buttonhole band bushes.

8 Work the soufflé bush (see Stitch

Glossary, page 154) in 1-ply 890 green pearl cotton and 6-ply 369 green floss for the tent stitches.

9 Work the web stitch (see Stitch Glossary, page 152) in 1-ply 988 and 367 greens for the alternate rows.

10 Work the diamond lattice (see Stitch Glossary, page 155) in the arch, starting level with or above the divide between the 6th and 7th, 17th and 18th flowerbeds. Use 1-ply light beige pearl cotton for all stitches over 3 and 1 threads and 6-ply medium beige floss. Work compensation stitches next to the soufflé and web stitch areas.

terned darning I (see Stitch Glossary, page 155) in 6-ply sky blue floss,

▲ *This detail shows the top left-hand corner. Notice how the stitches for the different bushes are carefully fitted together and the way the forsythia bush is worked over the other stitches.*

◀ A straight-on outdoor view was chosen for the center of this sampler because these work best in needlepoint.

taking the stitches down into the spaces left by the diamond lattice.

12 The laburnum tree is worked on top of existing stitchery. Work the trunk and branches in 6-ply deep brown floss for the basic chain stitch, whipped with 1-ply 471 green pearl cotton (see Stitch Glossary, page 155). Work the blossoms in French knots (see Stitch Glossary, page 149) in yellow.

13 Work the forsythia bush in stem stitch (see Stitch Glossary, page 156) in 6-ply 986 green floss and French knots in the two yellows in 4-ply (see Stitch Glossary, page 149).

14 Work the sundial following Chart B, using 3-ply yarn in the paler gray for the straight Gobelin base and vertical crosses and 2-ply yarn in the darker gray for the small crosses and ties on the vertical crosses and the basket-weave tent stitch. (See Stitch Glossary, pages 156 and 144).

15 Work diagonal Florence (see Stitch Glossary, page 156) in 2-ply of the beige/brown shades of yarn; mix them at random, but keep the deeper combinations for under the bushes (for shadow) and behind the sundial. Do not forget to leave a space for the puffed couching.

16 Work the last bush in puffed couching using a mixed selection of green floss stitched in place with 2-ply 367 green floss. Let the loops hang over the surrounding areas (see Stitch Glossary, page 156).

17 Work the sundial marker in buttonhole band in 6-ply, yellow 727 or 743. (See Stitch Glossary, page 153).

If you plan to have the piece framed, the outer row of cross stitches is extremely difficult to get precisely straight, so work a row of lop-sided herringbone stitch (see Stitch Glossary, page 157), using 1 strand of 890 green pearl cotton and 1 strand of 320 green pearl cotton alternately. Start each side in line with the outer edge of

▲ This detail of the outdoor sampler shows the bushes to the left of the arch, the sundial and gravel (with a darker mixture of yarn for shade under the bushes). Note how the color of the bushes is deeper at the back to add depth.

▼ Chart B shows the sundial, which is worked in straight Gobelin stitch and straight cross stitch.

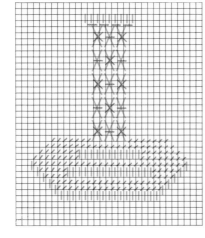

the original cross stitch outlines, leaving the corners ready for the pinwheel stitch (see Stitch Glossary, page 157). Work the first 4 stitches of each pinwheel stitch using 1 strand of 890 green pearl cotton, the second 4 stitches using 1 strand of 503 green pearl cotton, and the 8 tie stitches in 6-ply scarlet floss.

Finishing

Refer to "Finishing."

Variations

Color can help give a feeling of depth, so give this aspect careful thought if you wish to alter the Outdoor Sampler. For example, to place two green bushes, even worked in the same stitch, in different places in space, work the front one in a lighter shade and it will look closer. Notice that the color mixture for the back wall above is done in deeper shades than that used for the front wall to take advantage of this effect.

If you wish to change the colors in

the border, use the balance of colors of the original piece as a guide; that is, use a dramatic contrast in the corners and use another contrast, but probably not so striking, in the center at the top and bottom.

You can work some of the stitches used in the original design or others from elsewhere in the book – use your imagination to decide what is appropriate for the elements of your view. Chapter 6, "Free Embroidery," should provide you with the stitches you will need to make any flowers, bushes, and plants come to life.

To help you choose, bear in mind some of the following points. Big areas can take bigger stitches, so areas in the foreground of a view should be worked in larger-scale stitches than those in the background. An example of this is the bush on the left of the arch, worked in leaf stitch; whereas the smaller-scale diamond leaf stitch is used for the bush through the arch and bordering the path toward the back. You can, however, use the same stitch in near *and* far areas, but work them over different thread counts to accentuate the sense of perspective. For instance, the brickwork around the arch is worked in the same stitch as the wall right at the back, but in different sizes.

Also, balance the scale of the stitches you choose across the design. For example, web, wickerwork cross, Smyrna, mosaic, and tent stitches are all worked over two canvas threads and so balance each other well.

Most free embroidery stitches, chain stitch in particular, look best worked on top of areas that have already been stitched. The brickwork over the arch was completed and the right-hand tree worked before the chain stitch was worked on top.

SAMPLERS

+ + + + +   + + + +

$\mathcal{D}$ESIGNING YOUR OWN

If you want to design your own sampler, you may wish to look at other old and new ones for inspiration, and you will notice that there are two traditional layouts to which most samplers adhere – three horizontal sections: a lower one with a building, a central one with a verse and/or name, and a top one with small motifs, flowers, plants, etc. The wedding sampler is this type. When planning this type of sampler, keep the most solid motif (usually the building) at the bottom. The second layout has one large motif taking up most of the design area – a family tree, a map, or a scene such as the Outdoor Sampler incorporates.

Selecting and balancing the motifs

Part of the fun of working a sampler is to incorporate a number of objects that are relevant to the occasion, and you might like to copy or adapt a few on this page. Always try to balance two motifs that are level on the design with each other; do not stitch an elephant one side and hope that a ladybug on the other side will look right! If you cannot find two compatible motifs, it is a simple matter to reverse something – two angels holding up a garland, two horses facing each other; work out the reversal on graph paper. Similarly, use complimentary colors for items you want to balance; a brown dog will be fine with a black cat, but a pastel flower will not work with a dark sprig of holly.

Borders

Often matching borders run up the sides, with a different one across the base and two narrow ones between the horizontal sections. Changing the border along the base does mean that no difficult corners have to be worked out! Sometimes it is easier to work a large repeat border first (as for the Wedding Sampler) and then center the motifs inside.

Do not choose too straight a border for a piece that is to be framed; select instead a curved outline, again like the Wedding Sampler or an open-work one like the Outdoor Sampler. A border with a dominant outer edge can be tricky to mount squarely against the straight edge of a picture frame.

Colour

Pastels are particularly suitable for a birth or christening sampler. You can stitch some of the design in mixed shades and wait until you know the sex of the baby before stitching the name in pink or blue together with "feminine" or "masculine" motifs, although many parents today appreciate non-stereotyped colors and motifs – judge your audience. Wedding anniversaries can be made more appropriate with a little silver for the 25th, perhaps a border with ruby flowers for a 40th, and some gold stitching for a 50th.

Lettering

Names, dates, even a few bars of music, give even the most simple piece a really personal touch. Plan out lettering carefully on graph paper.

Dates are worth including, although I do think that Roman numerals are kinder on a birth or christening sampler – not quite so easily deciphered in later years; ordinary dates are perfectly acceptable on wedding samplers.

Marking

Plan out the larger motifs on graph paper and then transfer the overall dimension to the fabric again with a basting thread. On a work-in-progress photograph of the Wedding Sampler, the area that the two names will take has been plotted out.

▼ ▶ *Choose the motifs for a sampler carefully and repeat and reverse them as necessary.*

CHAPTER 4

STITCHERY

Stitchery is possibly the most exciting form of needlepoint. It can be defined as "textured stitches that produce geometric shapes and cover the canvas." Stitches vary in size and therefore durability, but all are square- or diamond-shaped, or have a strong linear effect. Thus stitchery works very well in geometric shapes: each stitch fills its area perfectly. In consequence, there is little or no background to work. In the projects in this chapter, you will see how square stitches, like crossed corner stitch and Smyrna stitch, have been used in square design areas, and diamond stitches, like 2-4-6-8 stitch and eggs-in-a-basket, have been used in diamond-shaped areas.

+ + + + + **STITCHERY · PROJECT 1** + + + +

MALTESE TILE CUSHION

Although the stitches for stitchery are almost limitless, it is very difficult to confine yourself to one technique in one design. I do not design like that – if a design requires a stitch from another section, I will include it. Maltese Tile is no exception; while it is mainly stitchery, both skip tent stitch and pulled eyelet stitches have been worked in the original. However, if you prefer to work a solid basketweave tent stitch background to the central square or not to pull the eyelet stitches, it will also be attractive.

Preparation
Mark the center of the canvas and mount the canvas on a frame.

Working the design
Chart A shows the whole design so you can see how the stitched areas fit together. Each stitch area is given a capital letter. Chart B shows the central design area and should be used to see how the stitches fit together.

Start in the center of the canvas and work outward. This means that you will not need to mark the canvas with pencil, which is important because some of the design is worked in skip tent stitch in pale colors, and any marks would show through.

1 Work the Maltese cross motifs, Area A in Chart A. Use 2-ply apricot pearl cotton, cutting the opened-out skein of pearl cotton at one end only. Hold the cut ends of one strand together to find the center point and thread the needle with the folded thread. Although you would usually cut the skein of pearl cotton at each end to obtain the correct working length, in this design two strands are needed for all stitches except the eyelet stitches, so cutting the skein just once makes it much easier to thread.

Start by working the central Maltese cross motifs in four-way Florentine

MATERIALS
1 hank Appleton's crewel yarn, chocolate 3
Pearl cotton no 5 in the following quantities and colors:
   1 skein 754, pale apricot
   1 skein 841, chocolate
Embroidery floss in the following quantities and colors:
   9 skeins ecru
   3 skeins 353, deeper apricot
2 size 20 tapestry needles
14-in (35.5-cm) square frame
14-in (35.5-cm) square piece of white 14-mesh plain mono canvas

Chart A

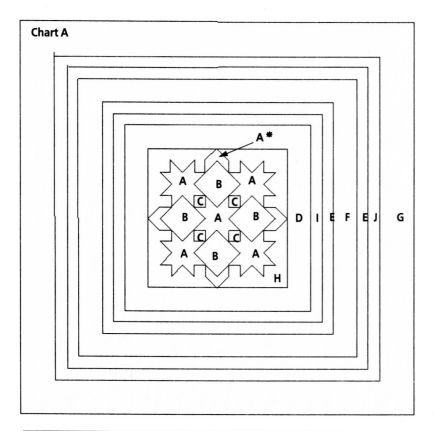

Chart D

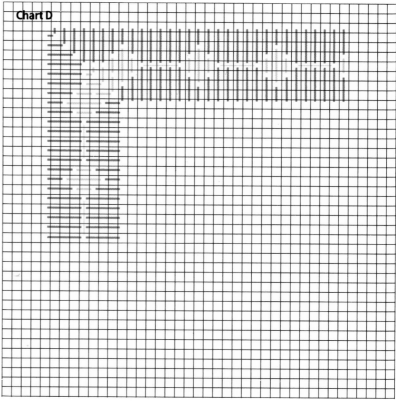

Chart B

◀ *Chart A shows the different stitch areas to be worked as detailed in the text.*

▲ *Chart D shows the border (area D on Chart A) that is worked immediately around the central area.*

stitch over the number of threads shown in Chart B and in the positions shown in Chart A, indicated by the letter A. The four crosses are linked by seven stitches worked in the same color on the outside edges (marked A* in Chart A). Work these only when you have completed all four crosses.

2 Next work area B in Chart A in satin stitch (see Stitch Glossary, page 146). Work a small diagonal star in the center of the diamond as shown on Chart B and surround it with four-way satin stitch. Repeat this for each of the four diamond-shaped areas labeled B in Chart A. Use 2-ply chocolate pearl

◀ *Chart B shows the central area of Maltese Tile: the five stars (A), the four diamond areas (B), and the four eyelet stitches (C).*

cotton for the star and 9-ply apricot floss for the satin stitches forming the diamond. Work over the number of threads shown in Chart B.

3 Work the large eyelets (see Stitch Glossary, page 157), area C in Chart A. Use 1-ply chocolate pearl cotton cutting it in half. Work each eyelet over six threads clockwise or counterclockwise, but always going down into the central hole. Following the order of stitching given in the Stitch Glossary on page 157 will always produce the best results.

4 Work the straight and Hungarian stitch border (see Stitch Glossary, page 158), area D in Chart A. Thread your needle with 4-ply chocolate yarn to work the background of Area D, and 12-ply ecru floss to work the Hungarian stitches. Start the straight stitches at the midway point of one side of the central motif (the point of A* in Chart A), with a stitch over two threads of canvas.

When you have finished working the yarn background and the Hungarian stitches, work a backstitch over four threads to join each of the Hungarian stitches together, using 9-ply ecru floss. Chart D shows the completed border on the right and the vertical section awaiting the finishing touch of the back stitches.

5 Work skip tent stitch (see Stitch Glossary, page 144) in area H in Chart A. Thread your needle with 4-ply apricot floss and work the background area H in skip tent stitch. It is important to have as little thread as possible on the reverse side of the canvas so that it does not show from the front, so never finish off and start a new thread in the middle of a row.

6 Work basketweave tent stitch (see Stitch Glossary, page 144) in Area I in Chart A. Work four rows of basketweave tent stitch using 6-ply ecru floss.

7 Work small eyelets (see Stitch Glossary, page 157) in area E in Chart A.

Using 6-ply apricot floss, work the eyelets as before, but this time over four threads instead of six. Start at the corner of the border to make sure that the row of eyelets fits correctly and follow the stitch sequence given in the Stitch Glossary on page 157 for perfect eyelets.

Count eight threads out and work a further row of these small eyelets in the same way. Make sure that this second row lines up with the first (refer to Charts A and E).

8 Work reversed cushion stitch (see Stitch Glossary, page 158) in area F in Chart A. In this eight-thread channel between the rows of small eyelets, work two rows of reversed cushion stitch using 6-ply ecru floss, slanting each square in the opposite direction to the previous one. When the reversed cushion stitch border is complete, work a single diagonal stitch over each square in the opposite direction to those forming the reversed cushion stitch, forming a diamond shape. Use one strand of chocolate pearl cotton cut in half for each group

◀ *The completed pillow front still mounted on its frame. The back of the work showing how care has been taken to finish threads off in their own area, except for the skip tent stitch, for which the threads have to be finished off in surrounding stitches.*

▼ *A detail of Maltese Tile in another color combination. When planning a color scheme, it is wise to work a segment like this to see how the colors look together in a particular sequence.*

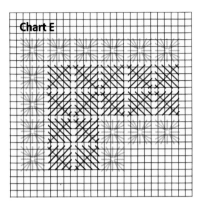

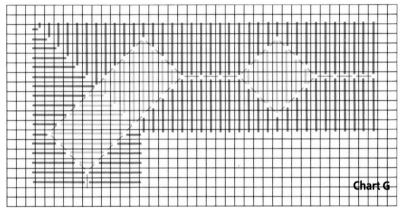

Chart E

◀ *Chart E (areas E, F, and E on Chart A). Work a band of basketweave tent stitch 4 threads wide beyond border D and then work the eyelets and reversed Scotch stitch as shown in this chart.*

▼ *Chart G. Work a further four rows of basketweave tent stitch and then work the final border detailed in this chart.*

Chart G

of four reversed cushion stitches.

9 Work basketweave tent stitch (see Stitch Glossary, page 144) in area J in Chart A. Work four rows in basketweave tent stitch using 6-ply ecru floss.

10 Work the final border, area G in Chart A. Follow Chart A and, as with area D, begin the border with a stitch

PICTORIAL STITCHERY

It is sometimes tempting to incorporate stitchery into pictorial pieces where curves and shading play an important part, but be careful, as a badly chosen stitch can easily finish up looking messy. The only instance in this book where a few textured stitches have been used in combination with a pictorial design is in the Tulip Pillow.

over two threads of canvas at the midway point of the central motif, aligning it with the point of an A* area. Use 4-ply chocolate yarn to work the straight stitches first, and then 12-ply ecru floss for the diamond motifs, working straight stitches over 2, 4, 6, 8, 6, 4, and 2 threads. Note, however, that at each corner you need to work 2 stitches, stepped, over 8 threads to make sure that there are no gaps (refer to the diagram). Use 1-ply apricot pearl cotton to back-stitch a line joining the diamond motifs, each stitch being worked over 2 threads, and to outline the diamonds, each stitch then being worked over a single intersection of threads. Chart G shows the border in greater detail.

Finishing
Refer to the chapter on Finishing for instructions on making pillows, with particular regard to the section on cording.

BOKHARA PILLOW

This design is worked in embroidery floss and pearl cotton in shades of rose. Any other harmonizing colors (all in one color family) could be used very effectively. Another option you might like to try is choosing your own color scheme and working it in crewel yarn. This would not only be attractive, but would mean that you would avoid the task of stripping the floss, and you would not have to lay the stitches so carefully. On 14-mesh canvas, you should use 4-ply yarn for the star and straight Gobelin stitches (see Stitch Glossary, page 145) and 3-ply yarn for all the remaining stitches.

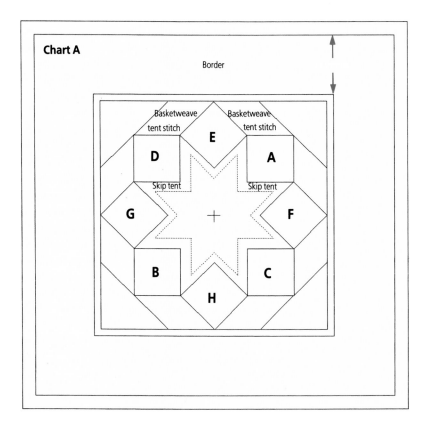

▲ *Chart A shows the way that the different stitch areas fit together.*

MATERIALS

DMC embroidery floss in the following quantities and colors:
  8 skeins 223, medium rose
  5 skeins 224, pale rose
  6 skeins 221, deep rose
  6 skeins 3023, gray-green
  8 skeins 822, stone
12- or 15-ply crewel or Persian yarn in medium to deep rose
1 skein DMC pearl cotton no 5 in 223, medium rose
16-in (40.5-cm) square 14-mesh white mono canvas
16-in (40.5-cm) square frame
Laying tool

Preparation

I suggest you only mark the center of the canvas with a small cross, and count out 20 threads diagonally in all four directions and then mark the inner corners of the square areas. At this stage it is not necessary to mark the canvas anywhere else. If you have not used floss or pearl cotton before,

refer to "Getting Started" for some tips on how to work with it to achieve the best results.

Working the design

Normally you would cut each skein of unfurled pearl cotton twice, once at each end, to obtain the correct working length, but in this design two strands are always needed, so cut the skein at one end only, hold the two cut ends of each strand together to find the center of the strand and thread the folded strand through the eye of the needle.

1 To work the star motif, working from the center out, follow the design as given in Chart B until you have worked the third ring. Use deep rose for the central star, pale rose for the second circuit and medium rose for the third circuit.

The spoon end of the laying tool is particularly good for controlling the

floss and preventing it from twisting. Note that each circuit has extra stitches in the corner, as this makes each round fit together well. Stop when you have completed the third circuit – the final circuit in deep rose is worked at a later stage.

Note: Come up, whenever possible, in an empty hole and go down into a filled one, one with a thread already occupying it. If the holes are occupied at both ends, choose to come up in the hole with the least number of threads in it and go down into the fuller hole.

Each area is 24 threads square, each

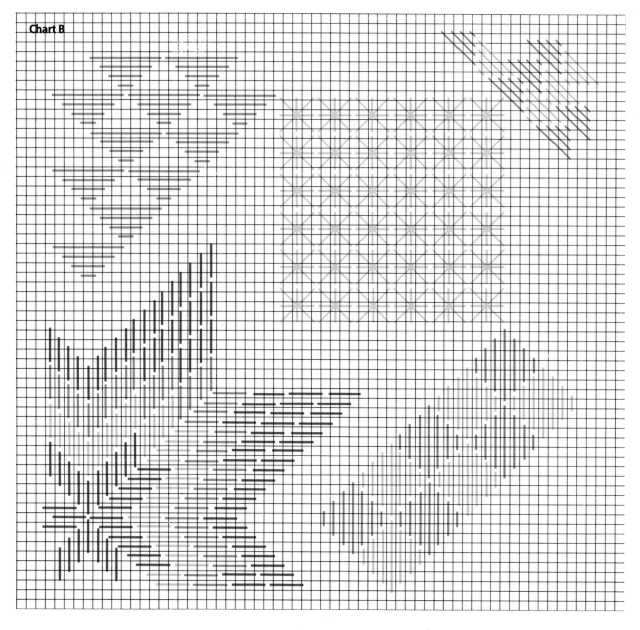

Chart B

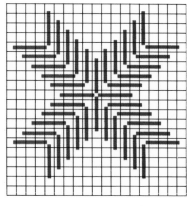

▲ *Chart B shows a corner of the star. Work it from the center up to the third circuit, and only work the fourth when the skip tent stitch area has been completed. Turn the chart around to match the stitches you are working as you do each circuit.*

◀ *This chart shows the central star of the design.*

stitch unit is over 4 threads, so there will be 6 by 6 complete stitches.

2 Work Smyrna stitch (see Stitch Glossary, page 147), in area A of Chart A. Work a 24-thread square in this stitch, using 2-ply of medium rose, as explained earlier, over 4 threads to produce 6 by 6 complete Smyrna stitches. Make sure that the horizontal

stitch of each Smyrna stitch is worked last.

3 Work crossed corners (see Stitch Glossary, page 145), in area B in Chart A. Work a 24-thread square using 2-ply medium rose as before, over 4 threads to produce 6 by 6 complete crossed corner stitches. You may have to change the stitch order given in the Stitch Glossary a little, but make sure that the top diagonal of the base cross is always worked in the same direction.

4 Work cushion stitch (see Stitch Glossary, page 148), in area C in Chart A. Work a 24-thread square in cushion stitch using 2-ply medium rose as before, and, once again, work 6 by 6 complete cushion stitches.

5 Work broad cross stitch (see Stitch Glossary, page 147), in area D in Chart A. Work a 24-thread square in broad cross stitch using 2-ply medium rose as before. I chose to work all the base stitches first so that I could do the base stitches quickly and then really concentrate on laying the top ones beautifully. You may prefer to complete each cross as you go. (See Stitch Glossary, page 147.)

6 Working the background areas. To make things easier later on, the backgrounds are worked at this point. You may have already experienced the difficulty of fitting tent stitch around Bargello or straight stitches when working other designs, wondering whether or not to stitch "under" the straight stitches because if you do not, the canvas shows most unattractively. By working the background first, you will not need to tuck your background stitches under, disturbing your beautifully laid straight stitches. Nor, with the charts here, is it difficult to do the backgrounds first.

To fill in the background behind the star, work both the inner and outer edges of this area, labeled on Chart A, in skip tent stitch (see Stitch Glossary, page 158) using 4-ply gray-green floss.

If you wish to outine the star, use only 1 ply for these guide stitches and then overstitch with the 4-ply when filling in the area – the extra thickness will not show.

When finishing a thread, you would

normally knot onto surrounding stitches, but here you do not have many, so bring any tail ends up in areas that will be completely covered later, such as the fourth round of the star or into one of the diamonds E, F, G or H.

To fill the background outside the square and diamond shapes, work areas S and Z on Chart A in basketweave tent stitch (see Stitch Glossary, page 144, or Chapter 1) using 6-ply stone floss, and match the stitches to the Smyrna stitches that you have already worked as shown on Chart A.

7 Work the corners only after the adjoining areas of basketweave tent stitch have been completed. Work the first row of Milanese stitch (see Stitch Glossary, page 165) in the right-angled corner using 9-ply medium rose floss. Use 9-ply medium rose and pale rose in alternate rows. (The diagram in the Stitch Glossary gives the correct diagonal direction for this corner, but when you are ready to work the other corners, simply turn the book so that the diagram matches the corner you are going to stitch.)

Continue to work the areas of basketweave tent stitch, then a corner in Milanese stitch, until all four corners are complete, and finish the skip tent stitch area behind the central star.

8 Work the final row of the star using deep rose floss, turning the canvas around a quarter as you work each segment. Bring your needle up into a hole occupied by skip tent stitch and down into a hole occupied by a stitch in medium rose. Don't forget that there are extra stitches in each corner, as shown in Chart B, and use the spoon end of your laying tool to produce lovely, neat stitches.

9 Work the diamond shape marked E in eggs-in-a-basket (see Stitch Glossary, page 159), using 9-ply medium rose for the "basket" and 9-ply pale rose for the "eggs". Start the pattern with a stitch over 8 threads sharing a hole with the top right-hand corner of the broad cross stitch square, and work a horizontal row of five full stitches so that the last stitch shares a hole with the Smyrna stitch square.

10 Work 2-4-6-8 stitch (see Stitch Glossary, page 159) in diamond F using 9-ply pale and medium rose in alternate rows. Start at the bottom right-hand corner of the Smyrna square and work the first row down to the top right-hand corner of the cushion stitch square.

11 Work 2-4-6-8 (see Stitch Glossary, page 159) in 9-ply medium rose and Hungarian stitch (see Stitch Glossary, page 158) in 9-ply pale rose in square G, starting at the bottom left-hand corner of the broad cross stitch square and working down to the top left-hand corner of the crossed corners square. Fill in the stitches on each side of this first row.

12 Work 2-4-6-8 variation (see Stitch Glossary, page 159) in the remaining diamond. The basic construction of this stitch is the same as 2-4-6-8 stitch used in diamond F, using 9-ply medium rose for the left half and 9-ply pale rose for the right half. The stitches do not share a hole with stitches on each side: the first upright stitch over 2 threads is 1 thread away from the crossed corners square, and the last stitch of this horizontal row is beside the cushion stitch rather than sharing a hole with it.

13 Work the first row of the border in straight Gobelin stitch over 2 threads (see Stitch Glossary, page 145), sharing holes with the Milanese and basketweave tent stitches already worked. Lay 3-ply yarn along the threads to be worked in Gobelin stitch, and work the Gobelin stitches over it in 9-ply deep rose floss.

14 Work the square crosses in 9-ply deep rose floss. Note that there is one more thread between the corner star and the last stars in each side.

15 Work the surround of each cross in 2-ply medium rose pearl cotton.

16 Work the linking areas between the crosses in 9-ply stone floss, following the chart. Note again that there is one more thread between the last cross in each side and the corner cross.

17 Now work the Continental tent stitch (see Stitch Glossary, page 144) in 6-ply deep rose floss on each side of the stitches just worked.

18 Finally work the remaining infill with 9-ply gray-green floss over 1, 4, and 6 canvas threads.

Finishing
Refer to the chapter on Finishing for instructions on making up a cushion, with particular reference to the section on piping.

◀ *In a border with individual motifs, work the central and corner motifs first and then space out the other ones evenly between them.*

◀ *After the third circuit of the star, work the square areas (steps 3, 4, and 5), then the backgrounds and the corners in Milanese, turning the chart in the Stitch Glossary to suit the corner.*

▼ *Chart C shows a corner of the border. Note (step 16) that there is one more thread between the corner stars and their neighbors than between the other stars.*

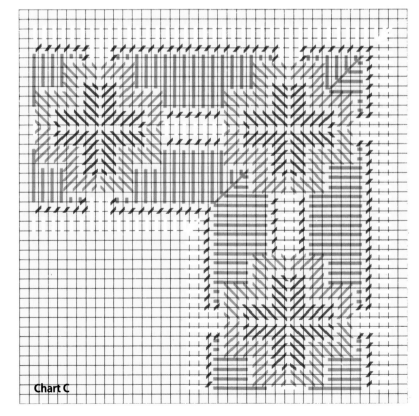

Chart C

STITCHERY

VARIATIONS

In addition to choosing from a vast number of stitches, it is great fun to take a traditional stitch and play with it – work it double size, use two or more threads for contrast, work it diagonally instead of vertically, combine two stitches together, or whatever else your creativity guides you to try. Refer to the Stitch Glossary to spark off your imagination.

LEFT *Cluny has diamond-shaped design areas, so all the stitches used in the areas are also diamond-shaped, i.e., triple cross stitch, 2-4-6-8 stitch and diamond eyelet.*

BELOW *The same design looks entirely different on a different size canvas, worked in different colors.*

ABOVE *A palette will keep your yarns neat and can be used to check the quantities you use. When a half-hank is used, check the area that has been worked to see that you have enough yarn to finish the project.*

RIGHT *Using different fibers, but all in a similar shade of ecru, allows for a large variety of different stitches, making it a very challenging project for an experienced stitcher who enjoys experimenting with many stitches.*

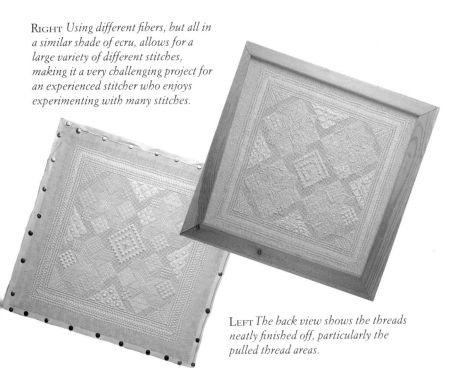

LEFT *The back view shows the threads neatly finished off, particularly the pulled thread areas.*

ABOVE *The two pinks used in the satin stitch flowers in this mirror frame are repeated in the braided border. The garlands between the flowers are used to introduce a new color and are similar to the garlands on the Christmas card in Chapter 7.*

RIGHT *Embroidery combines well with Florentine as can be seen in the throw pillow below.*

LEFT *Two layers of fabric, lace backed with silk, make a beautiful trim for a feminine cushion.*

CHAPTER 5

CANVAS AS PART OF THE DESIGN

The idea of leaving some of the canvas unworked originally occurred to me while stitching a very summery piece in thick white cotton on white canvas. The stitchery showed up so crisply against the bare canvas that even the smoothest tent stitch background would have the effect of reducing the texture I had worked so hard to create.

This chapter explores various ideas for combining stitchery with exposed canvas, but, if you prefer the canvas to be completely covered, the designs can easily be filled in. Some stitches are suggested; all you will need is a little extra thread in your chosen color.

+ + + + + **USING THE CANVAS · PROJECT 1** + + + +

MAYAN PYRAMID CUSHION

This is straightforward and quick to work, and is a good project for those who have not worked needlepoint before. You can work it in a variety of color schemes to suit any room.

To copy the design as photographed, you will need three colors of crewel yarn, all from one family, or two shades of one and a contrast.

Particular care must be taken when running threads from area to area where any canvas is to be left unworked, as they will show through the finished piece.

Preparation

Fold the canvas vertically and horizontally to find the center; mark this point in pencil, and mount it onto the frame.

Working the design

1 Work Rhodes stitch (see Stitch Glossary, page 160) over the center of the canvas over 12 threads using 3-ply green yarn.

MATERIALS

Appleton's crewel yarn in the following quantities and colors:
- 1½ hanks rose pink 2
- 1 hank rose pink 4
- 1 hank early English green 1
- 1 skein ecru pearl cotton no 5
- 14-in (35.5-cm) square piece of white 14-mesh plain mono canvas
- 14-in (35.5-cm) frame
- 1 size 20 tapestry needle
- (1 hank Appleton's crewel yarn or 2 skeins pearl cotton, both in ecru, if filling in the unworked areas of the design.)

2 Count up 8 threads and work straight Gobelin stitch (see Stitch Glossary, page 145) over 6 threads, leaving a gap of 2 threads, in 4-ply rose pink 4 yarn. Start halfway along one side, work toward the right with a long stitch behind the work and miter the corners as shown in the Stitch Glossary and Chart B overleaf.

3 Starting 2 threads out from the straight Gobelin stitches on the diagonal in a corner, work a square of boxes (see Stitch Glossary, page 161) in 3-ply rose pink 2. Whenever possible, come up in an empty hole and go down in an occupied one. Work the cross stitch (see Stitch Glossary, page 146) in the center of each box using 2 strands of ecru pearl cotton.

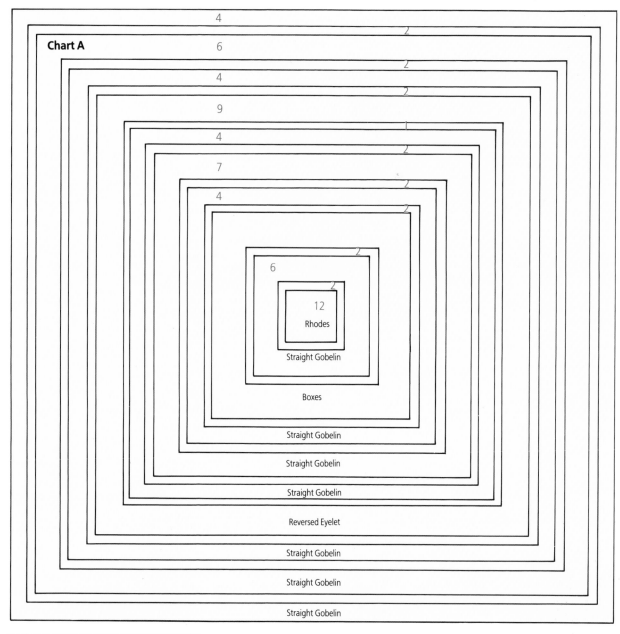

Chart A

4
2
6
2
4
2
9
1
7
2
4
2
4
2
2
6
2
12
Rhodes
Straight Gobelin
Boxes
Straight Gobelin
Straight Gobelin
Straight Gobelin
Reversed Eyelet
Straight Gobelin
Straight Gobelin
Straight Gobelin

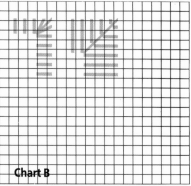

Chart B

▲ *Chart A shows the stitch count for each of the areas. Start by working Rhodes stitch in the middle of the canvas.*

◄ *Chart B shows corners worked in straight Gobelin: on the left 5 stitches over 2 threads share the inner corner hole; on the right, the stitches are mitered, and one stitch is worked over the miter.*

4 Count up 6 threads and work straight Gobelin stitch over 4 threads, leaving a 2-thread gap between this and the boxes, in 4-ply rose pink 2.

5 Count up 9 threads and work straight Gobelin stitch over 7 threads, leaving 2-thread gap between this and the previous using 4-ply rose pink 4.

6 Count up 6 threads and work straight Gobelin stitch over 4 threads, leaving a 2-thread gap between this and the previous row, using 4-ply rose pink 2.

7 Leaving a 1-thread gap, work 1 row of continental tent stitch (see Stitch Glossary, page 144), using 3-ply green yarn. Work from right to left with a long stitch behind the work. When you are working down the sides, do not turn the canvas and continue to work a long stitch behind the canvas. (Marking one side of the canvas on the masking tape will help you to remember which is the top.)

8 Again, leaving a 1-thread gap, work reversed eyelet stitches (see Stitch Glossary, page 161), using 3-ply rose pink 2 for the 24 stitches worked into the corners and 2 strands of ecru pearl cotton for the 8 stitches going down into the central hole.

9 Count up 3 threads and work straight Gobelin stitch over 2 threads, leaving a 1-thread gap, using 4-ply rose pink 4.

10 Count up 6 threads and work straight Gobelin stitch over 4 threads, leaving a 2-thread gap, in 4-ply green yarn.

11 Count up 8 threads and work straight Gobelin stitch over 6 threads, leaving a 2-thread gap, using 4-ply rose pink 4.

12 Count up 6 threads and work straight Gobelin stitch over 4 threads, leaving a 2-thread gap, using 4-ply green yarn.

Finishing
Refer to "Finishing."

Variations
Obviously, some of the canvas will show, so the canvas color should be considered along with the thread colors. For example, white cotton on white canvas looks very fresh; all shades of beige, ecru, and cream look good on antique canvas; pastels work well on natural linen-colored canvas. (If you have difficulty finding this shade, soak the canvas in a solution of strong tea overnight; then pin it onto the frame while it is still wet – you will be surprised how effective this can be.)

If you prefer, the gaps between the rows can be filled with tent stitch or long-legged cross stich (see Stitch Glossary, page 161).

CANVAS AS PART OF THE DESIGN

VARIATIONS

The colour of the canvas that is left exposed has, of course, to be taken into account when choosing the colour of the threads. Clean colours, such as the pink and green on the previous page go well with white; muted colours go better with a linen-coloured canvas, and ecru and corals are attractive with antique brown canvas.

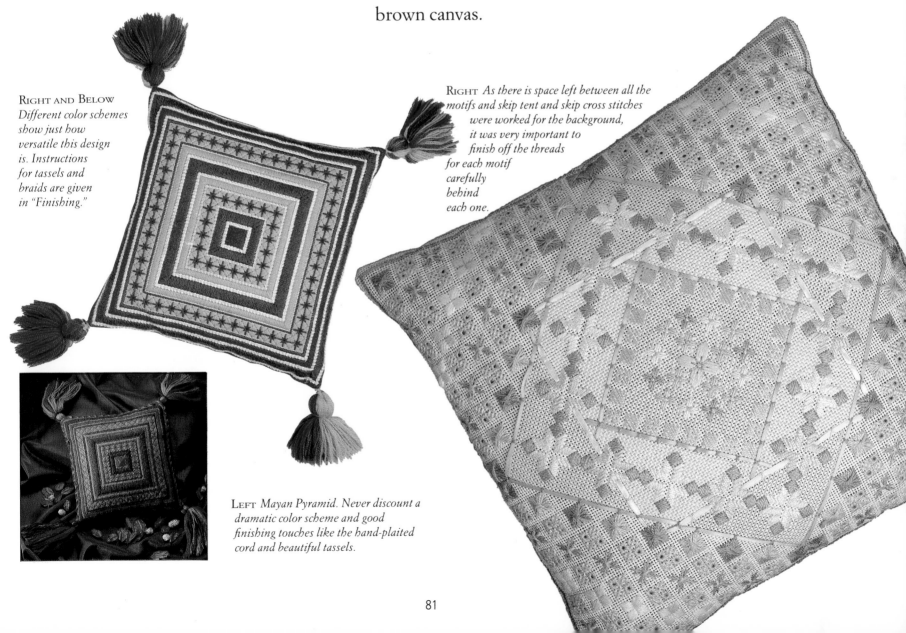

RIGHT AND BELOW *Different color schemes show just how versatile this design is. Instructions for tassels and braids are given in "Finishing."*

RIGHT *As there is space left between all the motifs and skip tent and skip cross stitches were worked for the background, it was very important to finish off the threads for each motif carefully behind each one.*

LEFT *Mayan Pyramid. Never discount a dramatic color scheme and good finishing touches like the hand-plaited cord and beautiful tassels.*

USING THE CANVAS · PROJECT 2

ℬIRD IN FLIGHT

This motif would also work well in other colors or on other backgrounds. For a box top such as this one, initials are good alternatives. For presents you can also needlepoint a message. Simply write a message (if it is long, the area will, of course, have to be bigger than that shown here), enlarge or reduce it to the desired size, and trace it onto the canvas. Work the letters in tent stitch, thickening up down strokes to add character, and refer to page 144 for details on how to connect stitches on the diagonal from lower right to upper left.

MATERIALS

DMC embroidery floss
    1 skein 813, blue
8-in (20-cm) square piece of
    24-mesh white plain
    mono canvas
8-in (20-cm) frame
size 24 needle

Working the design

Special care needs to be taken so that no threads trail behind areas that have been left unworked.

1 Work the bird in tent stitch, (see Stitch Glossary, page 144) in 6-ply blue floss following Chart A.

2 Choose initials for the letter in the bird's beak and chart, and work them.

3 Work the background in Victorian patterned darning (see Stitch Glossary, page 155) in 6-ply blue floss.

▼ *Chart A. In all our projects, the bird was worked in tent stitch. However, the same chart could be copied in cross stitch. The chart could be reversed to give two birds facing each other, making a pretty motif for a sampler.*
    Free embroidery

▼ *The same chart has been followed for these two pieces as for the project, but on different mesh canvas and with different background stitches, they look very different.*

▲ *The terracotta bird was worked on 18-count Aida cloth (it being softer for fitting into the wine coaster) with the background worked in patterned darning. The black version is on 24-mesh canvas; the bird shape is filled with skip tent stitch and the background is Jacobean couching.*

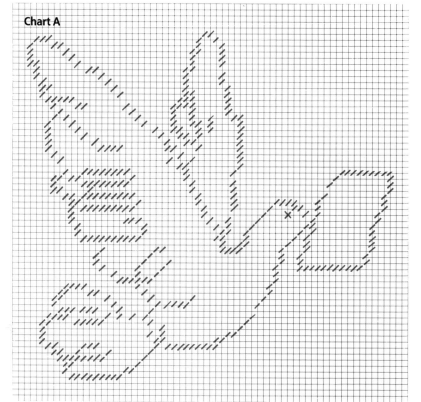

Chart A

CHAPTER 6

FREE EMBROIDERY ON CANVAS

Free embroidery, where the length of the stitches is judged visually rather than by counting out threads, provides all sorts of creative opportunities for realistic representations of a wide variety of subjects and is therefore fun and challenging to work.

The finer the mesh, the more satisfactory will be the end results, as soft curves are much easier to achieve. As with all Needlepoint, it is important to choose the right stitch for the focal point of the design, and to balance this with other parts of the design.

FREE EMBROIDERY · PROJECT 1

TULIP PILLOW

All the tulips are worked in long and short stitch. Therefore, first practice shading the design as described. This will only take a short while and will make your stitching of the piece itself much more enjoyable as you will make few mistakes, resulting in a professional finished embroidery. In fact, the shading exercise will be helpful to you when stitching any realistic subject in any stitch. If you have not tried working long and short stitch before, a little patience and practice is a good idea. Before you start, look at real tulips or seed catalogues for inspiration.

Blending the yarn

Shading calls for gradual changes in tone. Even with two close shades, a number of interim shades can be created. So, as 2-ply yarn and 18-mesh canvas is recommended for the pillow, with two close shades of one family, *one* intermediate shade can be created

MATERIALS

Appleton's crewel yarn in the following quantities and colors:
  1½ hanks early English green 3
  1½ hanks early English green 5
  ½ hank pastel 877
  1 hank flamingo 1
  1 hank flamingo 2
  ½ hank sky blue 1
  ½ hank sky blue 3
  2 hanks off-white
18-in (46-cm) square piece of white 18-mesh plain mono Zweigart canvas
Fine permanent marker
18-in (46-cm) square frame
Size 22 needles

for the 18-mesh canvas. Taking flamingo 1 and flamingo 2 as an example, you would get:
● first shade: 2-ply flamingo 1
● second shade: 1 ply each of flamingo 1 and 2
● third shade: 2-ply flamingo 2.

Shading

The diagram on page 90 shows an outline drawing of three of the tulips. At this stage, it is helpful to trace and color them with pencils. Enlarge or reduce the picture as necessary.
1 Take three colored pencils, preferably three shades of one color (felt pens are not suitable). These pencils will represent the pure yarn colors, i.e., pastel, flamingo 1, and flamingo 2. For ease, call the lightest "A," the middle

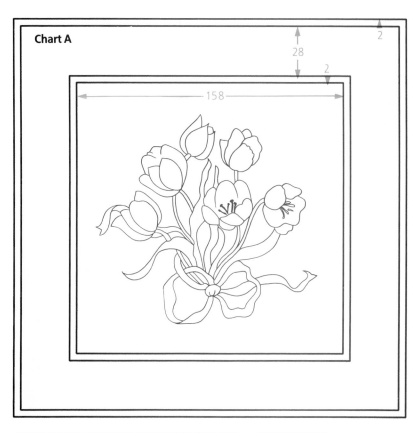

Chart A

▲ ▲ *Chart A shows, reduced, the complete design for the Tulip Pillow. Enlarge it as required.*

▲ *The stages of working a petal, then a flower, in long and short stitch. Note the careful way that the shades of pink are used to give a three-dimensional effect.*

shade "B," and the darkest "C."

2 At this stage you might even like to cut lengths of unblended and blended yarn in the right number of ply, and knot the ends of each strand. Lay them out in the following order:

- 2-ply pastel, which is pencil A
- 1 ply pastel + 1 ply flamingo 1, which is pencils A + B
- 2-ply flamingo 1, which is pencil B
- 1 ply flamingo 1 + 1 ply flamingo 2, which is pencils B + C
- 2-ply flamingo 2, which is pencil C.

3 Follow the diagram, coloring as shown. While you are coloring the tulips, remember:

- light colors tend to be on top
- shades get darker on underneath areas
- the inside of a flower will tend to be darker than the outside.

4 Start with the smallest tulip (at the top right) and take two pencils, B and C (being the flower most in the background). Remember that from the two pure colors, you get three shades – B, C and BC. Color in the whole petal nearest to you in space (the large central one) with the lighter of the two. For the small "crease" at the base of this petal, take the C pencil and make a little area of shadow above this line; this overlaid color is BC. You might also like to blend a little of this color in a small arc on the full part of this petal below the crease (not the edge) to give it a rounded shape.

5 Now think about the two side petals and use B and C, bearing in mind the two small tips right at the back for which you will need the darkest color, C: do not make the two petals so dark that there is no clear edge. Color the two tips at the back in C.

6 Finally, you may like to put one or two heavy dashes of C curving around the base of the two side petals. These, when you come to stitch, would probably be a single ply of the darkest shade of yarn overstitched after the whole flower has been worked.

7 Next, color the open flower. Since you can see both the inside and outside of the petals, remember that the centers of flowers tend to be darker than the outsides. Color the

petal nearest to you first (the central bottom one), and, as you see the outside face of the petal, color the whole area in A, adding some B at the base of the petal as it will be in shadow where it curves under. Do not bring the B coloring too much out to the sides, as you will then lose definition on the side petals.

8 Now color in the two petals on each side of it. Again you are looking at the outside faces of these, so color them in A first and add some B to represent the shadow that forms as they curve under toward the stem. As these two petals are also curving farther away from you on each side, add more B up each of their outside edges.

9 The inside petals are next. As they are darker than the outside ones, color an oval behind the stamens in B. The central back petal is lying on top of the petals on each side, so it will cast a shadow on them. Use A and B to color the central and side petals, adding more B where these shadows fall.

10 Now the only option left to you is A + B for the inside of the three back petals.

11 The third tulip on the left is large and has more petals than the two already colored. For this, we can use three close colors, A, B, and C that, blended, will give five shades alltogether. Think it through for yourself first, bearing in mind the layers, and then look at the diagram to see if you had thought of everything. There is the petal nearest you, one on each side of it, one to the left, two left and right behind, and one at the center back, which is farthest away. The nearest petal will be mainly A, the farthest C, and the ones in the middle blends of B and C.

12 The nearest petal is quite large, so it needs additional shading to prevent it from looking flat. Blend B lightly over about two-thirds of the area, echoing the overall shape; then color more heavily over approximately a third of this darker area, again echoing the shape (this will be pure B when you come to stitch).

13 Going down in layers, the petal on

the far left will have to be in pure B so the two petals on each side of the one just colored can only be A with some B over it representing the shadow cast from the first petal. Then color the petal on the far left in B. Add a hint of shadow in C at the very bottom of the petal.

14 The left-hand petal in the next layer away from you has to be B with shadow in C from the petal in front of it and down each side of the two creases at the top. That only leaves the back petal, which is farthest away and so needs to be colored in the darkest color in your range – C.

The logic of this process will help you tremendously to shade objects realistically when working long and short stitch.

Preparation

Whatever mesh canvas you are using, find the center as described in "Getting Started" and then count out 79 threads in all directions – this square will form the central design area. Then count out 2 threads, 28 threads, and finally 3 threads and mark these points. The 2- and 3-thread channels are for the straight Gobelin stitch, and the 28 threads are for the main "spire" pattern border.

Trace the outline of the bunch of tulips in Chart A and enlarge it to 8 in (20cm) across by 7 in (18 cm) high. Transfer it to the prepared canvas, as shown in "Getting Started," then go over the transferred outlines carefully with the permanent pen.

Finally, prepare a stitching card as described for the Ribbon Bow Box on page 40, preparing a number of lengths of each color – pure and mixed. Knot the ends and sew them to the card in a light-to-dark sequence.

Working the design

1 Stitch the flowers, starting with the central back tulip. Using a size smaller needle, work split stitch (see Stitch Glossary, page 162) along the outlines, stopping short of the base of each petal. (It is covered by the long and short stitches to give a smooth, padded edge to the finished petal). When one petal is outlined, fill the shape in with

long and short stitch (see Stitch Glossary, page 162).

In the open flowers, work some French knots (see Stitch Glossary, page 149) on single straight stitches for the stamens inside the flowers.

2 Next work the leaves. Start with one of the more vertical leaves and use 2 ply of the paler of the two greens to work knitting stitch (see Stitch Glossary, page 163) over two diagonal intersections. Then work backstitch on alternate rows in 1 ply of the darker green so that they sit in the angle of the 'V' formed by the knitting stitches (see Stitch Glossary, page 158).

3 When working the horizontal leaves, turn the Stitch Glossary diagram sideways so that the knitting stitches will be in horizontal rows.

Do not confuse the leaf with the ribbon that goes behind the left tulip and has a "square" end.

4 Work the flower stems in whipped chain stitch (see Stitch Glossary, page 155). Use 3 ply of the darker green for the whipped chain stitch. Work the whipping stitches in 2 ply of the lighter green.

5 Next, work the ribbon bow in Hungarian stitch (see Stitch Glossary, page 158), shading the ribbon as realistically as possible using the two shades of blue.

6 Next, work the border, using 4-ply yarn throughout. Following Chart B, work both squares of straight Gobelin stitch (see Stitch Glossary, page 145) over 2 threads where marked on the canvas using the darker green.

7 Work the "spire" patterns and linking stitches as shown on the chart using the paler green.

Work the stitches in flamingo 2 and in flamingo 1. Work all the remaining stitches in off-white.

8 Now work the background in Victorian patterned darning II using off-white yarn.

Finishing

Refer to the chapter on finishing.

◄ *In this detail of the completed pillow, the delicate effect of the background – in Victorian pattern darning, which leaves the canvas partly exposed – can be appreciated.*

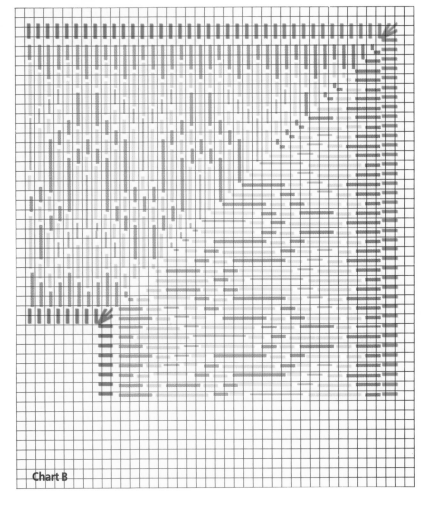

Chart B

▲ *Chart B shows a corner of the border, which is worked in a Bargello spire pattern often called Hungarian point (not to be confused with Hungarian stitch). Establish the pattern using the dark green; take care to change direction along the exact diagonal for a precisely mitered corner.*

FREE EMBROIDERY · PROJECT 2

*T*ULIP RUG

If you want to work this rug without having made the Tulip Pillow, read the notes on shading and practice long and short stitch before you start. Remember that since you are using 14-mesh canvas you will be using 3-ply yarn, which will give you:

• first shade: 3-ply bright yellow 1, pencil A

• second shade: 2-ply bright yellow 1 + 1-ply bright yellow 2, pencil A with light shading of B

• third shade: 1-ply bright yellow 1 + 2-ply bright yellow 2, pencil A with heavier shading of B

• fourth shade: 3-ply bright yellow 2, pencil B. Practice the coloring exercise, bearing in mind that you have two interim shades. You can achieve these four shades with the same two pencils by pressing harder for the darker of the two shades.

MATERIALS

To produce a rug 3 ft × 4 ft 6 in (91cm × 1.4 m)
Appleton's crewel yarn in the following quantities and colors:
  7 hanks off-white
  6 hanks coral 3
  1 hank each coral 1, 2 and 5
  4 hanks bright yellow 1
  1 hank bright yellow 2
  1 hank heraldic 1
  1 hank flamingo 1 and 2
  7 hanks pastel 877

15 hanks bright china blue 7
5 hanks sea green 2 and 5
5 hanks early English green
18 hanks bright china blue 9
40 in x 60 in (1.02 m x 1.53 m) piece of 14-mesh white plain mono Zweigart canvas
Size 20 and 22 tapestry needles
18- or 20-in (46- or 51-cm) square frame

Preparation

With such a large project, you may like to bind the edges (only the two cut ones need it) with webbing tape, machine-stitched into place.

Trace Chart overleaf and enlarge it to 54 in x 36 in (1.37 m × 91 cm). (The garland is approximately 48 in x 27 in (1.23 m × 67 cm) as described

▶ *Variations on the tulip design: here the original pillow is shown, along with the same design worked in soft pinks and greens and adapted for the richly colored rug.*

Chart C

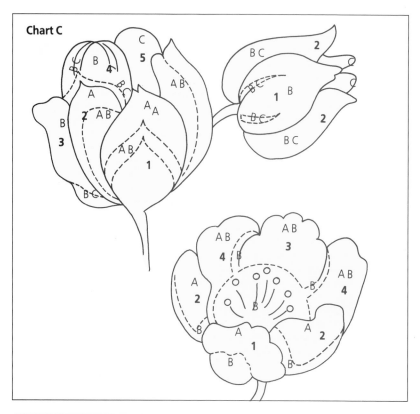

on page 24.) You will no doubt have to copy it in sections and then stick them all together.

For a background color as dark as this, you may like to paint the background a slightly lighter shade of the color of the yarn, which means that the canvas does not show between the threads. White canvas was used because antique canvas can affect the color of pale yarn. (Do not paint it the exact shade of the yarn, since it would be extremely difficult to see it well

◀ *Chart C shows the suggested shading for three tulips. The letters represent the color of the pencils; the numbers show the recommended order of stitching. The broken lines indicate, approximately, the changes of shade.*

▼ *Chart D shows the complete design for the rug. Enlarge it as required. The cross marks the exact center of the design; the numbers show the number of threads within the various sections of the rug.*

enough to stitch.) Follow the paint manufacturer's instructions and be careful not to paint too close to the flowers, as the wet paint can seep into adjoining threads.

Once the canvas is completely dry, find the center of the canvas as described in "Getting Started" and mark a horizontal and a vertical line from this point to the midway point of each of the four sides so you have equal quarters. This is easy to do before any stitching is done and helps a lot when you come to work the border.

Working the design

1 Work the flowers by blending off-white and the corals, the bright yellows and the heraldic, and the pastel and the flamingos to achieve the desired shading. When a tulip is finished, adding 1 ply of a rogue color adds to the effect.

2 Then work the leaves and stems in the same way as given for Project 1, the Tulip Pillow.

3 When you have done this, work the middle background in both shades of bright china blue. There will be a continuous circuit inside which will contain the large-scale Bargello stitch (see Stitch Glossary, page 163) that is worked in the middle of the rug.

4 Change to the small-scale Bargello stitch (see Stitch Glossary, page 163), also in both shades of bright china blue, behind the flowers and out to the marked border line.

If for some reason there is a gap in the garland, simply extend a leaf or stem to give the break line you need; this avoids the two Bargellos joining too obviously.

5 Start working the border at the midway point you marked along one of the long sides, working out from this point in both directions. Follow Chart F, working straight Gobelin stitches in the darkest background shade over 4 canvas threads.

6 Next, work the "spire" pattern and linking stitches, centering a spire on the central mark already on the canvas, in coral 5. These are all the stitches depicted as solid dark lines in Chart F. Follow this out in both directions until

Chart D

you are beyond the tulip garland approximately the same number of threads you are on the long side (probably 12 threads) and turn the corner as shown in Chart F.

7 Repeat for each side and corner until the border is complete.

Finishing

Block the rug as detailed on page 139; then back it as described on page 139.

Balancing colors

If you are going to work the rug or pillow in different colors, be sure to make a copy of the design on paper and experiment with colored pencils to see what effects the different colors have, or alternatively, in the case of the rug, work a loose knot of the selected yarn combinations in each flower head when it is drawn on the canvas to check that these colors will work. Before you commit your time and energy, it is best to make sure that, as far as possible, you will be pleased with the finished result.

Alternative colors and backgrounds

If you wish to stitch in a different color scheme, use any two greens for the leaves and border, two shades of the color (not too pale) for the bow on the pillow, a minimum of three shades for the tulips (whose tonal values are equally spaced – the sample I worked was in bright rose 1, 3, and 5; another good range might be bright yellow 1, 2, and 3. It would be very difficult to blend bright rose 1, 2, and 8, and it is better to take the three close shades and, if drama is needed, add 1 ply of a rogue shade).

There are all sorts of options for backgrounds – as you can see on pages 132-133. Whichever background you choose for the pillow, it is best to decide when you are planning the piece rather than at a later stage. Of course, you may change your mind once you see the design taking shape on the canvas, but there are some important points to bear in mind. For example, if you wanted to work Aili-sia's lace stitch (see Stitch Glossary,

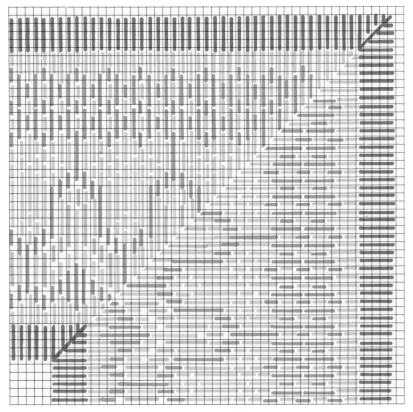

page 162) in ecru pearl cotton on brown canvas, you would obviously have to start out with Zweigart antique canvas. For a very dark background, painting it a shade lighter than the exact shade of yarn you are going to use is recommended (how you do this is fully explained for the rug). Equally, you might like to try a pulled thread background, a skip tent or skip cross stitch background – if so, it is essential that you leave no trailing threads in these areas. Even if you are working a basketweave tent stitch background, if it is a pale color, be careful about dark trailing threads; finish each area off within itself.

Substituting materials

If you want to work either the pillow or the rug design in a different brand of yarn or canvas mesh, remember the following:

● for 14-mesh canvas you will need 3-ply crewel yarn, but 4-ply for the straight Gobelin and Bargello stitches; 2-ply Persian yarn, but 3-ply for the straight Gobelin and Bargello stitches.

● for 18-mesh canvas you will need 2-ply crewel yarn, but 3-ply for the straight Gobelin and Bargello stitches; 2-ply Persian yarn, but 3-ply for the straight Gobelin and Bargello stitches; 6-ply embroidery floss or silk, but 9-ply for the straight Gobelin and Bargello stitches.

● for 24-mesh canvas you will need 4-ply floss or silk, but 9-ply for the straight Gobelin and Bargello stitches. If you want to use yarn, use 1-ply Medici for most stitches and 2-ply for Gobelin and Bargello stitches.

◄ *Chart E shows a corner of the border. Note that you should begin working the border at a midway point of the canvas.*

▼ *In this pink and green version of the Tulip pillow, the stitches are basically the same as for the project.*

FREE EMBROIDERY · PROJECT 3

PHOTOGRAPH FRAME

Photograph frames are very individual and decorative worked in needlepoint. The colors used in this project echo those of the photograph. The width of the left-hand and bottom margins are wider than the other two sides, and the canvas is painted before stitching to give a soft, marblized effect – all adding up to an innovative and attractive finished picture frame.

◄ A few butterflies worked to experiment with stitches and colors.

MATERIALS

DMC embroidery floss in the following quantities and colors:
  1 skein 841, brown
  1 skein 352, darker coral
  1 skein 353, medium coral
  1 skein 754, pale coral
  1 skein ecru
Twilley's Goldfingering WG10, pearlized white
12 by 14-in (30 by 35.5-cm) piece of white plain mono canvas
12 by 14-in (30 by 35.5-cm) frame
Size 22 and 24 tapestry needles
Fineline permanent marker pen
Pearlized apricot fabric paint

Preparation

There are a number of fabric paints available that can be used to paint canvas. They tend to be bold primary colors, but they can always be mixed with white to soften them or make pastel shades. Follow the manufacturer's instructions for applying the paint, but use a fairly stiff brush to stipple it well into the canvas threads for good coverage. The consistency of the paint should be similar to thick cream, and any canvas holes that get blocked can be cleared by blowing really hard when wet or piercing with a fine needle when dry.

With the two shades of pearlized fabric paint used here, test the paint on a scrap of the canvas you intend to use to see what amount works best – you can always increase the depth of a shade if necessary. Allow the piece to dry naturally or as instructed on the packet.

Once the canvas has been painted and mounted in the frame, make as few marks as possible. Use a fine marker pen to mark the flowers and the ribbon in Chart A, outlining the tendrils and leaves with a single line and only the body of a butterfly.

Working the design

1 Lay strands of the white Goldfingering vertically on the section of ribbon that cascades down from the top left group of flowers at 2-thread intervals. The result is long straight stitches (with long stitches at the back) ready to be couched down.

2 Use 2-ply brown floss to work the diagonal couching stitches (see Stitch Glossary, page 156) over 2 threads and the vertical stitches over 6 threads.

3 Immediately to the right of the flowers (before the ribbon twists over), work the same stitch but couch down 4-ply brown floss with 1-ply ecru floss and 1-ply light coral floss.

4 Work the large curve over the top right-hand corner in the same color combination as the left-hand ribbon.

5 Couch down 4-ply brown floss with mixed floss as before, and leave tail at the end.

6 Work stem stitch (see Stitch Glossary, page 156) using 2-ply brown floss to outline all the ribbon edges.

7 Next, work the three flowers on top of the ribbon, using 4-ply floss to work split stitch (see Stitch Glossary, page 162) around all edges and 4-ply floss to work long and short stitch (see Stitch Glossary, page 162) to fill in. Use light coral to work the largest flower, medium coral for the uppermost flower, and dark coral for the lower one.

8 Work the leaves and tendrils in braid stitch (see Stitch Glossary, page 163), turning into split stitch (see Stitch Glossary, page 162), using 4-ply brown floss. Start at the tip of each

leaf, working in braid stitch, and, when the leaf is the right length, continue with the same thread but work in split stitch.

9 Work the four flowers in the bottom right-hand corner in long and short stitch in all the shades of coral in 4-ply floss.

10 Next comes the body of the butterfly you marked on the canvas. Work a bar of raised needleweaving (see Stitch Glossary, page 164), using 9-ply brown floss, making sure any marks on the canvas are covered (a few French knots are worked later as a head, but are in addition).

11 Now, with 6-ply unstripped ecru floss, lay 5 bars on each side of the body that will form ribs for the wings. (Beware, do not be tempted to prepare and work one wing and then try to match the other one afterward – work both in tandem, stage by stage.)

12 Work backstitch using 4-ply light coral floss over these bars as described under raised bars in the Stitch Glossary, page 164. Start just beside the body, and bring the needle up just above the first bar, go back over this bar, under 2 bars, and back over one. Continue in this way until the fifth bar is reached, then take the thread down through the canvas and start again at the bottom. When a number of rows have been done (3 is a good number), work with the same color on the other side of the body.

13 Using 4-ply medium coral floss, work 3 more rows in the same way on each wing.

14 Continue in this way, using 4-ply floss in the following color sequence: brown, metallic (1-ply), darker coral. Pack each row firmly and work half rows where necessary, starting on the third bar, in order to bulk out the wider part of the wings. If necessary, fill in the wings in tent stitch in stronger coral.

15 For the head, work a cluster of French knots (see Stitch Glossary, page 149), using 4-ply darker coral floss and, for a neat pair of antennae, work split stitch using 4-ply darker coral floss.

◄ Different interpretations of the design elements in the photograph frame for you to copy and adapt. You might like to incorporate other elements which reflect the photograph your embroidery is intended to frame.

Finishing

Read the notes in "Finishing" for details.

Variations

For other ideas, look at the borders to the other projects in this book. Most of them could easily be adapted for photograph or mirror frames (in the case of the more complicated repeats, refer to the notes under Backgrounds and Borders in Chapter 10).

When choosing a color scheme, it is generally safest to select either a monochromatic or fairly subdued combination, so that the frame *enhances* the photograph rather than detracting from it. Some of the schemes that work well are tortoiseshell browns and beige and, for black and white prints, shades of black, gray, and white stitching look extremely stylish. If the frame is designed for a specific photograph, introducing some of the colors in the photograph into the stitching is very effective, as can be seen from this project, where the bridesmaid has a bouquet of apricot flowers, and both the dress and the voile curtains behind her are a creamy shade. Both these colors are used in the frame.

CHINESE BIRDS

I particularly like Chinese sources for needlepoint as they often have exotic flowers and birds, which are challenging to stitch, surrounded by tracery patterns that make very satisfactory counted borders. One of the great pluses in both the borders used here is the corner detail which is a typical Chinese feature. Fortunately, it also makes calculating the mathematical areas much easier than it would be if the borders were worked continuously on all four sides.

Illustrated here is one of a pair of panels shown, in progress, on the front cover of this book. The second one of the pair has the central motif reversed. To reverse a design is not difficult if it is originally drawn on tracing paper; all that needs to be done is to turn the tracing over and trace the new design onto the second canvas. It is best to work motif by motif, matching particularly the birds for, even with the most careful record keeping, it is difficult to remember exactly what was done when a whole canvas is complete. Among the stitches used are long and short stitch, stem stitch, French knots, and whipped chain stitch (see Stitch Glossary).

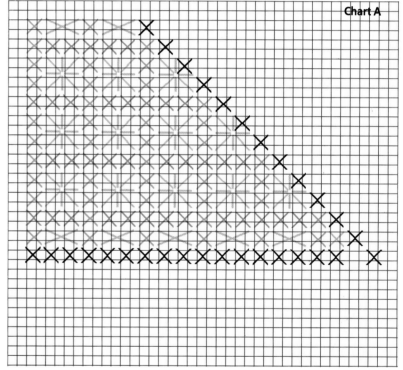

▲ *Chart A shows a corner of the border.*

▶ *The combination of free embroidery and counted thread work echo the free and formal elements in this picture. The colors in the border were chosen to compliment, but not compete with, the central images.*

CHAPTER 7

USING METALLIC THREADS

Embroidery in gold and silver has a long tradition all over the world, which is carried on by couturiers with the use of opulent metallic embroidery in their collections.

For the stitcher, there is an ever-growing range of metallic threads available — cheap and expensive, real and fake — and some are easier to use than others. They can all be grouped into two categories: those that can be stitched and those that have to be couched onto the surface of the work.

In this chapter you will learn how to make three pretty and useful projects and, in the process, the main techniques. I hope that you will continue experimenting yourself.

+ + + + + **METALLIC THREADS · PROJECT 1** + + + + +

CHRISTMAS CARD

There is something very special about making a card for Christmas that you can have as a simple card one year. Then you can add to it and remount it as a more sophisticated panel that can become a Christmas heirloom for years to come.

Sprayed canvas

Make sure that you follow the direc-tions on the particular can of the paint that you buy. If you plan to do a lot of spraying, make sure you take the right health precautions: do not inhale, use a mask if necessary, and ventilate the room you are working in or, do as I do, and pin the canvas on a clothesline and spray out-of-doors. Make sure, too, that you let it dry completely before you start to stitch.

A useful thing to remember, too, is that it is more economical to spray a large piece of canvas and then cut it into the sizes you need for individual projects than to spray little pieces individually. Also, the spray will go on better overall.

Using metallic materials

Only small amounts of each of the threads given under Materials are actually needed to complete the piece, but the quantities given are the smal-lest units that can be bought easily. If you choose to substitute anything in the list with materials you already

MATERIALS	
1 skein DMC embroidery floss 606, red	WG2, red
1 skein DMC pearl cotton 606, red	10 × 8 in (25 × 20cm) piece of 16-mesh canvas sprayed in gold
3 small sequin stars	Gold spray paint
1 spool Twilley's Goldfingering 234, blue-green	12-in (25-cm) square frame
1 skein Madeira, article 9810, color 357	Size 20 needles
1 spool Twilley's Goldfingering	

have, experiment first and watch carefully that the ply and texture you are using give the effect you want.

Working the design

Although all the details are given here to enable you to make the card completely yourself, if you prefer to buy a ready-cut craft card to frame your stitching, you may have to reposition or re-scale all or some of the motifs so that they look attractive in that space. To do this, first measure the opening carefully and mark the shape on the canvas using basting thread, then mark the position of each of the elements. The Christmas tree takes up about half the height of the panel, so mark that first and then position the presents, the swags, garlands, and the bells around it.

1 Work the Christmas tree in leaf stitch (see Stitch Glossary, page 153), using 1-ply blue-green Goldfingering for the side stitches and 2-ply red pearl cotton for the candles. Start at the top of the candle at the top of the tree in the center of the canvas.

(The size of the tree can easily be increased or decreased: simply work more or fewer horizontal rows of leaf stitch. Each row, as you work down, will then have one more complete leaf stitch in it.)

2 Work the tree trunk in straight Gobelin stitch (see Stitch Glossary, page 145) in the same Twilley Goldfingering.

3 Using 1-ply red pearl cotton, work the bucket in cushion stitch (see Stitch Glossary, page 148).

4 Work the horizontal swag next. Stitch a sequin star centrally above the top of the tree and then work the swag out in both directions following Chart A. Stitch the two side stars in place.

(If you want a larger design, these swags could be repeated to the required width and either worked in exactly the same way, descending to even lower stars, or reversed so that the fourth and fifth stars are level with the first.)

5 Work the bells according to Chart A, working areas of dark lines in tent stitch in red pearl cotton and the pale

ones in blue-green Goldfingering. Note the reverse angle of the tent stitch in the left-hand bell.

6 The side garlands: work these garlands (which could be increased or decreased to suit) centrally, following the outside stars from the top down in Madeira. The first 5 patterns have 3 lazy daisy stitches (see Stitch Glossary, page 150) and 2 diagonal stitches, all worked into the one hole, the next 3 patterns have 3 lazy daisy stitches placed closer together, and the side ones have the retaining loop stitch coming up and down into the same hole. The last 3 patterns are just 1 lazy daisy stitch. In between each pattern, work a French knot (see Stitch Glossary, page 149) in the red pearl cotton. The top 5 are worked using 2 strands of the pearl cotton, and the lower 6 have only a single strand, which gives a larger berry on the top than on the lower ones, adding depth.

7 Next, work the presents in cushion stitch and a variation of this stitch (see Stitch Glossary, pages 158 and 165), level with the base of the Christmas tree bucket and centrally on the garlands. (If you have increased the width of the design, you may wish to add some more parcels to fill the area between the tree bucket and these first two parcels.)

If you have followed the instructions exactly, the whole motif will measure 6 in by 3½ in (15 cm by 8 cm).

Finishing

1 If you are using a ready-cut card, simply anchor the canvas in place with the merest touch of fabric glue or attach it with masking tape, which will enable the recipient to remount the piece in a more permanent frame for future Christmases.

2 If you are making your own cut-out card, you will need two pieces of medium-weight cardboard of the same size – one decorative, one for the inside. Placing a piece of rich colored thick paper behind the canvas looks good – I used festive red. Cut the colored paper to the same finished size of both the front and the back of the card. Then, trim the canvas so that it

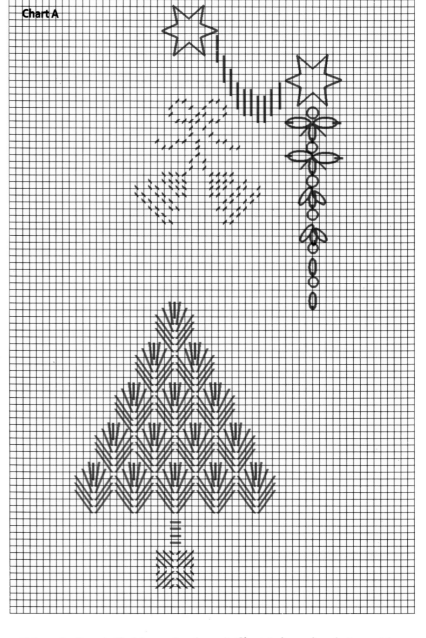

Chart A

will fit on the front half of the card and anchor it with masking tape along the edges; the tape will be hidden by the decorative card edges. Using tape rather than glue, as before, means the recipient can remove it later for more permanent mounting. Now, carefully, with a sharp scalpel, cut a hole 6½ in by 4 in (15.5 cm by 10 cm) in the front of the decorative card, line up the canvas design with the hole, and hold the two pieces of card together with a

▲ *Chart A shows the relative positions of all the elements in the Christmas card.*

decorative cord, with or without a tassel, depending on how fancy you want it to be.

Mounting it as a panel

The idea for the collage remounting of the Christmas tree panel came to me when I heard of a woman who collects

working on your sprayed canvas, because too much unpicking can rub some of the paint off.

It is important to use pieces worked on paint-sprayed canvas in a fairly rigid construction, such as a picture or panel, handbag, or belt – a pillow cover sprayed before stitching would not look good for very long. Also, the paint does not seem to fade, when used in a rigid item. I have worked two of these pieces in the past. Both are now about 12 years old; one is under glass and the other one is not protected in any way, and there is little difference between them; in fact, they have mellowed gently all over, which looks good.

This first project makes the most of lots of imaginative materials: the canvas is sprayed and unusual threads are combined with sequin stars, for example. This is one of the great things about purely decorative items for Christmas – you can use any thread or bauble that takes your fancy! The sequin stars on the Christmas tree are simply stitched on, and when the piece is mounted as a panel, additional beads can be used to hold the stars in place and a cord couched just inside the mounting board. Keep your eyes open when you are in department stores for "threads" of all sorts: you will find all kinds of exciting yarn in the knitting section, for example, and stationery departments have tying tinsel, rickrack and braid. Alongside all the usual beads in a specialist bead shop, you will also find minute silver bells or tiny charms that might look wonderful on another project – if it looks good, use it.

If you wish to use other brands that you already have, please experiment first. The Goldfingering used for the tree, however, is such a wonderful green with a blue shimmer to it – just like the marvelous blue spruce trees – that I would strongly recommend saving what you have left over from this for another project, so magical is the effect. Also, the Madeira metallic thread is quite thin and so is perfectly suited to the garlands, which could easily look too heavy.

▲ *The Christmas card in a different mount. These can be bought ready-cut or made at home.*

attractive candy wrappers and uses them to make beautiful frames, cards, and other decorative presents by mixing the papers together in collages. Gift wrapping has a practical edge over candy wrappers by not restricting me to a small unit size.

An attractive alternative would be a frame covered in patchwork or just one mini print fabric, echoing the colors in the piece. To make it look really good, cover the mounting board with a thin layer of padding such as batting, then cover it with the fabric.

The Christmas card project uses canvas that has been sprayed gold, but there is no reason why canvas should not be sprayed any color you like as long as you use the right paint. Don't

spray canvas you are going to use for pulled thread work, because when you pull the threads, you will expose unsprayed bits of canvas. With silver spray, I would advise taking care because of my own experience: the only time I ever worked on a "silver" canvas, it turned gray and looked remarkably dingy within a very short space of time.

I would also suggest that you work test motifs on unsprayed canvas before

METALLIC THREADS · PROJECT 2

CHRISTMAS PINCUSHION

Straight Gobelin stitch worked over two and four threads is used extensively in this design, so take a careful look at the Stitch Glossary, page 145, to see how to turn the corners neatly.

Also, re-read the section on working and couching ribbon in "Getting Started" to remind yourself of the best techniques for professional results.

One canvas thread is left unworked between each row of straight Gobelin stitch and two threads are left clear on each side of the second and third rows of the ⅛-in (3-mm)-wide ribbon, so check the chart carefully while you are working.

It is essential to buy double-faced satin ribbon, which is turned at each corner to achieve a crisp angle.

Preparation

Find the center of the canvas and mark it with a small cross in pencil. Then mount the canvas in the frame as described in "Getting Started".

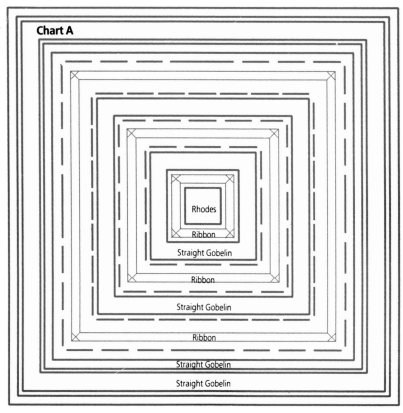

Chart A

Rhodes

Ribbon

Straight Gobelin

Ribbon

Straight Gobelin

Ribbon

Straight Gobelin

Straight Gobelin

MATERIALS

Appleton's crewel yarn in the following quantities and colors:
  ½ hank scarlet, 502
  ½ hank leaf green, 7
1 ball Twilley's Goldfingering, WG2
Offray's double-faced satin ribbon in the following quantities and colors:
  1 ¾ yds (1.5 m) ⅛-in (3-mm) wide cream
  1 ¼ yds (1 m) ¹⁄₁₆-in (1.5-mm) wide red, 250
  1 ¼ yds (1 m) ¹⁄₁₆-in (1.5-mm) wide emerald green, 580
  1 ¾ yd (1.5 m) Offray's decorative ribbon (8304-037-comb-05)
Small interior pad
8-in (20-cm) square piece of backing fabric
8-in (20-cm) square piece of white 14-mesh plain mono canvas
8-in (20-cm) frame
Size 20 tapestry needles

Working the design

1 Using 3-ply scarlet crewel yarn, work a Rhodes stitch (see Stitch Glossary, page 160) over 8 canvas threads, starting at a point 4 thread intersections diagonally away from the center of the canvas so that the stitch is central. See Chart A.

2 Couch the cream ribbon with cross stitches (see Stitch Glossary, page 146), worked over 2 thread intersections, 1 thread out from the Rhodes stitch, leaving 2 threads of canvas between each cross stitch, using 1-ply Goldfingering. Follow Chart A carefully, making sure that a cross stitch is

▲ *Chart A shows the central Rhodes stitch and the thread count for the surrounding squares of straight Gobelin stitch and couched ribbon.*

worked at each corner to hold the ribbon well.

3 Work a full square circuit in straight Gobelin stitch (see Stitch Glossary, page 145) over 4 threads of canvas, 1 thread away from the couched ribbon as shown in Chart G, using 4-ply leaf green yarn. Remind yourself of how to turn a corner for different scales of straight Gobelin.

4 Stitch the narrow red ribbon in straight, stabbed stitches 1 thread of canvas away from the straight Gobelin stitches you have just worked, leaving 2 threads between each stitch. Note that the central stitch on each side is over 8 threads, and on each side of this stitch the stitches are over 6 threads.

5 Count 2 threads of canvas out from the red ribbon just worked and couch the cream ribbon with 1-ply Goldfingering as before with 2 threads of

canvas between each cross stitch.

6 Work another square using the narrow red ribbon, stitching as before but over 5, 6, 6, 6, and 5 threads of canvas each side, leaving a 2-thread gap between it and the couched cream ribbon just worked.

7 Leave a 1-thread gap and work straight Gobelin stitch over 4 threads using 4-ply scarlet yarn.

8 Count 1 thread out from the straight Gobelin stitches just worked and stitch a square as before, but with the emerald green ribbon, and work each stitch over 6 threads of canvas with only 1 thread between stitches.

9 Count 2 canvas threads out from the green ribbon and couch the cream ribbon as before, but leave 3 canvas threads between each cross stitch and a space of 4 threads at the midway point along each side. Make sure, as before, that there is a cross stitch at each corner to secure the ribbon.

10 Count 2 canvas threads out from the couched ribbon just worked and work straight stitches in emerald green ribbon again, this time over 12 threads of canvas at the midway point along each side, the rest over 6 threads with 2 threads between each stitch.

11. Leave a 1-thread gap and work straight Gobelin stitch over 4 threads using 4-ply leaf green yarn.

12. Count 1 thread of canvas out and then work straight Gobelin stitch over 2 threads using 4-ply scarlet yarn.

Finishing

Refer to "Finishing" for details of how to make a pillow with ribbon edging. It can be filled with fiberfill stuffing or a rich, spicy potpourri.

CHRISTMAS STOCKING CUFF

Christmas would not be the same without stockings – some people even receive them from their children. A cuff can be quickly stitched and made into a stocking with ready-quilted fabric. Vary the motifs for each member of the family, stitching red poinsettias with a green trim, a person's name, or the garland from the Christmas card.

◄ ◄ *The canvas, removed from the frame, ready for the selvage to be removed and the upper edge bound.*

MATERIALS

1 ball Goldfingering WG 34, green
DMC pearl cotton No. 5 in the following quantities and colors:
    1 skein 910, green
    1 skein white
½ oz (12.5 g) Appleton's crewel yarn Scarlet 1
Strong red button and ordinary sewing thread
20 red beads
11 by 14-in (28 by 35.5-cm) piece of white 14-mesh plain mono canvas

11 by 14-in (28 by 35.5-cm) frame
½ yd (0.5 m) red quilted fabric
At least 1½ yd (1½ m) red wide (1-in/2.5-cm) bias binding
2 size 20 tapestry needles and a sewing needle whose eye passes through the hole in the beads
15 by 18-in (38 by 48-cm) piece of cardboard for patterne
red and green yarn for pompoms

▼ *A Christmas stocking becomes a cherished possession for any child (or child-at-heart); it is fun to find small presents during the year to fill it with – everybody enjoys unwrapping package. on Christmas morning.*

▶ *Chart A shows two holly leaves; five were worked on the cuff.*

Working the design

1 Work 4 holly leaves in cross stitch (see Stitch Glossary, page 146) as shown in Chart A. Note that half of each leaf is worked using 2 strands of green Goldfingering and half using 2

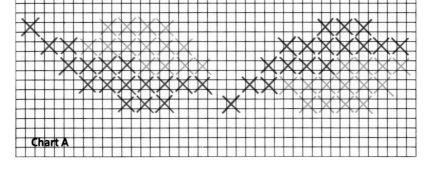

Chart A

strands of green pearl cotton.

2 Work the background in tent stitch (see page 144) using 1 strand of white pearl cotton, filling the area between the leaves and 3 threads above and below them to the same width as the top of your pattern, about 20 cm (8 in) wide.

3 Sew on 5 beads clustered together at the base of each leaf for the berries, using the sewing needle and the strong red thread.

Finishing

Remove the canvas from the frame and block (see page 139). Trim the canvas to six threads below the edge of the tent stitch, fold under half of this (so three threads can be seen) and work plaited edge stitch (see Stitch Glossary, page 164) using 4-ply scarlet crewel yarn, working each stitch over the 3 threads and through both layers of canvas. Repeat along the top edge.

Fold the quilted fabric in half and, using the template, cut out two stocking shapes. Bind the top edges of each shape with the red bias binding. Pin the cuff, right side up, in place along the top edge of the right side of one shape, aligning the top edges of both. Using red sewing thread stitch the cuff carefully to the stocking shape where the upper red plaited edge stitching joins the white tent stitches.

Pin the 2 stocking shapes together, wrong sides facing, and, with the back of the stocking uppermost (the one without the cuff attached), machine- or hand-stitch the binding in place around the edge. Turn it over the seam to the front, making sure that it covers the seam, and sew it in place neatly, either top stitching with the machine or catch-stitching invisibly. Make a hanging loop using bias binding.

To make the pompoms, see page 141; then attach them with a cord or next to the hanging loop.

Variations

For a larger stocking, work extra leaves or insert larger spaces between the leaves.

USING METALLIC THREADS

$\mathcal{V}$ARIATIONS

The use of gold thread in embroidery goes back into earliest recorded history: from the fine apparel of Solomon's attendants to the famous English ecclesiastical embroideries of the 13th century, Opus Anglicanum, worked for the Church, which employed a great deal of both silk and gold thread.

Real gold and silver threads are now extremely expensive, but, there is an ever-growing choice of metallic threads available to stitchers. Experimentation is the only way of discovering which ones are most enjoyable to stitch while giving the best effect.

BELOW *This Chinese panel is silk cloth embroidered with silk and couched with gold. The gold serves to highlight the beauty of the embroidered birds and is also a beautiful part of the design.*

RIGHT This experimental piece was worked purely for the embroiderer's own reference.

A number of techniques mentioned elsewhere in this book are demonstrated – the silk was mounted on strong cotton fabric and, after cutting away the area behind the silk, the whole piece was mounted onto the frame (see Chapter 8). Keeping the canvas or any ground fabric really taut is also important; a sharp needle and silk creates great pressure during stitching.

Numerous different couching techniques are shown: in the top left-hand corner, rows have been couched close together with a stitch taken at the end of each row to guarantee a sharp crisp turn; to the right of these, single string has been couched with the holding stitches made close to the string; below are pairs of pieces of string couched down centrally in the gaps to give a more undulating effect.

Under the leather "button" in the middle, the domed effect is created by three layers of felt, each one slightly larger than the one below.

These abstract designs created with many different metallic threads worked in different stitches are, LEFT, a small picture and, RIGHT, the base of a glass paperweight.

CHAPTER 8

SURFACE WORK

Applying objects, threads, or other pieces of embroidery to needlepoint creates interesting variations in texture. Beads, extensively used in Victorian embroidery, can be used by themselves or with various threads, including metallics.

Counted thread work can be stitched on a finely woven ground by basting canvas to it, working the design, and then removing the canvas threads with care.

A motif or section worked on canvas of a fine mesh can be stitched on canvas of a different mesh to achieve finer detail and a different scale. Threads can be couched around the edges to give a neater finish. And, of course, couching can be used alone or over padding to give raised work.

+ + + + + **SURFACE WORK · PROJECT 1** + + + + +

*B*EADED PILL BOX

Chart A

▲ Chart A shows the four-way Bargello flower for the pill box.

MATERIALS

DMC embroidery floss in the following quantities and colors:
- 1 skein 776, light pink
- 1 skein 899, dark pink

Small package of beads in mixed shades of pink

8-in (20-cm) piece of white 24-mesh plain mono canvas

8-in (20-cm) frame

1 size 24 tapestry needle and 1 size 10 straw needle

Silver-plated readymade pill box

Laying tool

Working the design

The finished size of the piece is 1¾ in (4 cm) square.

1 Follow Chart A, working four-way Bargello stitch using 4-ply dark pink embroidery floss and 4-ply light pink floss. Use the laying tool to get the stitches really smooth for a very professional look.

2 When these stitches have been worked, stitch the beads on individually with 1 ply of light pink floss using the straw needle. Fill the hole in the center of the flower and continue to add beads, clustering them in a small mound (14 beads should be about right).

Finishing

Follow the manufacturer's directions to insert the embroidery into the pill box, but as acetate should not be used on such a raised design, color the small piece of white cardboard that should also be included with a pink felt pen. It will show through the unworked canvas and match the flower.

▶ *The pill box in the foreground is available from embroidery supply stores; however, the other two holders are flea-market finds, a bone napkin ring and a mug.*

The flower worked in beads is copied from one in the Victorian flower picture on page 113, and the napkin ring has small curtain rings covered with buttonhole stitch and ribbed spiders worked on Aida cloth.

NOTES FOR WORKING THE PROJECTS

In each of the projects, an 8-in (20-cm) piece of canvas and an 8-in (20-cm) frame have been listed under Materials; but as none of the designs is more than 4-in (10-cm) square, if you prefer to be more economical, use a smaller piece of canvas and sew the small piece of canvas to an 8-in (20-cm) piece of closely woven cotton such as an old sheet. Mount the fabric in the frame as usual, and then cut a panel from the sheet where the stitched area of canvas will be.

The two beaded designs are mounted in boxes with only a tiny amount of padding under the design and so are worked on ordinary canvas. The Domed Pincushion worked in raised work is mounted in a very domed shape, so Aida cloth is used because it is softer and therefore more pliable. Each of the designs are interchangeable, so if you like, you can work the raised piece, but mount it flat and work it on ordinary canvas.

Quantities given are the smallest amounts that can be purchased, but you should find that you have enough material left over to make other projects and objects.

Needles for beading are very long and fine, and a needle threader (the fine, wire variety is the only one that can be used) is recommended. A fine "straw" needle can be used for larger beads.

+ + + + + **SURFACE WORK · PROJECT 2** + + + + +

*M*UG WITH BEADED FLOWER

This flower has been copied from one of the flowers in the beadwork picture in Variations. Extremely small beads and fine canvas were popular in the Victorian period. This flower is worked on 18-mesh canvas and is twice the size of the original.

▶ *Chart B. Each square on the chart represents one bead attached with a tent stitch. Start with one of the central vertical rows down the center of the canvas and work – in rows – out to each side.*

Working the design
Stitch on each bead individually with silk, using a tent stitch (see Stitch Glossary, page 144), each time, using the chart for guidance on color. For

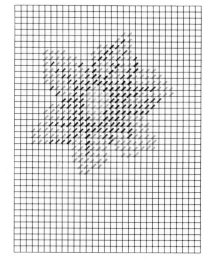

the center, two shades of gold were used on the design photographed, and both are shown on the chart. However, one color is enough unless you already have a few gold beads of different shades. Work in straight vertical rows; when one row is complete, take the needle and thread and run up through all the holes of the beads with one continuous stitch to align the beads and anchor them more securely.

Complete the background with Parisian stitch (see Stitch Glossary, page 165) using 7-ply (1 strand) of purple silk.

Finishing
Stuff the chosen receptacle firmly with batting; trim the canvas to within 8 threads of the finished work, place in position and tuck the unworked edges down inside the rim.

+ + + +   + + + +

DOMED PINCUSHION

Aida cloth is used in this project because a more flexible fabric is needed to fit over the dome and down the sides of the napkin ring. This means that a lacy background stitch can be used, in this case Victorian patterned darning III.

Preparation

Gently push the napkin ring into the block of florist's foam and, following the impression made by the napkin ring, cut all the way through the block. Trim the florist's foam away on all sides until it is smooth; then, gently, with the sharp knife, shave the edges

MATERIALS

1 skein Marlitt 053, turquoise
DMC embroidery floss in the following quantities and colors:
   1 skein 353, light coral
   1 skein 352, dark coral
8-in (20-cm) square piece of natural 18-count Aida cloth
8-in (20-cm) frame
Napkin ring
Small cube of florist's foam
Strip of thin white cheesecloth for lining
2-in (5-cm) square of sticky-backed felt for trimming the bottom
Pack of curtain rings, approximately 1 5/8 in (1.5 cm) diameter
A flat washer
Sharp knife
Basting thread
A number of size 24 tapestry needles

of the top down to form a gently domed shape. The dome should extend about a third of the way down the florist's foam (see Chart C).

Cover the florist's foam with the square of Aida cloth and push it up into the napkin ring (it will make a few pleats, but this is all right). With a needle and basting thread, run a line of stitches around the top edge of the napkin ring, taking care not to stitch into the florist's foam (it will flake). Leave tails at both ends of the thread to help you remove it eventually. Remove the Aida cloth from the ring, flatten it, and mount it on to the frame.

Run a second row of small basting stitches using 2-ply Marlitt approximately ⅜ in (1 cm) outside the first row. Again, leave a tail at each end, as this second row will be used to gather up any small pleats in the fabric, and you will need the tails to help you pull when all the design is complete.

Working the design

1 Using 2-ply Marlitt, start working Victorian patterned darning III (see Stitch Glossary, page 165), across the center of the circle and finish each line outside the inner circle, placing the turning stitch immediately beyond the second circle. This means that the pattern fills all of the area when it is mounted. Finish the threads on alternate sides to avoid unnecessary bulk.

2 When the background is complete,

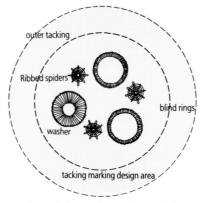

▲ *Chart C shows the stitches and the curtain rings.*

use 1 ply of the appropriate thread to baste 2 curtain rings and 1 washer in place: use light coral for 1 ring, turquoise for the second, and dark coral for the washer. These stitches will not show under the decorative stitches (3 or 4 stitches should be sufficient).

3 Work buttonhole stitch over ring 2, using 6-ply light coral. The stitches going around the curve of the ring will have to be closer together on the inside edge than on the outside. As starting a new thread in the middle of a buttonhole stitch is tricky, use a longer length than usual – 24 in (61 cm) will complete the circuit comfortably.

4 Work buttonhole stitch over ring 1 using 4-ply Marlitt.

5 Work buttonhole stitch over the washer using 6-ply dark coral stranded cotton. You will find that you need to

be even more careful to make sure that it is covered completely.

6 Fill the center of ring 2 with French knots (see Stitch Glossary, page 149) worked in 6-ply (unstripped) dark coral floss, with a few worked in light coral in the center.

7 Work ribbed spider stitch (see Stitch Glossary, page 166) using 4-ply Marlitt (shown as B in Chart C) over 4 canvas threads and the 2 further ones in 6-ply unstripped dark coral floss over 3 canvas threads.

Finishing

Cover the florist's foam with the cheesecloth, gathering it if necessary. Remove the inner basting thread, pull up the second one to gather the fabric enough to fit over the cheesecloth-covered florist's foam dome neatly and make any gathers as even as possible. Push the napkin ring down into place.

Trim the bottom edge of the material flush with the base of the napkin ring.

Lay the square of sticky-backed felt felt side down on the table, put the pincushion on top, and draw around the pincushion. Cut the shape out, cutting fractionally inside the line and smoothing the shape.

Peel off the backing and carefully stick the felt in place on the bottom of the pincushion, going around the edge slowly, easing in all the fabric for a neat edge.

SURFACE WORK · PROJECT 4

INITIALED CARD BOX

The technique of mounting a piece of canvas onto a woven ground fabric, using it to work accurate stitches, and subsequently removing it, is useful, fun, and decorative, without the amount of work usually associated with needlepoint.

Ordinary 18-mesh mono canvas was used quite satisfactorily. However, a special waste-canvas, which is dampened and withdrawn when the work is complete, can be used.

MATERIALS

2 skeins DMC embroidery floss 606, red
1 skein Madeira 5014, old gold
10 by 5-in (25.5 by 13-cm) piece of white 18-mesh plain mono canvas
¼-yd (20-cm) dark green flannel
8 by 12-in (20 by 30-cm) frame
Card box
Size 24 tapestry needles and fine sewing needle
Dark green sewing thread

Preparation

Re-read the sections on stripping embroidery floss and handling metallic threads in "Getting Started".

Mount the flannel on the frame, taking care to place the thumbtacks well beyond the area that will show on the finished box top. Baste the canvas to the flannel in the center where the initials and motif are to go.

Working the design

The less you handle the ground fabric the better, therefore if you are not certain about the positioning of your particular letters, if you wish to work more initials, plan the overall design on graph paper or a scrap of canvas, as unpicking may leave marks on the ground fabric; with a trial piece, you will be able to unpick and/or move letters until you have gotten them right without having to worry about any damage you do.

The pad in the top of the box I used is soft and therefore absorbs any knots behind the work, but if you want to cover a hard box, do not leave any knots on the wrong side as they will make bumps when the piece is mounted.

While stitching, support the fabric as you stitch, placing the index and middle fingers of your non-stitching hand on each side of where the needle is coming up so as to strain or stretch the fabric as little as possible.

▶ *Chart A shows the central motif.*

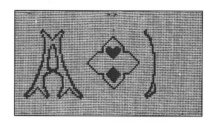

◀ *The canvas basted in place on the flannel with the motif partly worked.*

1 Follow Chart A, here, using appropriate letter(s) from the alphabet on pages 58-59 (or any alphabet of your choice). Start in the center with the diamond, heart, spade, and club motif, working the outline, heart, and diamond in continental tent stitch (see Stitch Glossary, page 144) in 6-ply red

◀ *The diamond motif behind the "A" was unpicked when it became evident that it would not be effective behind the "P."*

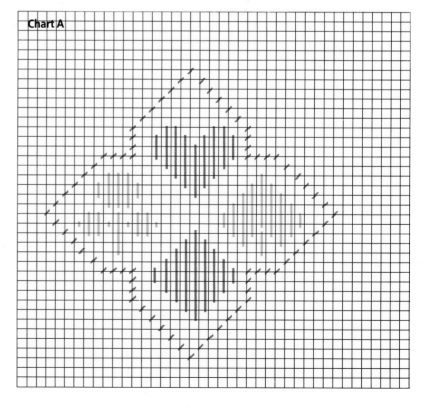

Chart A

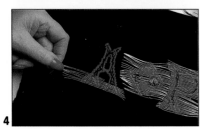

▲ *Unravel all threads beyond letters on all four sides*, **1**. *Then take out vertical threads to left and right of the first letter*, **2**, *cut horizontal threads just beyond the first letter*, **3**, *and pull them out. Continue to remove first vertical and then horizontal threads*, **4**, *around each letter, always leaving a tail long enough to pull on.*

floss and the club and spade using a strand of the Madeira metallic yarn.
2 Then work the letters on each side in tent stitch in 6-ply red floss.
3 When the piece is finished, unravel the canvas, thread by thread, around the design.

Take out the vertical threads on the right of the first letter (next to the central motif) so that there is a tail just

▲ *The canvas threads have now been removed, and the cloth is ready to be wrapped around the top of the box.*

long enough to get hold of. With tweezers, pull each vertical thread out, holding the remaining canvas in place with the other hand so that there is as little strain on the stitches as possible. Cut just beyond the first letter and pull out the horizontal threads from behind the letter. Cutting close to the letter means less drag on stitches and gives you long enough tails to pull for the

second motif when you come to it.

Finishing
Take the fabric off the frame, taking extreme care not to rip the fabric in the process.

Unscrew the pad from the card box, position the fabric centrally on the box, and hold it in place with a few fine dressmaker's pins, and, after checking that it is centered exactly, trim off any excess fabric. With the matching sewing thread and a sharp needle, gather the fabric with one or two rows of small running stitches to help the two curved ends to lie flat and catch them to the lower edge of the pad with little stitches. Then screw the pad back in place.

▲ *The back of the drop-in top of the card box, with the cloth sewn in place.*

SURFACE WORK

*V*ARIATIONS

Three pieces are shown here to give you further ideas for beadwork, from a pillow decorated with less than 250 pearl beads, to a Victorian piece covered entirely with many thousands of minute beads. If you find an old piece of embroidery in a very bad state of repair, but with some beads still attached, you could unpick the beads for future projects – they can add sparkle to many decorative pieces of embroidery.

LEFT *In this Victorian beadwork picture, a spray of flowers was worked entirely in minute beads on perforated paper with an embossed border on the panel. A detail shows the blue flower worked on the mug in this chapter.*

ABOVE AND LEFT *This circular pillow design is a* tour de force *worked in tiny beads, French knots, and continuous cashmere stitch. The stitcher has collected antique beads for many years and has enjoyed using some of them in this piece.*

RIGHT *Antique brown canvas was stitched with shades of ecru pearl cotton, embroidery floss and double-sided ribbons. The design is highlighted with small and medium-sized pearls.*

CHAPTER 9

PULLED THREAD WORK

Pulled thread is a technique that, traditionally, has been widely used in English and Danish embroidery and is usually worked in white thread on fine evenweave linen to produce extremely beautiful pieces. Pulled thread work is, literally, pulling worked stitches so tightly that the threads of the ground fabric are distorted into lacy, open holes. Frequently, it is the spaces created by the pulled stitches that form the pattern, rather than the stitches themselves. Canvas is a natural medium for this counted thread technique and results, rather surprisingly, in relatively hard-wearing pieces.

+ + + + + **PULLED THREAD · PROJECT 1** + + + + +

PINCUSHION

Pincushions have always been popular: in portraits of ladies at a dressing table, there is almost invariably a pincushion. Since pins and needles were extremely expensive, a well-filled pincushion was a sign of wealth.

Pincushions are a perfect gift either for use or decoration. They can be co-ordinated with the décor of the room for which they are intended, or made in seasonal colours like the Christmas pincushion in Chapter 7. They can be stuffed with batting or pot-pourri.

Before you start

If you wish to trim your pincushion with a decorative ribbon, or with fabric that has been pinked, scalloped, or gathered, it is wise to match the stitching threads to the trimming fabric or ribbon of your choice – there are many more shades of embroidery floss available than there are fabrics with just the right combinations.

Working the design

1 Find the center of the canvas and mark it discretely with a pencil; then mount the canvas taut on the frame (see "Getting Started"). To have the canvas taut is always important, but even more so with pulled thread, because since the work distorts the canvas threads, you need something to "pull against" which keeps the stitches even.

2 The surrounding stitches are work-ed before the pulled thread areas. Begin with the padded straight Gobelin stitch (see Stitch Glossary, page 145). Chart A shows the "garden walls" of stitches. Start in the center of the canvas and follow the chart carefully, using 3-ply crewel or 2-ply Persian yarn in green laid under 9-ply

MATERIALS	
DMC embroidery floss in the following colors and quantities: 3 skeins 776, pink 3 skeins 704, green 1 skein white **Yarn (crewel or Persian) in the following colors and quantities:** 1 small skein pink (similar to 776) 1 small skein green (similar to 704)	**¼ yd (0.5 m) ¼ (3 mm) wide white double-sided satin ribbon** **2 size 22 and 1 size 20 tapestry needles** **8-in (20-cm) square piece of white 18-mesh plain mono canvas** **8-in (20-cm) frame**

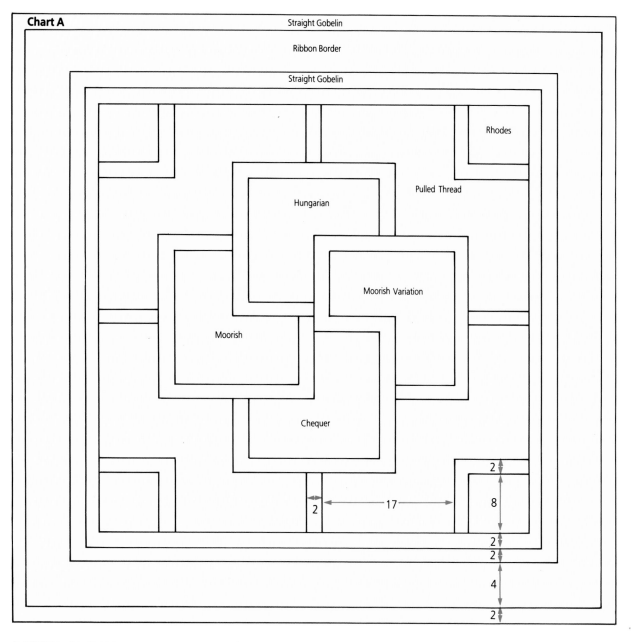

Chart A

Straight Gobelin

Ribbon Border

Straight Gobelin

Rhodes

Pulled Thread

Hungarian

Moorish Variation

Moorish

Chequer

2

2

17

8

2
2

4

2

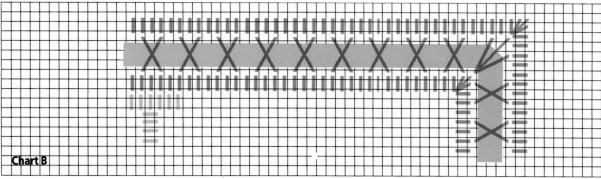

Chart B

green floss for the stitches charted green. Work the pink areas on the Chart in the same way. See the Stitch Glossary, page 145, for helpful tips on how to turn the many corners in this design neatly.

3 Having completed the areas worked in straight Gobelin stitch, work the square Rhodes stitch (see Stitch Glossary, page 160) in the 4 corner squares using 9-ply pink floss.

4 Work Hungarian stitch (see Stitch Glossary, page 158) in the top part of the Celtic cross in the center of the design. Work in horizontal rows in 9-ply floss – first pink, then green. Start at either the top left corner or the top right corner.

5 Work Moorish stitch (see Stitch Glossary, page 166) in the left-hand part of the horizontal bar of the cross. Work the stitches over 1 and 2 threads in 9-ply pink floss and the tent stitch component in 6-ply green floss. Start stitching in the lower left-hand corner.

6 Work the Moorish variation stitch (see Stitch Glossary, page 166) in the right-hand bar of the cross in small boxes over 1, 2, and 1 threads in 9-ply pink floss. Then work the "step pattern" over 2 threads in 9-ply green floss to fit in with the stitches already worked. In each case, start in the upper right-hand corner.

7 Work checker stitch (see Stitch Glossary, page 166) in the bottom arm of the cross, working the boxes over 1, 2, 3, 4, 3, 2, and 1 threads in 9-ply pink floss, and the squares of 16 tent stitches in 6-ply green floss.

Check the back of the work for any trailing threads: if there are any, they must be anchored and hidden in the surrounding stitches. To fiinish very short lengths, try using the "lasso" method: take a short length of any handy thread with no knot in it, weave

◄ *Chart A shows the straight Gobelin "garden walls" to be stitched first.*

◄ *Chart B shows the ribbon couched with cross stitch between two rows of straight Gobelin stitch.*

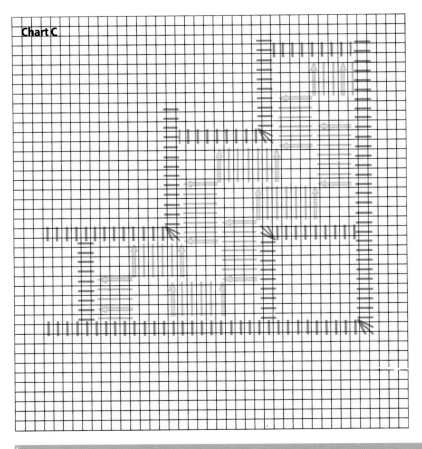

Chart C

◀ Chart C

◀ *Chart C shows the pulled thread stitches to be worked in the lower right-hand corner of the design; follow the arrows for the direction of the stitches. Turn this chart to match the other corners as they are worked.*

through the back of a few stitches close to the end you wish to finish off neatly, wrap the new thread around the end of it – lassoing it – and return through the same stitches, pulling the end with you.

8 Having set up a framework of firm, unpulled stitches, you are ready to work the pulled thread stitches. Use the back of existing stitches to ánchor the thread to be pulled (anchor it firmly, as there will be far more pull on it than there would for a normal stitch). Use 4-ply white floss, double wrapping each stitch. (Read the tips for best results).

Chart B shows the lower right quarter of the design, so work that area first. Follow the arrows in each group of stitches for the direction of your stitching, starting at the bottom left and working up to the top. Then

work from upper right down again to the bottom.

Now work the other areas, turning the chart to match the shape being worked. Where necessary, use the "garden walls" to run the thread along, out of sight, to the next group of stitches. This also keeps the tension even.

9 Between the completed pink "garden walls" of straight Gobelin stitch already worked, couch the ribbon, using 6-ply pink floss to work upright cross stitches (see Stitch Glossary, page 169). Start midway down one side, leaving a 1 in (2.5 cm) tail to the left and couch it down toward the right. The first cross is 1 thread away from the center of the side. Work a cross stitch (see Stitch Glossary, page 146) in each corner to hold the ribbon in place, which is turned over before continuing along the next side (hence the need for double-sided ribbon). When the ribbon border has been completed, simply overlap the two layers of ribbon on the surface and couch down as one.

TIPS FOR GETTING THE BEST RESULTS WHEN WORKING PULLED THREAD STITCHES ON CANVAS

- Use a larger needle than the one normally recommended for the mesh of canvas; it will automatically enlarge each hole as it is worked (if a very lacy look is desired, a stiletto or the point of sharp embroidery scissors can be used to enlarge each hole even more).

- Use *half* the number of ply recommended for the mesh, but repeat each stitch twice – this will give the same coverage, but means the same canvas threads are pulled twice (in the instructions this is called double wrapping).

- Practice unfamiliar or tricky stitches

on a small piece of spare canvas; unpicking pulled thread is not easy. (If stitches do need to be taken out of your piece of work, do it immediately and realign the individual canvas threads before working the alternative stitch.)

- The order and direction in which pulled thread stitches are worked is very important for a beautiful, lacy look, so follow the numbers and/or arrows given in the charts for the best results. (This means you will not have the working thread passing behind a hole, so, when you are trying a stitch

for the first time, play with the order until you are satisfied that there will be no threads trailing under the work. Sometimes it is necessary to make a "holding" stitch into the surrounding embroidery both to maintain the correct tension and to get a new starting point without trailing, hence the importance of working the pulled thread stitches last.)

- If your pulled thread work results in areas that are not as lacy as those in the illustrations, do not worry – the important thing is to keep the tension in each area constant.

- Pulled thread stitches do not work on interlock canvas.

- Monochromatic effects – white on white (see the Pincushion), ecru on antique canvas – tend to work well, but if colors are used, keep the extent small so the stitches are the focal point of the design, as in the Mirror Frame.

- When the piece is complete, consider mounting it on a colored background that will enhance the holes – you will find that quite a strong color is needed for the pattern to "read" well.

PULLED THREAD · PROJECT 2

MIRROR FRAME

This second project is first and foremost an attractive decorative item that can be copied exactly or made larger or smaller according to your requirements. The mirror is useful and can be an eyecatching addition to a guest bathroom, a hall, or a bedroom. The finished size, following the directions below, is approximately 14 in (35.5 cm). At the end of the instructions for making the project are notes that will help you adjust the size of the mirror, and at the end of the chapter, there are more ideas for using the design in other ways, for example, worked with a central panel to make a lovely pillow cover front, a panel to hang on the wall, or a tray insert, protected with glass or plastic. Refresh your memory on handling and preparing embroidery floss, pearl cotton, and metallic threads by re-reading the pages in "Getting Started."

MATERIALS

4⅜ yd (4 m) ½-in (9 mm) wide jade Offray double-sided satin ribbon
5 skeins Marlitt 811, green
DMC embroidery floss in the following quantities and colors:
　　5 skeins 964, light turquoise
　　5 skeins 958, dark turquoise
　　5 skeins 701, green
DMC pearl cotton no. 5 in the following quantities and colors:
　　4 skeins 336, navy
　　3 skeins Balger 019 08, pewter
18-in (47-cm) square piece of 18-mesh white plain mono canvas
18-in (47-cm) frame
1 size 22 tapestry needle
1 size 20 needle
1 sharp sewing needle
Basting thread
16½ by 17 in (41 by 43 cm) mirror
Clear, strong glue

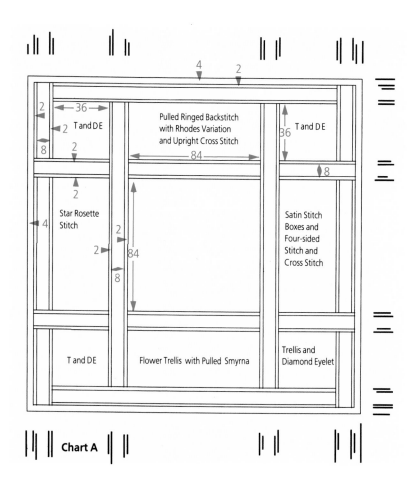

Chart A

36
2
T and DE
Pulled Ringed Backstitch with Rhodes Variation and Upright Cross Stitch
84
T and DE
8
Star Rosette Stitch
Satin Stitch Boxes and Four-sided Stitch and Cross Stitch
84
T and DE
Flower Trellis with Pulled Smyrna
Trellis and Diamond Eyelet

Preparation

When you mount the canvas in the frame be extra careful to stretch it really tightly, as this is especially important for good results in pulled thread work.

A great deal of the design is worked in pulled thread and in pale colors, so marking the design areas where they will be worked is not practical. Chart A shows the pattern that the ribbons and the long-legged cross stitch on each side of them makes; this is the framework of the design. Notice the marks *beyond* the design with thread counts in between. Make these marks on the edges of your taut, mounted canvas with a hard pencil or permanent marker that you have tested and is definitely waterproof.

◀ *Chart A shows the marks that should be made outside the design area in order to demarcate the canvas correctly without making marks which would show when the work is finished. The numbers give the thread count for each part of the design.*

Working the design

1 Cut 8 lengths of the ribbon, each 15 in (38 cm) long. Stretch out all the horizontal ribbons in their positions first, basting the ends to the canvas with a sharp needle and some sewing thread in the center of the "off stage" 8-thread tramlines. When the ribbons are mounted in one direction, turn the canvas and mount the others, weaving them over and under each other as shown in the layout diagram. When all the ribbons have been mounted, held taut at each end in this way, they will naturally follow the line of the canvas.

2 Using 2-ply Balger, work spaced Cretan stitch (see Stitch Glossary, page 167) along the length of one ribbon at a time, not stitching the areas where that particular ribbon passes under another. It is easiest first to work the ribbon that does not go under others very much. As soon as one ribbon is secured to the canvas, work the row of long-legged cross stitch (see Step 3) along each side of it. Refer to Chart B for how to work spaced Cretan stitch where the ribbons intersect. It is important to note that the needle goes *down* into the outer edge of the ribbon channel and *up* 1 thread inside it.

3 Work a row of long-legged cross stitch (see Stitch Glossary, page 161) on each side of the ribbon in the 2-thread channels, stopping the stitch when the ribbon goes under another one and stitching into the ribbon when it goes over another one, as shown in Chart C. Use a strand of Marlitt (4-ply, stripped and dampened). At this stage, a laying tool is useful to help you get each stitch worked in embroidery floss really smooth.

4 Work trellis stitch, without pulling, and pulled diamond eyelet stitch (see Stitch Glossary, page 167) together. Use 12-ply lighter turquoise floss for the trellis stitches and 4-ply darker turquoise floss for the pulled diamond eyelet stitches.

Work the pulled diamond eyelet stitches with 8 stitches down into the central hole, starting with the top vertical stitch and working clockwise around the diamond. Double wrap

each stitch as it is made, to give a really good pull and to keep the tension constant. When one eyelet is complete, move horizontally on to the next one, running the thread through the existing trellis stitches to avoid trailing it behind any lacy holes and again to hold the tension.

5 Work satin stitch boxes, four-sided stitch and cross stitch combination (see Stitch Glossary, page 168) on the right-hand side of the design. Use 6-ply light turquoise floss to double wrap the satin stitch boxes and 4-ply dark turquoise floss to double wrap the four-sided stitch and cross stitch. Work the satin stitch boxes first, then the four-sided stitches, with the cross stitch in the center of each box. Pull all the stitches firmly.

6 Work pulled ringed backstitch, pulled cushion stitch, and upright cross stitch, (see Stitch Glossary, pages 168, 170, and 169) along the top panel of the design. Use 6-ply light turquoise floss to double wrap the ringed back-stitches, worked over 3 threads (to fit the stitches properly into this area, start the ringed backstitch with stitch 5 and 6 – see Stitch Glossary diagram, page 168 – so that it will balance at each end; examine the photograph on the previous page where it is clearly visible in the top segment), 6-ply dark turquoise floss for the Rhodes variation stitches (see Stitch Glossary, page 160), worked over 4-threads, not pulled, and 6-ply dark turquoise for the upright cross stitches, worked over 2 threads, not pulled.

7 Work flower trellis stitch with pulled Smyrna stitch (see Stitch Glossary, page 170) along the bottom panel of the design. Use 4-ply light turquoise

▶ *Chart B shows the method of working spaced Cretan stitch over ribbon. Note that the stitch is interrupted where one ribbon will be crossed by another.*

▶ *Chart C shows the stitches in the top right-hand corner of the mirror.*

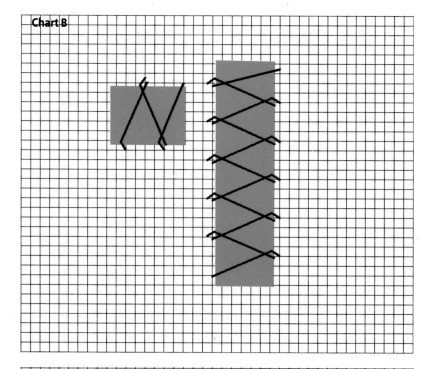

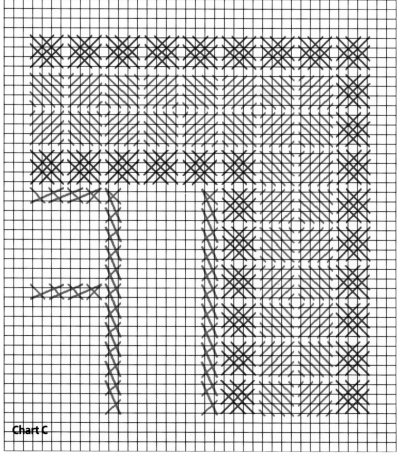

floss to double wrap the upright crosses and 4-ply dark turquoise floss to double wrap the Smyrna stitches.

8 Work star rosette stitch (see Stitch Glossary, page 170) in the left-hand panel of the design. Use 4-ply light turquoise floss to double wrap the stitches numbered in the diagram in the Stitch Glossary and 4-ply dark turquoise floss to double wrap the stitches given letters in the diagram.

9 Work the broad cross stitch (see Stitch Glossary, page 147) border using 1 strand navy pearl cotton. Work a single row of broad cross stitch over the 4 threads marked on all 4 sides of the existing design, trimming off the excess jade ribbon as you reach each end of ribbon so that they are hidden under the stitches and held in place by them. Using the sharp needle for these stitches will enable you to pierce these ends and thus hold them in place.

10 Count 8 threads out and work a second row of broad cross stitches using 1 strand of navy pearl cotton.

11 In the 8-thread channel, work 2 rows of pulled cushion stitch (see Stitch Glossary, page 170), using 6-ply green floss, single wrapped. Work each pulled cushion stitch square over 4 threads and alternate the direction of the diagonal stitches.

12 Finally, work 3 rows in basketweave tent stitch using 1 strand of navy pearl cotton along all 4 sides to give the framer smooth stitches to lay the mount over.

Finishing

Remove the finished canvas from the frame and cut a hole in the central unworked area 16 threads square. Make four straight cuts from this hole out to the middle of the inside edges of the worked area. Unravel the canvas threads back to the embroidered edges and, threading each canvas thread in turn, weave them back into the back of the stitches on each side of the ribbon and then trim them off neatly.

Take off the masking tape from the edges of the canvas and trim the canvas (if it is more than 12 threads) on all sides.

Apply glue very sparingly to the back of all the ribbon areas and wherever there are solid stitches; then carefully lay the canvas centrally on the mirror. The mirror in this instance replaces the board that is normally recommended for pictures or panels.

Once the glue has dried, glue thin board or strong paper to the back of the mirror to protect it, as any scratches on the back will show on the front. Once this has dried, the mirror can have the mount added.

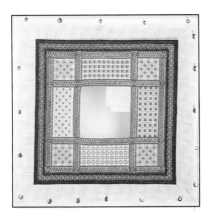

▲ *Finishing the inner edges. First, a small square 16 threads wide and deep is cut away; then the canvas is cut into four quarters; here three of the quarters have been finished.*

▼ *Here the canvas threads are being unwoven.*

▼ *The canvas threads are darned into the back of the work. The long ends are then trimmed.*

PULLED THREAD WORK

$\mathcal{V}$ARIATIONS

These motifs can be worked in a variety of different stitches, which must be carefully chosen to compliment the border stitches. Depending on the motif you want to work in the center of the shape, you may need to change the shape and size of the border and center. Make a pattern and plot the thread count on graph paper.

Adapting the mirror frame design for other projects is fun. Motifs can be worked in the center to make a pillow cover or tray insert.
RIGHT An experimental drawn thread center. In drawn thread work, the threads are cut and removed. Before the threads that are to be removed can be cut, it is necessary to surround them with firm stitchery to hold the remaining threads in place.

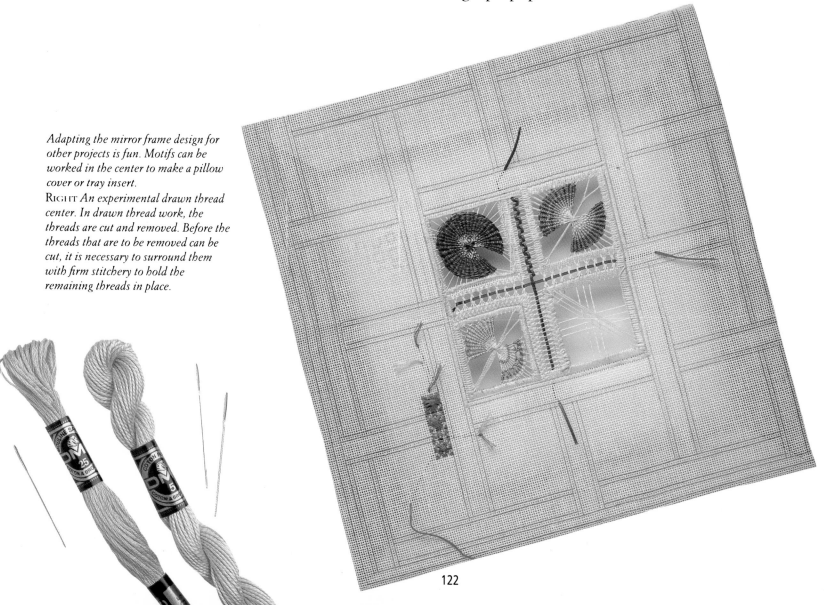

The butterfly motif (LEFT) is worked using traditional canvas stitches and free embroidery stitches.

The petals in the flower motif (ABOVE, LEFT) are good examples of pulled thread stitches, as is the lacy patterned darning stitch worked as the background. To define the flower, outline stitch is used (it also serves to cover any pen or pencil marks).

ABOVE Two variations of the first project in this chapter.

CHAPTER 10

DESIGNING YOUR OWN NEEDLEPOINT

There are times when you cannot find a design in a book or as a kit that is exactly what you are looking for, or when you want to make something really personal. It may be a present, it may be something to go in a room where you want to adapt or coordinate with an existing fabric; it may be that you want to make something that appeals and you want to experiment. What is the best way to go about it?

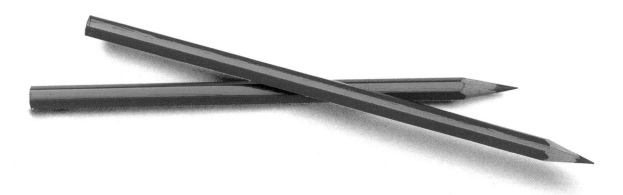

If you have changed any colors in the projects you have worked from this book, if you used a different mesh canvas that suited you better – for example, you may have worked the Doll's House Rug on a coarser mesh canvas to make a pillow cover – if you worked your own initials for the Card Box project, then you have already started designing your own needlepoint. At the end of each chapter, ideas for variations have been included, and I do hope that they have given you some idea of the endless possibilities of needlepoint. How do you start from scratch?

Before you embark on a design that is wholly yours, here are a few tips that will help you make sure that your finished piece turns out to be what you wanted when you started it.

● The more detail you want to portray, the finer mesh canvas you will need to use.
● The greater the number of different stitches you want to incorporate, the fewer colors should be used.
● Small stitches should be used for small areas; large ones for larger areas.
● Where possible, create areas where stitches will fit; for example, if you want to use crossed corner stitches over four threads, make sure that the area they are worked over is divisible by four; likewise, if you plan to work cushion stitch over three threads, the area should be divisible by three.
● Embroidery projects are most successful when the stitches are allowed to form their "own" pattern, so do not try to put diamond-shaped stitches such as Hungarian and diamond eyelet into square-shaped areas; likewise, do not put square-shaped stitches like crossed corners or broad cross into diamond-shaped areas, and so on.
● Have a piece of scrap canvas on hand to try out stitch or color combinations, particularly if you are using sprayed canvas or pulled thread stitches, or where test stitching could otherwise distort or mark the canvas threads.

As for the designs themselves there are three main sources of inspiration for successful designs:
● Copying or adapting a repeat pattern or an architectural detail can be fun, though I hope you will *adapt* rather than *copy*.
● Incorporating motifs, such as flowers from wallpaper or fabric in a room, into a design to link the piece with its surroundings.
● Working from nature, which could involve preparing artwork, taking photographs, or simply recognizing something that will translate into needlepoint stitches.

Throughout the book, there are numerous examples in which I have used one of these ideas as my starting point, but three specific examples of each are shown here.

▶ *The Flower and Trellis Rug shown with the original curtain fabric, and a drawing of a basic design unit.*

DESIGNING YOUR OWN · PROJECT 1

*B*ARGELLO STOOL

Covered stools like this one provide useful additional seating and a pleasing complement to the matching fabric. The pattern would also be suitable for other items where long wear is needed, since none of the stitches is longer than four threads. This is important to bear in mind for upholstery.

The Bargello stool was inspired by the curtain fabric shown with it. Once the right shades of the colors were chosen, it was comparatively easy to work out the proportions of each color used in the fabric and therefore decide the width of each line of stitching. A more ambitious alternative would have been to work the diamond shape in a four-way pattern.

When translating any Bargello-type

▼ *A 4-way variation of the same pattern quickly stitched on scrap canvas as an experiment, to use for reference in a future project.*

design for working on canvas, always remember that a soft curve will be created by big groups of stitches and small jumps between each group, whereas angular patterns will be created by working single stitches over a greater number of threads with a jump of at least half that number of threads between each stitch.

This concept works universally, whether your Bargello pattern is one-way, two-way (such as when it is reversed in the middle to incorporate initials), or four-way. Examples of both sharp and soft curves are shown in the diamonds and circles of the

dining-room chair seat cover in Chapter 2. The Bargello stool here has a diamond repeat motif, so single stitches climbing regularly reproduced the original best.

▶ *Choosing colors for upholstered pieces requires care, because they are a fixture, unlike pillows, which can be removed or put away at will to suit your mood or the season.*

▼ *The chart shows one diamond shape. The color sequence in each unit could be varied either in horizontal rows, diagonally, or even at random.*

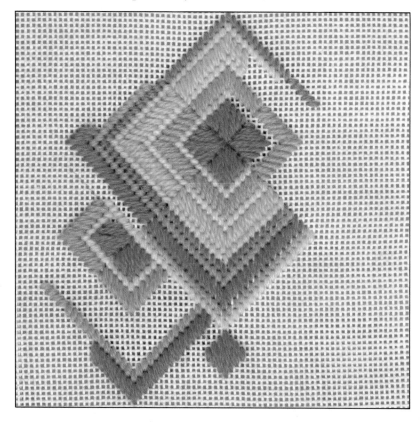

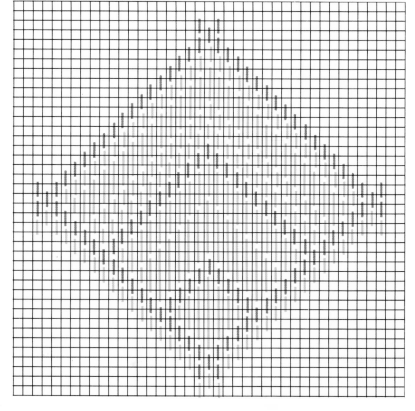

DESIGNING YOUR OWN · PROJECT 2

*F*LOWER AND TRELLIS RUG

This rug is an example of the second type of inspiration. It relies on motifs taken from a curtain fabric that have been regrouped and placed in a scheme appropriate to the size and mesh of the rug and the potential of needlepoint.

The fabric pattern has wide panels of baskets of flowers and a strong vertical trellis pattern with smaller flowers growing up between the bushets. An adaptation of the trellis was used to make a stunning border, and flowers like those in the fabric were strewn in a loose group in the central area, since keeping the baskets as part of the design would have immediately made it directional, which would not have worked as it is viewed from all angles.

The finished rug lies in front of a fireplace, and at the design stage a pattern of the proposed size was put in position and viewed from every angle to check that it balanced the fireplace and fitted the scale of the room.

The border pattern is very exact. Each band of the trellis had to be identical and the spaces between all bands the same, although the position of the flowers in the center did not have to be worked out to the thread. The border pattern therefore was calculated and test-stitched on a spare piece of the same mesh canvas, trying a number of potential stitches until the most attractive were found.

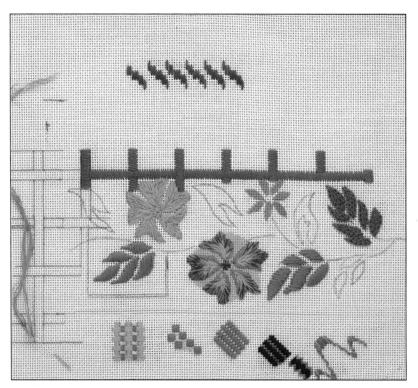

◄ A collage of flowers arranged on a large sheet of strong paper the size of the rug, ready for tracing on the canvas.

Tracings of individual flower heads were made from the fabric and duplicated so that there was a wide choice of flowers for the central design.

Next, a large sheet of paper, the size of the rug, was prepared. The border pattern was marked, and a collage of the flower heads was made – these were grouped, moved about, and regrouped until they looked right, and only then were they glued down. Then the design was carefully marked on the canvas and worked.

◄ An essential prop when designing any project from scratch – a piece of canvas the same mesh as the project on which to try stitches, colors, and motifs. There is an added bonus in recording ideas like this – you will have a record of the idea for the future!

The blue trellis pattern was counted and worked first as it is easier to count bare canvas. The other elements were worked around it. After that, basketweave tent stitch was chosen as the background for the trellis area. However, web stitch was selected for the main area to give a tight texture and because it is faster to work than tent stitch.

▶ A well-advanced corner with some of each of the elements worked to see the overall effect.

DESIGNING YOUR OWN · PROJECT 3

+ + + + + + + + +

ℋYDRANGEA RUG

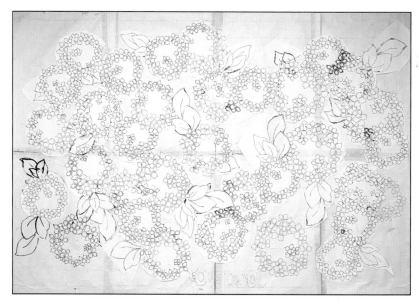

◀ *The rug was worked on 14-mesh canvas with a background of double brick stitch outside the flowers and tent stitch inside each cluster; the pillow was worked on 18-mesh canvas.*

▲ *More than thirty flower heads were arranged and then glued in place in preparation for tracing. Overlapping the flowers and particularly letting them "fall" onto the border gives the desired informal look.*

The rug has been in constant use for about ten years and has worn very well, even with the fairly long stitches. It would also make a beautiful wall-hanging if you feel that you cannot let people walk on your hard work. Make sure that you place it where it can be fully appreciated.

The Hydrangea Rug was inspired by nature, but was planned much in the same way as the flower and trellis rug.

Instead of tracing the motifs from fabric, however, I drew flower heads from plants in my backyard. I also pressed some of them for reference, and made notes about the colors and the way the tiny buds formed in the centers of each flower head. Then I matched the yarns to recently gathered flowers, as pressed flowers lose their color over time.

When I had made a number of drawings of the flower heads, I made a collage of them in much the same way

as I did for the flower and trellis rug, and when I was satisfied with the arrangement, I glued the drawings to the larger piece of paper and traced it on the canvas. The final link with the setting for the rug was to represent the design of the brass fender of the fireplace close to which it would finally be placed, in a Bargello motif in the border designs.

These basic principles can be followed time and time again for different designs.

To find your own floral motifs, look at flowers in the country, at florists, or in farmers' markets. Get into the habit

of looking at almost anything around you with a view to converting it into a motif, pattern, or design for needlepoint. It is a good idea to carry a sketchbook for noting down ideas as they come to you, from which you can select or experiment with ideas at a later date. You will soon find that you can never accommodate all your various inspirations.

▶ *All the flowers in the Hydrangea design are worked with straight stitches and blended shades of yarn.*

DESIGNING YOUR OWN

BACKGROUNDS AND BORDERS

Both borders and backgrounds should be thought about right from the initial planning stages. I have mentioned the need to choose the color of the canvas carefully, as you may wish to leave areas bare. I have also talked about marking the canvas as little as possible and covering any drawing lines you do make carefully so that you can choose a background you *want* rather than have unremovable marks that you have no option but to cover.

BACKGROUNDS

Several designs look good with the canvas as a background, but when a background is to be stitched, interesting textured stitches that are quick to work and add to the overall effect without overpowering the main design work well.

The color of the canvas

White and antique canvas are neutral, and these colors are the easiest to find, but Christmas colors are available. You can also spray-paint the canvas to get precisely the shade you want.

▼ *The color of the background is an integral part of this design.*

Selecting the stitches

The degree of durability you need from the finished piece helps you decide which stitches to use. It is unlikely that any stitch will be quite as hardwearing as basketweave tent stitch worked well in high-quality yarn. For a background worked around a motif, join the tent stitch at the narrowest point.

If durability is not high on the list of requirements, it must be better to finish a piece and enjoy it by using slightly larger stitches, such double brick stitch (used in the Hydrangea Rug), Bargello and Ailisia's lace. Very long stitches are not practical for upholstery pieces, where they could be caught and pulled loose.

Beware, too, of working large areas of background in stitches with a strong diagonal pull in just one direction. Milanese stitch is one of the stitches to avoid. This effect is exaggerated if a central area is worked in a similar diagonal stitch, but spreads out in four different directions – the center is almost bound to be distorted, it will not be rectifiable.

Selecting the color

The color you choose for the back-

▲ *Ailisia's lace gives a textured feel to this pillow.*

ground will often be dictated by your décor. Obviously, darker colors are more practical than pale ones.

Although it is best to, do not feel that you *have* to select the background yarn when you are planning all the other colors. A particular case for delaying the choice of background color is when many colors are used in the design. Indeed, it is often best to finish working the central motif and then test stitch some shades, both dark and pastel, in small background areas

to see which effect you like the best.

A background does not, of course, have to be all one color. The Bargello stitches used in the Tulip Rug in Chapter 6, for example, are worked in two similar shades, and the background the beaded piece in Chapter 8 is worked in different colors *and* stitches.

Shaded backgrounds work well for any floral design. Because the color is dark at the bottom, lightening all the way up to the top, the stitch chosen needs to work well in horizontal rows such as Hungarian, Parisian, and (double) brick stitches. A gradual color change can be achieved by introducing one shade paler, one ply at a time. When the changes are subtle, the finished result is beautiful. Adding a ply or two of embroidery floss or even a fine metallic thread (the thickness of a sewing thread) to the yarn gives the area a sheen or discreet glint.

For inspiration for patterned backgrounds, take a look at natural materials such as wood, granite, marble, and other stones that have veins of amazing colors running through them. Look, too, at sponged, dragged, or rag-rolled wallpapers, and experiment until you get the effect you want.

▲ *A dramatic change in the background makes it an integral part of the design.*

Materials

Use threads that have a sheen and work stitches at different angles to add interest to a background area. The different parts of the stitches will reflect the light differently.

Backgrounds worked in more than one stitch

This is very effective when the background area is quite large and the central design is in, say, tent stitch depicting fine detail. If a decorative stitch were to be worked right up to the detailed central motif, the background would tend to dwarf or overpower the subject. However, if a shape is created around the center and basketweave tent stitch is worked inside the area and a larger stitch is worked in the same color outside the area, this frames the central panel, but you also have an interesting background. The Chinese birds in Chapter 6 are another example of how well this works. The birds needed a plain area around them, but an additional texture was also needed to buffer the dramatic border.

Some designs have a scroll, ribbon, flower garland, or other pattern separating the background to a central motif from a second background outside of it. In such instances, it is easy to change both the color and the stitch. The Tulip Rug in Chapter 6 illustrates this very well.

Some stitches that work well in a

variety of situations to fill background areas are: basketweave tent stitch (see Stitch Glossary, page 144), skip tent stitch (see Stitch Glossary, page 158), skip cross stitch, Ailisia's lace stitch (see Stitch Glossary, page 162), Parisian stitch (see Stitch Glossary, page 165), brick stitch, Bargello patterns (see Stitch Glossary, page 144), patterned darning (see Stitch Glossary, page 155), and web stitch (see Stitch Glossary, page 152).

BORDERS

Almost every piece of needlepoint is improved by the right border. If, however, you plan to use cord, ribbon trim, ruffles, or lace on a pillow cover, for instance, then you will either not need a border at all or, at most, a simple one. The function of the border is to balance and frame the design.

Colors

To generalize, many designs are worked using two colors with white or a pastel. Using the two strongest shades (featured in the main design) together with a pastel shade often works better than introducing other colors.

The effect of surroundings

If you have made a coral and green pillow cover for a chair upholstered in coral, make the border predominantly green so that it will not simply disappear against the chair. If a rug is going to lie on a darkish carpet, stitch the border in either paler or much darker shades.

▼ *The garland marks the change in scale of the background stitch.*

Scale

If you look through the designs in the book, you can see that the border for the Wedding Kneelers is almost two-thirds of the whole of the design, for example, whereas at the opposite end of the scale is the tiny border for the Kelim Rug in Chapter 2. Let the piece itself dictate the size of the border.

Ideas for designs

I keep a record of border ideas stitched on canvas, and tent-stitch samples for each project.

There are three types of border design:
• row(s) of stitches that will fit any size of canvas;
• large stitches that can be placed at intervals suited to the dimensions of the piece;
• pattern repeats that need to fit the length exactly.

The first type can be extremely simple, such as a row of straight Gobelin stitch. You can make this a bit more sophisticated by using two colors to work straight Gobelin stitches, such as on the Doorstop in Chapter 2, or work groups of stitches alternately in two colors as was done in the Kelim Rug in the same chapter. Also, wide Bargello borders can fall into this group, as Bargello valley and mountain patterns (like those used for the background in the Tulip Rug in Chapter 6) can be mitered successfully at any point.

The second type is demonstrated in the Bokhara project in Chapter 4, where a large stitch is used as an individual unit and positioned where it is needed. The central and corner motifs were worked and only then were the intervening motifs plotted out – in fact, there is an extra thread on each side of the corner one, but only stitchers will know. Rhodes stitch is another attractive stitch to work in this way.

The third case is different – it has to

fit exactly to look good. The boxes and reversed eyelet stitches in the Mayan Pyramid pillow cover in Chapter 5 fit each side and, equally, there are no compensation stitches in the border to the Mirror Frame in Chapter 9.

How to work an accurate border

It is wise to plan – and, frequently, even stitch – a border of the third type described above before centering and working the design inside it.
• Find the center of the canvas and mark it. Mark, too, the central points on the outer edges of the canvas (this is a good idea as they will never be covered by stitching and so will always be visible to help you).
• Count the pattern repeat of the motif you want to stitch (for example, a Maltese cross is 32 threads across) toward the top right-hand corner, for example. Where the two intersect, stitch your corner motif.

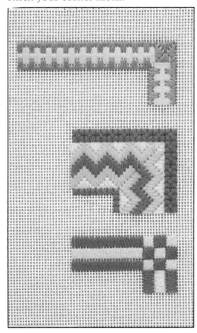

▲ *Samples on scraps of canvas are a good record for the future.*

There are occasions when you can make breaks in the border, such as with the Chinese birds in Chapter 6 and the Hydrangea Rug, illustrated in this chapter, where some of the leaves encroach into the border design.

FINISHING

Whether or not you make up your needlepoint, it can only help to know which finishing touches look good and how these styles can be achieved. A scrapbook for needlepoint ideas has been suggested already for ideas for finishing in magazines and home furnishings books: even if you give the piece to someone to finish for you, a photograph of what you wish to copy is of tremendous value.

I always recommend that, if you can afford to, have your work finished professionally. With so many hours of work in a piece, it is sensible to have it completed by someone who has all the right equipment and is finishing canvas pieces regularly. This said, there are times when it is easiest to finish an object yourself. Or you want the fulfilment of knowing that the finished article is all your own work. Therefore, read on for details about basic blocking and finishing techniques and appropriate finishing touches, including cords and tassels.

Note that all the following instructions apply to evenweave canvas, which is the canvas recommended for all the projects in the book.

PILLOWS

Even a simple pillow can be made or marred by the finishing. The following will give you a few examples of how pillows are constructed and some suggestions as to which methods suit particular designs.

PANELED FRONTS

Even a small piece of canvas work can be made to look important by mounting the completed piece in a panel of coordinating fabric. Probably the quickest and cheapest way is to buy a ready-made pillow cover.

Alternatively, you can easily make a pillow cover yourself and then apply the panel to it. If so, it is usually better to make the front of the pillow cover from one piece of material to which you sew your canvas, rather than attaching a strip of fabric to each side of the canvas, mitering the corners. However, a striped fabric that enhances the needlepoint, for example, with its corners carefully mitered so that the stripes matched exactly to frame the piece could look fabulous.

WINDOW MOUNTS

One fabric to avoid as the backing fabric for a panel is velvet. The pile makes it extremely difficult to sew anything on flat or tidily. If, however, you have set your heart on a heavy velvet, window-mount your panel. If your panel is square or rectangular, draw the finished window size in the center of the pillow cover on the wrong side of the fabric, drawing diagonal lines from opposite corners. Then,

▲ *Ruffles look good on small pieces, especially when the colors in the ruffle pick out the colors of the yarns. Cording* *between the pillow and the ruffle gives a nice sharp edge.*

insert a sharp pair of scissors in the center, and cut along the diagonal lines. Trim off the flaps, leaving about ¾ in (2 cm), turn this allowance in to the wrong side, and press just the edge on the wrong side using a damp cloth.

Lay the window over the canvas panel, pin it in place and then, using small, invisible slipstitches, pick up a few threads of canvas, then pass inside the edge of the velvet window, and carefully attach the velvet to the panel. You will have to work extremely carefully, though, to achieve neat edges and crisp corners. If the edges are not neat enough, you could sew some cord along the edge of the window, which would also help frame the work nicely.

CRISP EDGES

To get a crisp edge on a piece of needlepoint that is to be mounted on a panel, block the work as usual, trim the unworked canvas border to about eight threads, and carefully unpick the horizontal canvas thread running along right next to the worked area on all four sides (be assured, the stitches are firmly in place and will not move). Fold the border to the back of the work, folding the corners down first, and run your fingernail along the fold. Herringbone-stitch the raw edge to the back of the embroidery. Place the panel centrally on the ground fabric and slipstitch it into place.

▲ The same design with very different finishing styles; when using two different colored ruffles for a piece (as on the right), experiment to find the color that looks best framing the work and the one that is best as the secondary color. A lace ruffle gives a very light look.

SMALL PIECES

A really small piece of needlepoint might need to be edged to make it stand out. Lace can either be slipped just underneath the prepared edge of the canvas before slipstitching it to the background; or carefully slipstitched to the edge once the panel has been attached, and a thin cord can be sewn to the edge of the canvas, covering the seam. A thicker matching cord sewn to the edge of the pillow or piped into the seam can look very good.

If you want to edge a round panel with lace, simply remove the plain center of a ready-made linen doily of the right size and replace it with the needlepoint for a perfect lacy edging.

KNIFE-EDGE PILLOWS

This is the technical term for untrimmed pillows and is the best solution when there is an interesting border to a design as in the Tulips design in Chapter 6.

◀ Trim the excess canvas away and, with the right sides together, machine-stitch along three sides and around the corners of the last side (leaving a gap long enough for the zipper) as close to the needlepoint stitches as possible. In the case of a directional design, such as the Tulips, make sure that the side left open is the bottom one.

◀ Fold the seam allowance down to the back of the needlepoint, mitering the corners, and, using a sharp needle and strong thread, work herringbone stitch to attach it to the back of the needlepoint stitches. Pierce the canvas threads that are at right angles to the raw edge rather than taking stitches through the canvas holes.

◀ As the stitching is worked, fold the corner down, one side in and then the other, to miter the corners. Sew the folds of the corners together, too, to prevent raveling.

◀ Then simply turn the pillow cover right side out, hand-sew the zipper in place and add tassels or whatever other finishing touches you had in mind.

▶ A wide border such as this one is best finished with a simple knife edge.

HERRINGBONE STITCHING

The border of unworked canvas left on all projects once the tape has been trimmed off should be turned to the back of the work and fastened to it with herringbone stitch. Even if you are making a rug from squares to be joined together, the borders of each square are still stitched to the back in this way before they are joined to each other.

BOX PILLOWS

Making a pillow in a box shape gives it a tailored look and allows all the canvas to be seen, as the worked area is displayed flat rather than curved over the pad as with the other methods we have seen so far (you will, of course, need to buy a box-shaped pad). If you make the sides, or upstands, from a coordinating fabric, they can be flat, box-pleated, or ruched, and about 2-in (5-cm) deep. If you are feeling more ambitious, you can also needlepoint the sides, but be sure to pipe the seams between the top and sides and down the vertical seam at each corner using tightly woven fabric for neat, attractive joins.

▲ *A box cushion displays your work effectively. Here the sides have been tucked.*

▲ *Cording gives a very neat edge to set off your work. Here, the color has been carefully chosen to match the central panel, which unifies the look of the whole pillow.*

◄ *This piping fabric was cut on the bias and was therefore sewn on the bias, having been stitched around the edge of the pillow.*

◄ *Make sure you have enough piping cord to overlap the ends.*

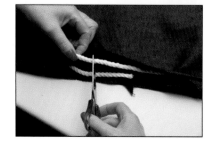

◄ *Align the two overlapping ends of the piping cord, trimming them if necessary so that they are both the same length (about 2-in/5-cm).*

PIPED PILLOWS

Make sure the piping cord you purchase is preshrunk. Cut the piping fabric either straight or on the bias – the results will be almost identical. Interweave the two ends of the cord as shown below to give a really neat tailored join.

◄ *Separate the three ply of one end and snip the 2-in (5-cm) overlap from one of these ply.*

◄ *Twist the three remaining ply – two from one end and one from the other – together to form one neat cord.*

◄ *Then stitch through the cord to make sure it won't pull apart over time, using matching thread (colored thread has been used here so that you can see the stitches).*

◄ *Fold the fabric back over the cord and neatly slipstitch the folded edges together.*

◄ *This really neat piping is the result.*

NEEDLEPOINT FOR UPHOLSTERY

Remember that finished canvas work is frequently thicker than upholstery fabric and so it may be necessary to shave a small amount of wood off each side of the drop-in seat frame before fixing the needlework. I speak from practical experience – one of my chairs had too thick a canvas fixed and it sprung the whole chair frame!

UPHOLSTERED PIECES

Fixing the cover for a drop-in seat is comparatively easy, and directions for making a simple pattern is explained on page 22; stretching a shaped piece is shown on page 139.

To fit the stretched, trimmed canvas (do not cut off the corners, just trim the overall shape to about twelve threads of bare canvas): center the pattern on the seat, place the canvas correctly along the front edge underneath the seat and nail it in place. Pull the canvas firmly over the seat and nail it in place along the back. Tuck in and trim any excess on the corners, then nail the sides, keeping the canvas taut and the design central.

PICTURES

Use masonite for mounting all pieces except very small ones, in which case strong cardboard will be strong enough. If the design leaves a great deal of the canvas bare, you may like to cover the board with colored fabric or cardboard. Framers have a wide selection of mounting boards that are suitable for this purpose and come in a wide choice of colors. If there are ends of metallic or thick, couched threads at the back of the work, cover the board with a piece of cotton batting or interlining to accommodate the lumps (without it they will push up the surface of the work). If this shows through the work, cover it with matching or contrasting felt. If you decide to have glass, make sure that it is specially mounted so that it sits well away from the stitching, particularly for raised stitches. This can be achieved either by having an extra thick mounting board (a bevelled edge to

◄ *Lace a needlepoint picture over thin board by working long stitches (using a strong thread) from side to side and top to bottom, pulling and holding each one taut as you work. Start and finish the thread carefully.*

the window looks good) or, if a mount is not appropriate, by having the framer insert a narrow strip of wood between the work and the frame itself.

THREE-DIMENSIONAL PIECES

Objects such as brick doorstops, tissue-box covers, a three-dimensional model of your house, need to look very tailored around their filling, which is always firm. If you cover a brick, it will need additional wrapping. Make sure the seams and corners are very crisp.

◄ Smooth any loose bits from the brick, fill out any hollows or holes with some interlining, then cover the whole brick with interlining, and sew the edges together neatly to produce a smooth outline.

◄ With right sides together, firmly hand-stitch each corner with strong buttonhole thread through the canvas threads (as close to the needlepoint as possible, but not through the stitches themselves), matching any pattern carefully.

◄ Cut away the excess canvas along these seams to about six threads away from the needlepoint.

◄ Open the trimmed seams and run your fingernail along them.

◄ Use herringbone stitch to attach the seam allowances to the back of the work.

◄ Then, simply slip the canvas over the brick, giving it a firm pull to make it fit snugly.

◄ Turn the lower edges of the canvas in over the bottom face of the brick and lace back and forth to pull the canvas taut over the edge, going first from end to end, then from side to side.

◄ You then simply slipstitch a panel of felt (cut to the exact size of the bottom of the brick) neatly over the lacing around the lower edge, catching canvas threads rather than needlepoint stitches as you go, to give a neat finish to the base.

RUGS AND CARPETS

To finish a rug, block the piece (or each individual piece) with the aid of a large T-square or set square to guarantee that the sides are straight and the corners are square.

Alternatively, if you have a blocking board as shown on page 139-140, you could use it for this job.

If you have worked your rug in squares, turn the borders of unworked canvas to the back of each individual blocked piece and use herringbone stitch to sew them to the back of the work. Then join the squares together using a strong buttonhole thread and zigzag stitch, stitching through a thread on the left-hand side, then the right-hand side and so on up the seam, pulling the thread every three stitches to abut the edges together well. Make sure that the stitches go through the *canvas threads*, not just the needlepoint stitches as they would pull and there would be no strength in the seam.

If you wish to interline your rug with industrial felt, cut the felt about ⅜ in (5 mm) smaller all around than the finished measurements of the rug, so that the edges of the rug turn to the back easily and no backing shows from the right side. Lay the interlining over the back of the rug (still on the blocking board), and pin it in place every 4 in (10 cm). Use a curved needle and strong buttonhole thread to baste the interlining to the rug with running stitches, taking care to catch only the back of the rug with these stitches. Work from end to end and then from side to side until you have a crosshatching of stitches holding the interlining firmly in place.

Miter the corners of the canvas by turning the corners in, first in such a way that the raw edges form a right angle and the fold joins them on the diagonal; then, when you fold in the sides, the seam forms a perfect mitre. Turn the unworked edges of the canvas over the edge of the interlining and secure them to the felt with herringbone stitches worked in carpet thread. Run your finger along the edges to flatten them.

I have found that Irish Linen Holland makes the best lining. This time, cut a piece that is 1½ in (3 cm) *larger* all around than the rug itself. Lay the lining over the interlining, and pin it in place and baste as you did for the interlining. Turn the allowance under and, using a curved needle and matching thread, slipstitch the lining just inside the edge of the rug in little invisible stitches. Be sure to pick up the canvas threads rather than the yarn.

▲ *A corner of the Hydrangea Rug turned over to show the backing fabric. To keep it lighter, this rug has not been interlined – worth bearing in mind if you carry your work around.*

WALLHANGINGS

To finish a wallhanging, block and line it like a rug, without interlining, stay-stitching the lining directly to the back of the needlepoint stitches to prevent the lining from drooping down when it has been on the wall for a while.

Stitch the two side seams of any items that you intend hanging on the wall, such as bell pulls, from top to bottom.

If the design allows, turn your piece to hang the other way up every six months so that the minimum pull in any one direction due to the weight of the embroidery occurs.

GENERAL TECHNIQUES

BLOCKING

For blocking you will need the following:
- a thick board large enough to take the flat canvas (plywood is best, but whatever wood you use, it should not be painted, stained, or varnished, and it must be soft enough to push tacks into)
- rustproof tacks (or ordinary thumbtacks if they are inserted well away from the worked area and will not be dampened)
- small spray bottle, like those used for misting plants, but kept scrupulously clean and solely for blocking
- clean water, distilled if necessary
- an old sheet, if you have not prepared a board as described below.

Tacking needlepoint on a board and dampening it is the most effective way to block it. However, if you have used silk congress cloth that has some unstitched areas, painted canvas that is not waterproof, pens that are not waterproof, or satin ribbons, tack a wet but well wrung-out towel or piece of cheesecloth over your blocking board and pin your piece to that, or even simply tack it on the blocking board and leave it in a humid place for a short period before allowing it to rest, still pinned down, somewhere else for a day or two.

For all other projects, using the blocking board as described, it is simple to line up any square or rectangular design, as you can see the guide lines through the border of canvas. Leaving the masking tape or stitched edges of the canvas intact, tack the work in place: pull and tack one side of the canvas in place, then the opposite side, then the other two sides, pulling the edges straight and the corners square as you do so. Spray the work with clean water using the spray bottle until the threads, but not the canvas, are wet.

If your project is a shaped piece, prepare a blocking board as before, but leave

RIGHT SIDE UP OR DOWN?

Block pieces worked in tent stitch right side down (to even out the texture) and pieces worked in any other stitch right side up (it is especially important to remember this with textured stitches that would be flattened if blocked right side down).

out the guide lines and draw around your original pattern instead. Dampen your finished piece as described, and mount it on the board, but pull it to fit the pattern instead, pulling opposite sides. It will probably be necessary to move the positions of the tacks as you work around the shape to get it to fit the pattern exactly.

When you are satisfied with the shape, allow the piece to dry naturally for a day or so in a horizontal position. When it is completely dry, remove it from the board and trim off the masking tape and excess canvas to within about 8 to 12 threads of the stitches.

Once you have blocked your project, you will need to deal with the raw edges.

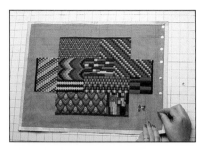

◄ Cover a large square 2-ft (60-cm) piece of plywood with cotton lining fabric, securing it with thumbtacks on the back, keeping the fabric taut as you do so. Then draw guide lines at 1-in (2.5-cm) intervals using a waterproof marker pen. It is essential that the surface of the board is completely smooth.

◄ Pin the completed tent-stitched piece of needlepoint out, right side down, with thumbtacks, leaving the masking tape in place and not trimming any canvas away. Use the lines on the blocking board to get the corners square and the sides straight.

◄ For a shaped piece, draw around the paper or fabric pattern on a blocking board prepared as before, but without the guide lines drawn in.

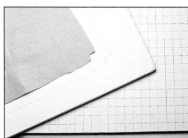

◄ Mark any corners or areas not worked, but do not cut them out.

CORDS

Cords made from the same yarn used to stitch the piece add greatly to its finished appearance. In different thicknesses, they lend themselves to numerous applications: thin ones can edge a mounted canvas or curtain tiebacks, medium ones look great edging pillows, especially if they are color-coordinated to a thinner one around a central mounted panel, or to tassels, and really thick ones can be used to suspend a wallhanging from a decorative pole.

Twisted cord is straightforward to make, but, for the best results, you need two people.

1 Measure the length of finished cord that you will need and multiply by three.

2 Cut two lengths of yarn to this measurement, either in the same or contrasting colors. (You can make thicker cord by cutting more lengths of yarn, but add the same number of lengths to each of the two original lengths.) Knot the ends together (trim them for neatness); this makes a large loop.

Both people then pull the loop with the knot halfway between them.

3 Then put a pencil, or a long, smooth stick, through the inside of the loop at each end and, keeping the yarn taut throughout, each person twists the yarn by rotating the pencils clockwise at the same speed as the other person.

4 When it is quite tightly twisted, take hold of the knot and give your end to the other person, keeping the yarn taut as you do so.

5 Then pull the knot until 2 in (5 cm) of yarn is released and twist counterclockwise. Move one hand along to the end of this section, keeping the other on the knot, and pull 2 in (5 cm) more yarn out and smooth it down.

6 Bring the hand that was holding the knot along until it is behind your other hand, and continue to pull this amount out; smooth it, and move your other hand up until you have worked the whole length. You will find that the lengths twist themselves into a neat cord ready to be used after the first section is twisted.

BRAIDS

An even easier decorative edging, which you can make single-handed, is the eight-strand braid.

It is difficult to estimate how long the threads need to be to make a certain length of finished braided cord, as everybody has their own particular tension. However, on average, you will need to multiply your desired finished length by three. Preferably your lengths of yarn should be the same weight (although you can make a thinner yarn up to the same bulk by adding more lengths of yarn) in four colors. The more lengths you have, the thicker the final plait will be.

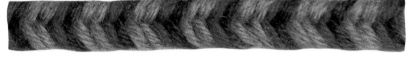

◄ Gather your lengths of the four colors together, aligning the ends, and fold them in half. Tie them together firmly with a short length of thread at the midway point. Secure them at this point to a pillow with a large safety pin and group the strands of the same color together, fanning them out from the pin.

◄ To braid, pick up the lengths of yarn (all one color) on the far left and place it in the middle of the two groups, then pick up the lengths on the far right (which will be the same color) and place them over the other lengths.

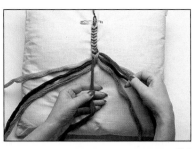

◄ *Continue in this way, always picking up the lengths of yarn on the far left first and then those on the far right. Vary the pattern by laying out the colors in different sequences, and use only two colors instead of four.*

◄ *Cut the loops along the bottom edge of the cardboard, putting one blade of the scissors between the two cards and cutting the loops so one side is not longer than the other. Remove the cardboard.*

TASSELS

Tassels are quick to make and can be used to embellish all kinds of projects – the corners of pillows, the ends of bell pulls and bolsters, and so on. They can be made in one or more colors. You can use yarn, pearl cotton, metallic threads, or even narrow ribbon. You can keep them simple, just binding the heads, or decorate them with embroidery or beads.

◄ *If you are using more than one color for your tassels, the best way to avoid the finished tassel having clumps of one color is to divide each color a number of times and then to gather each division up randomly with the other divided colors. Uncut yarn is best for making tassels, but do long lengths will do.*

◄ *Cut out two rectangles of stiff cardboard, at least ½ in (1 cm) longer than the length you want your finished tassel to be. Wrap the yarn around the length of them until you have the right sort of thickness. If matching tassels are needed for the four corners of a pillow, count the number of times you wrap the yarn around the cardboard.*

◄ *When you have the required thickness, pass a, approximately 6-in (16-cm) long, length of strong yarn of a matching color beneath the loops, and lift it so it lies under the loops along the top edge of the cardboard.*

◄ *Then, bring the ends of this length of yarn together, gathering up the loops, and tie them together tightly with a double knot.*

◄ *Cut a 10-in (25-cm) length of yarn in one of the colors used, and wrap it neatly and quite tightly around the tassel about ⅕ to ¼ of the way down from the tied end a number of times to form a head and neck.*

▲ *Lay the end of the binding yarn in a "u" shape, and then bind, leaving the end of the yarn above the binding and a loop, below. Pass the other end through the loop, and pull the end above the binding point until the other end is pulled through. Then, simply cut both ends off close to the binding.*

◄ *Buttonhole-stitch the wraps together immediately under the head as shown. Trim the ends evenly, and comb them with a large-toothed comb to fluff them up a bit. Decorate further if desired.*

POMPOMS

Pompoms are used to trim the Christmas Stocking in Chapter 7.
1 To make a pompom, cut two identical cardboard circles the desired size of the eventual pompom; then cut holes in both circles (the size of the hole will determine how much yarn you are able to use, so a large ball will need a large hole. More yarn tends to make a better pompom).
2 Thread a number of long strands (half the hank if you've already cut it, or a hank cut only once is even better), into a large blunt needle and bind the yarn over and over the cardboard ring, distributing it evenly.
3 When the hole is full or you think there are enough wraps, cut all the loops around the edge of the circle with sharp scissors, slipping the scissors between the two pieces of cardboard.
4 Thread a long matching thread between the cards and tie firmly.
5 Remove the cardboard and shake the pompom vigorously to fluff it out. Finally trim it into a perfect shape with small snips of the scissors. For the stocking, three different sizes were made.

STITCH
GLOSSARY · + · + · +

The stitches, each one illustrated with
a photograph, are grouped according
to the projects they appear in. The
method for each one is described, with
a diagram for clarity. You can use this
section to find alternatives for the
stitches suggested for each project, or
you can use it as a source of inspiration
and information when you move on to
designing your own work.

Basketweave tent stitch

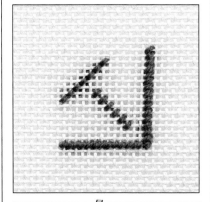

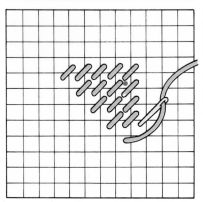

The name of this stitch comes from the look of the back. It is the only way of working tent stitch that does not distort the canvas and is therefore excellent for backgrounds and other large areas.

Start in the top right-hand corner of the canvas, at the spot shown on the diagram. Bring the needle up 2 horizontal threads down for downward rows, and 2 horizontal threads out for upward rows.

Work down the canvas from top left to lower right when the horizontal canvas thread is on top and up the canvas from bottom right to top left when the vertical canvas thread is on top (see Chapter 1, Tent Stitch).

Continental tent stitch

This version of tent stitch should be used for working a single row. Follow the diagram, starting at the spot, and stitch from right to left for a horizontal row (turn the book upside down if you want to work from left to right). A long stitch is created at the back of the work, which makes it very hardwearing.

If you need to work a row of Continental tent stitch, from lower right to upper left, run a thread underneath the stitches to join them together.

Continuous cashmere stitch

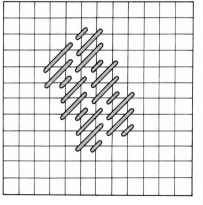

This is a diagonal stitch worked over 1, 2, and 2 threads diagonally across the canvas. It can be worked in one color or alternate rows can be worked in a contrasting color. It is a good stitch for filling in backgrounds.

When worked in one color, the first row is worked from the top left-hand corner down to the bottom right-hand corner, then the second row is worked back up along the first, the third back down along the second, and so on, with each row slotting into the previous one with one of the long stitches sharing a hole with the short stitch of the previous row as shown. This is the only traditional canvas stitch that forms an angle other than 45 degrees.

Bargello stitch

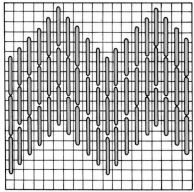

Also known as Florentine or Irish stitch, this is generally an upright stitch worked over 4 or 6 threads with a jump up or down between stitches. Many variations can be worked by altering the length of stitch, the number of stitches worked in a group, and the size of the jump between groups. The particular Bargello patterns used in this book are diagramed within the Bargello chapter.

Straight Gobelin stitch	**Crossed corners stitch**	**Wheat stitch**	**Sloping Gobelin stitch**

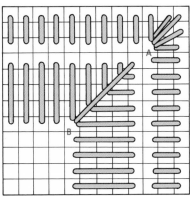
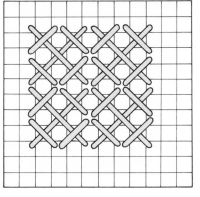
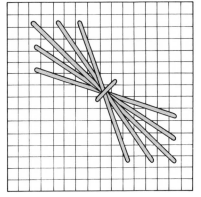
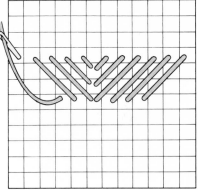

This is an upright stitch that can be worked over almost any number of canvas threads, but 2, 4, and 6 threads are the most usual and are the ones shown here.

Work it in rows as an area filler or to outline a square or other straight-sided shape. When working the stitch over 2 threads, follow the numbers in diagram A to turn a corner neatly. If you are working straight Gobelin stitch over more than 2 threads, follow diagram B for a mitered corner, working a single stitch over where the stitches merge, diagonally from the inside corner to the outside point of the corner to finish it neatly.

Threads can be laid on the canvas, and straight Gobelin stitch worked over them for raised stitching.

This stitch can also be worked by diagonally stepping each stitch down one thread from the previous one.

First work a large cross over 4 threads of canvas and a small diagonal stitch across the tip of each corner in turn. Always work the large cross in the same order, so that the top stitch is on the same diagonal.

This stitch looks effective worked in different color combinations, whether it is worked completely in one color, worked alternately in two colors to give a checkerboard effect, or with the large base cross worked in one color and the tips worked in a contrasting color.

When stitching in two colors, use one needle for each color.

This is a decorative stitch that can be worked in one colour or with a contrasting color or thread used to work the short stitch binding the wheatsheaf in the centre.

Work a long diagonal stitch over 12 thread intersections first, followed by 2 stitches on each side of that 1 thread away from the first stitch, then 2 stitches on each side of these, 2 threads away, working them all cross-stitch fashion and so that the ends of the stitches form right-angled corners. Finally work a short stitch over 2 thread intersections on the opposite diagonal to the first stitch.

Four wheat stitches can be worked together, and a backstitch, in the same color thread as the short stitch across the center, can be worked between each sheaf.

Work straight stitches diagonally over 2, 3, or 4 thread intersections in horizontal or vertical rows to fill an area or outline a straight-sided shape.

When working a single row as a border stitch, maintain the same slant for all the stitches (see diagram). The angle may be reversed at the central point on each side of the design.

You can try using two colors alternately and sloping each row on opposite diagonals.

Cross stitch	**Half-cross stitch**	**Chain stitch**	**Satin stitch**
		 (top) 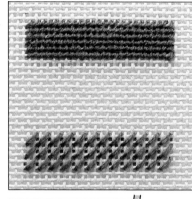 (right)	
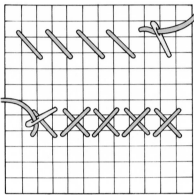	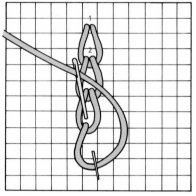	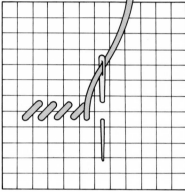	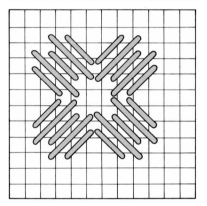

The stitch can be used to outline an area or as a narrow border; it can also be a feature in itself used in concentric squares. It is a good stitch to use for bold lettering. Basic cross stitch is always worked over 2 threads.

Cross stitch can be worked in two ways: either work all the diagonals in one direction first, and complete the cross on the return journey, or complete each cross before moving on to the next stitch. The stitch behind the work is short and vertical. For very open motifs on a sampler, it is probably best to work each stitch separately. Whichever method you use, always work the top diagonal in the same direction.

From the front of the work, this stitch looks like tent stitch, although the back is different, being rows of vertical stitches.

Work the rows from left to right, with each stitch over one diagonal from bottom left to top right, as shown in the diagram.

To work the stitch, bring the needle and all the thread up at 1, form a loop and hold it; re-insert the needle at 1, pass it under 2 threads of canvas, in line with 1, and bring it up at 2, holding the looped thread below the point of the needle. Pull the thread gently through to form the first loop.

Always put the needle back in the hole it has just come out of inside the last loop. To finish a row, make a little stitch over 1 thread just outside the final loop.

This is a good stitch for creating a curve, either as a shape or an outline, and can be combined with rows of continental tent stitch to make a filling stitch.

Satin stitch is a traditional crewel embroidery stitch. In this book, the term satin stitch has been used for stitches laid side by side, but, unlike straight and sloping Gobelin stitch, the stitches are of different lengths.

Stitches on one diagonal can be superimposed on another diagonal or vertical stitches on horizontal ones.

Double cross stitch

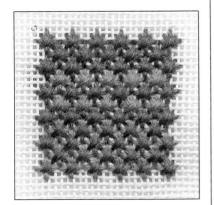

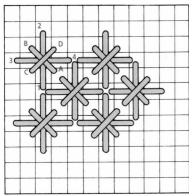

Work an upright cross stitch over 4 threads (stitches 1/2 and 3/4 in the diagram). Work a basic cross stitch over 2 threads (stitches A/B and C/D in the diagram) over the upright cross.

This stitch can be worked in horizontal rows in one color, or two colors used for alternate rows. It can also be worked with all the base crosses in the contrasting color and the basic cross worked in the second color (as shown). It is best then to use two needles, one for each color, and complete the crosses in each row rather than trying to fill in the diagonal crosses later on.

Smyrna stitch

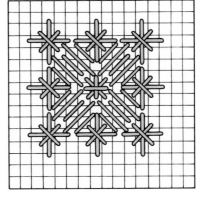

This is a traditional embroidery stitch.

First work a base diagonal cross stitch (stitches 1/2 and 3/4 in the diagram) over four threads of canvas, then a vertical and, last, a horizontal stitch (stitches A/B and C/D in the diagram) as shown. Two colors are frequently used, giving very different appearances, as the photograph shows. Complete stitches can be worked in alternating colors to give a checkerboard effect, or the base cross can be worked in the first color and the upright one in the contrast.

This stitch can be made smaller by working it over 2 threads.

Satin flower combination

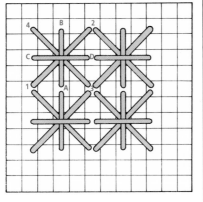

Work 8 double cross stitches as shown in the chart.

Next, work the petals in diagonal satin stitches as shown (see page 146) over 2, 3, 2, 3, and 2 intersections.

Complete the flower by working a small-scale Smyrna stitch over 2 threads in two colors.

Broad cross stitch

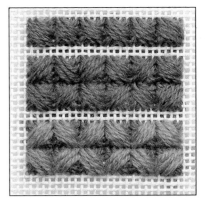

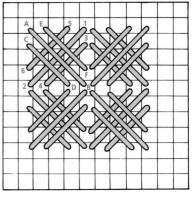

Work a diagonal stitch over 4 threads from upper right to lower left (stitch 1/2 in the diagram), then work a stitch over 3 threads on both sides (stitches 3/4 and 5/6 in the diagram). Next work a diagonal stitch over 4 threads from upper left to lower right (stitch A/B in the diagram) and a stitch over 3 threads on both sides of this one (stitches C/D and E/F in the diagram). Work all the stitches in the same order so that the direction of the top stitches is uniform.

The angle of the 3 base stitches, and thus the 3 upper stitches, can be worked on alternating diagonals. You can also work the stitches in two colors in alternating directions.

Outlined double cross stitch	**Cushion stitch**	**Fan stitch**	**Fan stitch with double cross stitch**
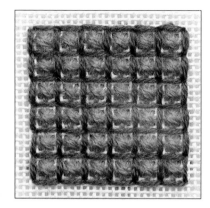			
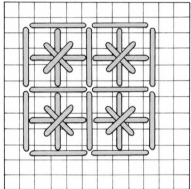	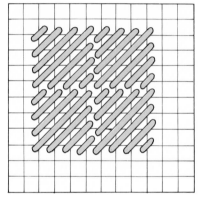	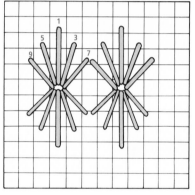	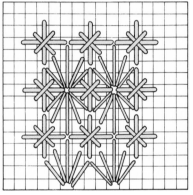

Work double cross stitches (see page 147), then work straight stitches over 4 threads horizontally and vertically as shown in the diagram.

This is a traditional embroidery stitch.

A group of diagonal stitches are worked to form a small square. Stitches can be worked over 1, 2, 3, 2, and 1 threads all in the same direction, or over 1, 2, 3, 4, 3, 2, and 1 threads, or small squares worked alternating the diagonals – large squares can also be worked in this way.

Frequently, the pattern is worked in two contrasting colors with two squares of one color worked on the same diagonal before the other two squares in a contrasting color on the other diagonal are stitched. Different scales, color combinations, and directions are also possible.

Work this stitch in horizontal rows, working 5 straight stitches in the order given in the diagram to form pairs of fans, each made up of 5 stitches sharing the same central hole. The longest stitch of the fans in the second row shares a hole with the longest stitch of the previous row.

An upright cross (see page 169) can be worked in a contrasting color in the spaces between the fans. Alternatively, four double fans can be worked as a four-way motif.

First work the double cross stitch (see page 147). Now work fan stitches in the spaces between the double cross stitches. Working the 2 outer stitches, then the 2 inside those, then the vertical stitch last (stitches 1/2, 3/4, 5/6, 7/8, 9/10 in the diagram), gives a neat finish.

Mosaic stitch	**Mosaic stitch with tent stitch**	**French knots**	**Bouquet variation I**
			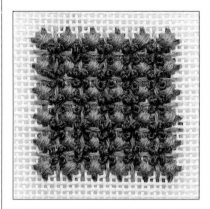
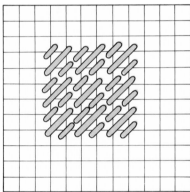	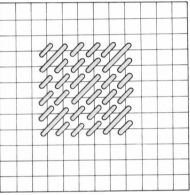	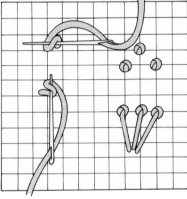	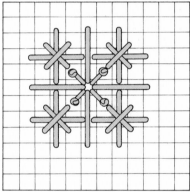

Mosaic stitch

Three diagonal stitches are worked over 1, 2, and 1 threads to form a small box.

These boxes can be worked horizontally or vertically across the canvas, or in diagonal rows.

Mosaic stitch with tent stitch

Work the 3 diagonal stitches as above, then work 4 basketweave tent stitches (see page 144) beside them to form another small square. Alternate the squares of mosaic and tent stitches across the canvas. When working the second and subsequent rows, work a square of tent stitch under the mosaic square and vice versa.

An alternative method of working this stitch is to work a diagonal row of mosaic stitch squares, then a diagonal row of tent stitch squares. Generally slope both the tent and mosaic stitches, on the same diagonal, from lower left to the upper right, but, if required, the mosaic stitch squares can slope on the other diagonal. Never slope the tent stitch squares the other way. When working in two contrasting colors, it is easiest to use two needles.

French knots

Bring all the thread through, hold the needle horizontally and pointing to the left (if you are right-handed). Wrap the thread around the needle once, and turn the needle so that it is vertical, pointing upward. Take it back through the canvas one thread above and to the right of the original hole.

Wrap the thread around the needle once only. For a larger knot, use thicker thread.

French knots on stalks are excellent for the stamens of flowers. Work a French knot as before, but re-enter the canvas 3 or 4 threads away to form a knot on the end of the stitch.

Bouquet variation I

First work double cross stitches (see page 147) over the whole area. Then work vertical and horizontal stitches over 4 threads, over where the tips of the double cross stitches share a hole, pulling them firmly. Finally, work French knots on stalks, radiating out from where the vertical and horizontal threads share holes as shown in the diagram.

| **Large and straight cross stitch** | **Cross stitch and Smyrna stitch** | **Lazy daisy stitch** | **Lazy daisy stitch and double cross stitch** |

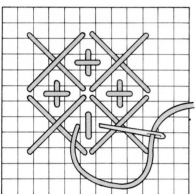
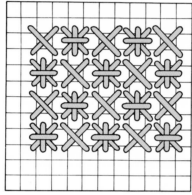
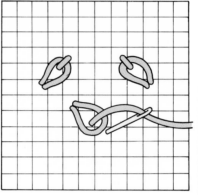
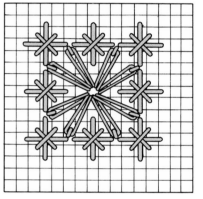

First, work large-scale cross stitch over 4 threads over the whole area. Then work small upright cross stitches over 2 threads of canvas with the horizontal stitch on top. Complete each cross as you go.

Only work the small cross stitches in complete spaces between the large cross stitches – do not work half cross stitches around the edge of an area. The diagonal and upright cross stitches can be worked in contrasting colors if desired.

Work small-scale Smyrna stitches (see page 147) over 2 threads, leaving 2-thread gaps between each one, alternating the gaps checkerboard fashion. Then with a contrasting color, work basic cross stitches over 2 threads of canvas in the gaps between the small-scale Smyrna stitches.

This stitch is sometimes called detached chain stitch.

Bring your needle and thread up at the required position, re-enter the hole you came up through to form a loop, and hold it with your other hand. Bring your needle up inside the loop a few threads away (how many threads depends on the length of the daisy petal required). Anchor the loop down with a small stitch taken over it and over one thread of canvas (do not pull the loop too taut so it forms a petal shape).

Work 8 double cross stitches (see page 147) as given in the chart below.

Work 8 lazy daisy stitches, all radiating from the hole in the center of the square of double cross stitches and anchor them down between the double cross stitches as shown.

Triple cross stitch

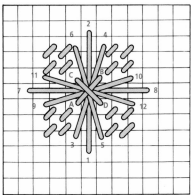

Work a base cross of 6 stitches (stitches 1-12). Next, work a small basic cross stitch cross (stitches A-D). Subsequent stitches fit over these.

Groups of 4 basketweave tent stitches (see page 144) can be worked in the spaces.

The small basic cross stitches are often worked in a contrasting thread or color.

The stitch can easily be worked in different sizes.

Byzantine stitch

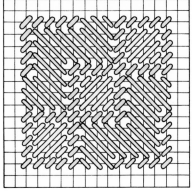

This consists of straight diagonal stitches worked over 3 or 4 thread intersections in a step pattern. The chart shows the stitch worked over 4 threads in steps of 6 stitches (the pivot, or corner stitch, is counted twice).

This can be worked over more or fewer threads, and works well over both even and odd numbers of threads.

The stitch can be worked so the steps and stitches go up to the left or the right.

Byzantine boxes

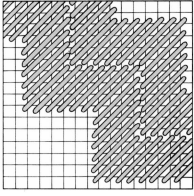

This is a variation that combines Byzantine stitch with continental tent stitch.

Work two diagonal stepped lines in continental tent stitch (see page 144) to form boxes from upper right to lower left, making each step 5 stitches (counting the pivotal stitch twice).

Work Byzantine stitches in steps of 5 stitches down (the pivot is counted twice) over 3 thread intersections above and below the lines of tent stitch, following them, but sloping the stitches the opposite way.

Work 2 diagonal lines of continental tent stitch to form boxes, as before, above and below, before working the Byzantine stitch steps again, above and below these.

When the area has been filled in this way, fill in the tiny boxes of bare canvas with diagonal straight stitches in the same direction as the continental tent stitch over 1, 2, 3, 2, and 1 thread intersections.

Bargello variation

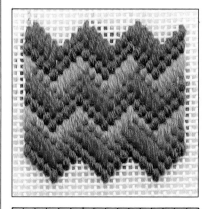

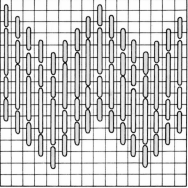

Start with a row that is worked over 2 threads along its length. The next 2 rows, though, are 4 stitches over 2 threads and 4 stitches over 4 threads (work these in horizontal rows to avoid confusion). The design then repeats the row worked over 2 threads of canvas.

Use an extra ply for the rows with stitches over both 2 and 4 canvas threads.

Satin stitch flower with double cross stitch	**Wickerwork stitch**	**Multiple cross stitch**	**Web stitch**
		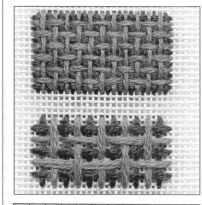	
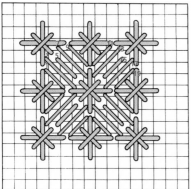	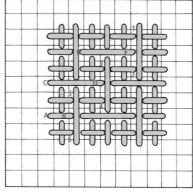	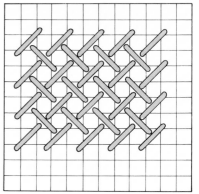	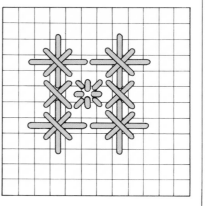

Work double cross stitches (see page 147) where shown in the chart. When these have been worked, work satin stitch petals between the double cross stitches as numbered in the chart.

Work upright cross stitches (see page 169), each over 2 threads, first. Work back and forth across the canvas to make it easier.

When this stage is complete, work long vertical stitches between them over 4 threads, working diagonally down across the area (follow the numbers and arrows in the diagram).

Finally, work the long horizontal stitches (follow the letters in the diagram). It is easy to quarter-turn the canvas and work as before.

The stitch can also be worked over 4 and 8 threads.

Work double cross stitches (see page 147) as shown. Then, work basic cross stitches over the arms of the double crosses. Finally, work 8 stitches over 1 thread, going down into the central hole, pulling these very firmly.

First work a row from left to right of diagonal stitches sloping to the right over 2 threads with a straight stitch behind the work.

Work the second row from right to left, slanting the stitches the opposite way to those of the first row, tucking them up into the previous row of stitches (see diagram). Continue to work back and forth across the rows, alternating the slant of the stitches.

If you want to use two colors, always start one color from the left side and the second color from the right, and fasten off at the end of each row, or, if it is not far to the correct starting point, use the back of the stitched area to get you back neatly.

Leaf stitch

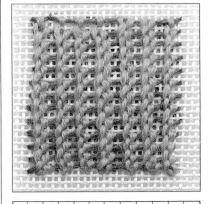

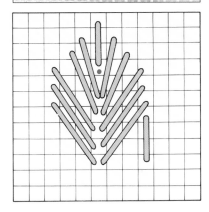

Start stitching at the spot in the chart, and work the central top stitch over 3 threads, then work sloping stitches down one side, leaving the hole immediately below the starting point empty. When one side is complete, return to the top and work down the other side, missing the same hole again.

The second row can either be interlocked, starting the top stitch in the center below the last stitch of each side of two "leaves," as shown in the chart, or as individual rows with the top stitch of the leaf sharing the hole occupied by the pair of bottom stitches of the previous row.

Raised buttonhole band

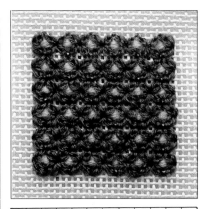

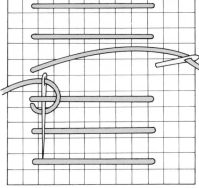

The horizontal bars are formed by working straight stitches over 2 threads worked 2 vertical canvas threads apart. Work these from side to side across the area with a long stitch behind the canvas.

When the bars are complete, bring the needle to the front of the work at the left-hand end of the area and immediately below the top bar. Work buttonhole stitch over the bars in turn, working down the rows and not going through the canvas. Do this by forming a loop of thread, sliding the needle under the top bar, and up through the loop, pulling it firmly. Repeat this over the second bar and continue until the bottom bar has been covered. Then, anchor the loop of the last stitch to the canvas with a little stitch.

Bring the needle behind the canvas and up to the front beneath the top bar as before. Work a line of stitches as before, and continue in this way until the band has been completed.

In a shaped area, complete the bars from edge to edge across the whole shape. Start at the left-hand side, and work in vertical rows as normal filling in the shape.

Daisies

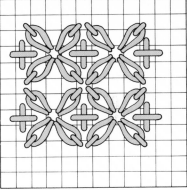

First work the upright cross stitches (see page 169) in the positions shown in the chart below.

Then work groups of 4 lazy daisy stitches (see page 150) radiating out from one central hole between the upright cross stitches as shown on the chart. When stitching each loop down, come up inside the loop one diagonal hole away from the central hole and go down over the loop through the next diagonal hole (2 canvas intersections away from the center).

Diamond leaf stitch	**Bouquet variation II**	**Bouquet variation III**	**Soufflé stitch**
		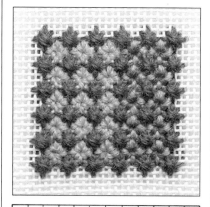	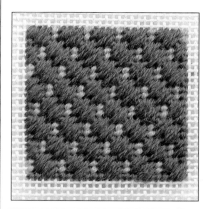
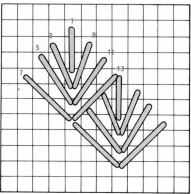	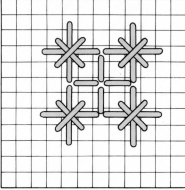	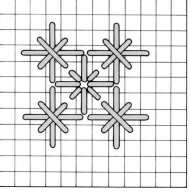	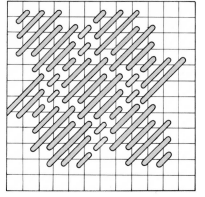

This is like leaf stitch, but on a smaller scale, and forms an attractive diamond shape.

Work the stitch as numbered in the diagram, starting with the top stitch, then work down one side into every hole, then down the other side, from the top.

Start the second leaf with the top stitch, coming up in the hole of step 13 of the first leaf.

Work double cross stitches (see page 147) in the positions shown in the chart.

Then work 4 straight stitches down into the center of each area between the double cross stitches.

As with bouquet variations I and II, work the double cross stitches (see page 147) first in the positions shown in the chart.

Next, work small vertical and horizontal stitches, each over 2 threads, and finally the 4 diagonal stitches over 1 thread intersection, all down into one central hole, between the double cross stitches where shown in the chart.

Up to four different colors can be used to work this variation.

Work in diagonal rows with stitches over 1, 2, 3, 2, 3, 2, and 1 thread intersections, as shown in the diagram.

When starting the second and subsequent rows, note from the diagram how the stitches interlock and that 2 tent stitches (see page 144) are worked in the gaps in either a contrasting thread or color.

154

Diamond lattice stitch

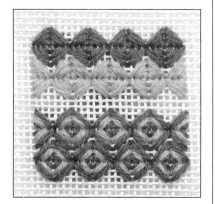

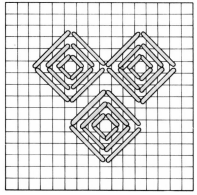

This stitch involves working horizontal rows of diamond shapes, first over 3 threads, second over 2 threads, and last over 1 thread as shown.

Stagger the second row, starting stitching 2 threads, below the bottom corner of the outer diamonds of the first row.

Two or three colors can be used to work this stitch, and the diamonds can be worked over more threads to give a larger pattern.

Victorian patterned darning

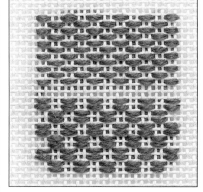

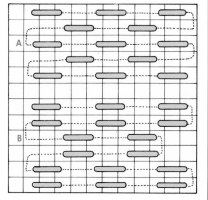

There are many darning patterns that are excellent for needlepoint pieces.

The principle with any patterned darning is that the thread behind the canvas as well as on the surface forms part of the pattern; therefore every thread has to be started right at the beginning of the row and taken all the way to the end. In order to achieve this it is necessary to work any **border** or surrounding stitches first, then use the back of these stitches as turning points. It is important that the thickness of the thread fills the channels that it is to lie along.

Variation I

The first design is simply over and under 2 canvas threads; the subsequent rows are staggered.

Diagram A shows the first row starting on the left, going under and over 2 threads horizontally to the right (the dotted lines indicate the thread behind the canvas showing through

the unworked spaces).

The photograph shows a holding stitch at the end of each row; there is no border in which to anchor the threads.

Variation II

The second design is worked in the same way, but 2 rows are worked over the same threads before staggering the next 2 rows, whereas the first pattern staggered every row.

As before, the thread under the canvas is indicated by dotted lines.

Whipped chain stitch

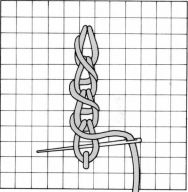

Work a row of chain stitch (see page 146). Then, using a thread of a contrasting color, bring it up through the canvas beside the thread and at the top of the first chain stitch. Bring the needle diagonally across the first chain stitch, and pass the needle under the loop of the second chain stitch. Repeat this movement, not piercing the canvas, until all the chain stitches have been worked over. The loops can be pulled tight to make a narrow raised cord effect, or less tightly depending on the desired effect.

Stem stitch	**Vertical cross stitch**	**Diagonal Florence stitch**	**Couching**

  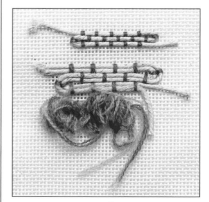

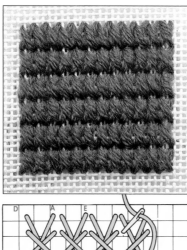 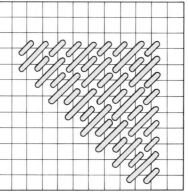 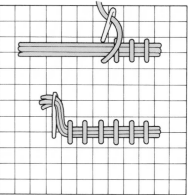

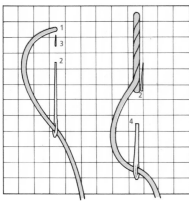 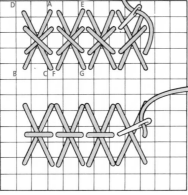

Stem stitch

This is a good stitch for outlining embroidered areas to increase definition (it can be worked first, with long and short stitch worked over it, to give a smooth padded edge). Alternatively, rows of stem stitch can be packed close together as an area filler.

Work the stitch by bringing the needle up at 1, down at 2, usually 2 threads away, but not necessarily in a straight line if the stitch is being used to outline a curve.

Before pulling the thread down on to the canvas, bring the needle up at 3 (halfway between 1 and 2), holding the thread to one side. Pull the thread snug to the canvas.

Go down at 4 (stitch 3/4 is the same length as stitch 1/2), and come up at 2 before tightening the thread.

The thread can be held to either left or right of the needle when working in a straight line; when working a curve, it should be held *outside* the curve.

Vertical cross stitch

The base cross looks like a stretched basic cross stitch, as it is 2 threads wide and 4 threads high. A basic cross stitch can then be worked over the center base cross, or a row of backstitch may be worked over 2 threads over the center of the base crosses.

If either of these secondary stitches is worked in a contrasting color, it is easier to use two needles, one for each shade, and work a complete stitch at a time. The letters in the diagrams enable you to come up in an empty hole and go down into a filled one when working from left to right. When working the second row back from right to left, the *direction* of the stitches is reversed, but the order in which the stitches are worked remains the same.

These two versions can be mixed, say working them in alternate rows, and they can be worked smaller or larger.

Diagonal Florence stitch

Work this stitch diagonally across the canvas over 1, 2, 1 threads.

Work the second row beside the first, with the stitch over 1 thread of the second row sharing a hole with the stitch over 2 threads from the previous row, as shown in the diagram. Also see how, at the top, a compensation stitch needs to be worked to get a straight edge.

Couching

This is used to attach a thread or ribbon that is too thick or fragile to stitch up and down through the canvas.

Lay a length of the thread to be couched along the surface of the canvas. The thread must be longer at each end than the area to be couched. With 1 ply of couching thread, come up on one side of the thread to be couched, bring the couching thread up over it, and go back down through the canvas on the other side, not pulling the couching thread too tight. When the couching has been completed, the couched thread is "plunged," that is, a large-eyed tapestry needle is pushed up halfway through the canvas in the same hole as the last couching stitch, the extra length of the couched thread is passed through the eye and the needle is gently pulled down, bringing the thread to the back of the canvas to be finished off. If the couched thread is too thick for any needle, make a "lasso" with another thread by coming

Lopsided herringbone stitch	Pin-wheel stitch	Eyelet
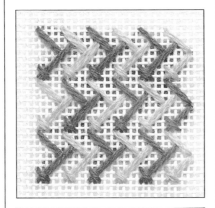	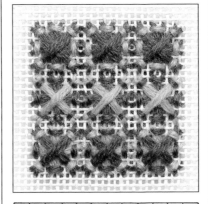	
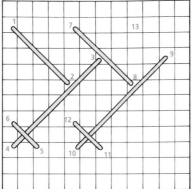	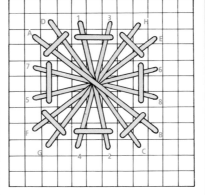	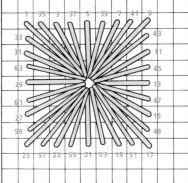

up through the canvas in the last hole, going over the couched thread and back through the same hole, and gently pulling the thread through to the back.

If you want to couch around a corner, place a couching stitch over the corner itself to give a neat, sharp turn.

For Jacobean couching and spaced Cretan stitch over ribbon, see pages 161 and 167.

Work the stitches as indicated by the numbering in the diagram, working straight diagonal stitches in opposite directions.

If two colors are used, use separate needles for each, but still follow the numbers as indicated, changing needles for stitches 7 to 12, back to the first color for stitches 13 to 18, and so on. It helps to take the needle with the unwanted color up in the correct hole for the next stitch in that color before working the stitch in the other color, that is, ready for its next turn. After working stitches 1 to 6, come up at 13, ready for the next stitch in that color.

This stitch can be worked larger or smaller, or in a thicker thread, if denser coverage is required.

Work 4 stitches over 8 threads, following the numbers. Then work the 4 stitches shown in the diagram following the letters. These stitches can be worked in the same color or a contrasting color to the base stitches. Stitch G-H must be worked last.

The tie stitches shown can be worked in the same color as the base stitches or in another contrasting color.

This forms a square shape with all stitches going through the central hole. By working the stitches in the order numbered in the diagram (the even numbers are where the thread is stitched through the center), thus making two trips around the center, the final appearance is much neater than if every stitch is worked as you go around.

The stitch can easily be made larger or smaller over almost any even number of threads.

The pulled-thread version of eyelet stitch is worked in the same way, but the thread is given a tug after working each stitch, so when the two circuits have been completed, the central hole is enlarged.

Hungarian stitch	**Skip tent stitch**	**Back stitch**	**Cushion stitch variation I**
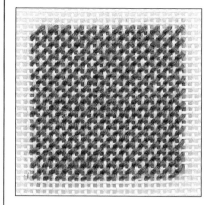	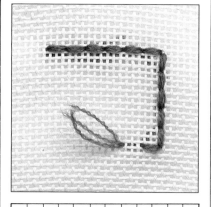		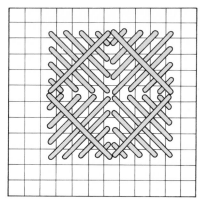
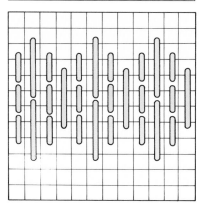	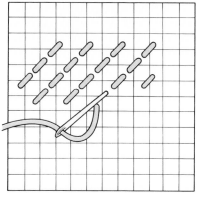	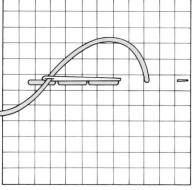	

Work this stitch in horizontal rows in groups of 3 stitches over 2, 4, and 2 vertical threads, with a gap of 2 threads between each group. Repeat.

For the second row, fit the stitch over 4 threads into the 2-thread gap between the groups in the previous row. Work compensation stitches at the top and bottom edges of an area to achieve a neat edge.

Alternate rows can be worked in contrasting colors.

Before working any area with this stitch, be sure that there are no trailing threads behind it; it does not completely cover the canvas, and so they would show. A light, lacy look is part of the beauty of this stitch.

Follow the diagram below carefully, starting at the dot. There is very little thread behind the work, and the second and subsequent rows form a diagonal line across the canvas.

Before starting a line of skip tent stitch, always check that you have enough thread to finish it, and anchor it in surrounding solid stitchery, as any finishing or starting thread left loose would show through.

This stitch is usually worked over 1 or 2 threads and is often used for outlining.

As shown in the diagram, bring the needle up at 1 and down at 2, make a long stitch behind the canvas, going back on yourself, and come up at 3, ready for the second stitch. Continue in this way, going down at 4, up at 5, down at 6, and so on as necessary.

Work four squares on alternate diagonals as shown. Then, using a contrasting color thread, work 1 stitch over each square on the opposite diagonal to the satin stitch squares.

Eggs in a basket	**2-4-6-8 stitch**	**2-4-6-8 stitch variation**	**2-4-6-8 stitch and Hungarian stitch**

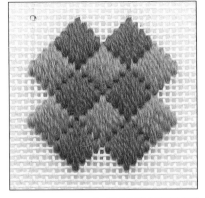

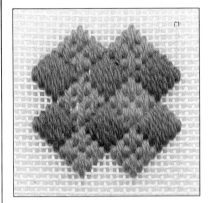

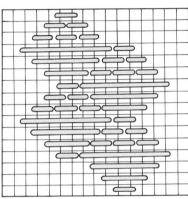
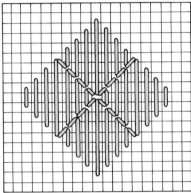
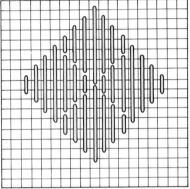
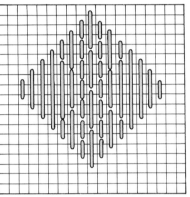

The "basket" is formed by 4 horizontal stitches over 8, 6, 4, and 2 threads of canvas. There are six "eggs" in each basket, each over 2 threads of canvas.

This stitch looks good in two contrasting colors. It is best worked unit by unit, with two needles, horizontally across the canvas. The second and subsequent rows fit into the spaces formed by the previous row.

This stitch can be rescaled to form a smaller basket (using 6, 4, and 2 threads) with three eggs in it as shown.

This stitch consists of large diamond shapes formed by working vertical stitches over 2, 4, 6, 8, 6, 4, and 2 threads of canvas. Work the diamonds in horizontal rows, leaving 2 threads of canvas between each group. On second and subsequent rows, the diamonds fit in the gap left by the first row – the stitch over 2 threads sharing a hole with the stitch over 6 threads of the previous row and so on.

When the whole area has been worked, backstitches (see page 158) can be worked along the edges of the diamond shapes, which works best if fewer ply or a thinner thread is used.

This stitch is worked in the same way as 2-4-6-8 stitch, but the left-hand stitches over 2, 4, 6, and 8 threads are worked in one color, while the rest of the stitch is worked in a contrasting color.

With two needles, work vertical rows of 2-4-6-8 stitch and Hungarian stitch (see page 158) alternately.

Milanese	**Border satin stitch cross**	**Rhodes stitch**	**Rhodes stitch variation**
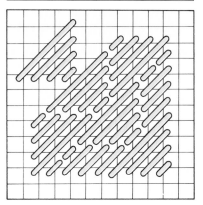			
	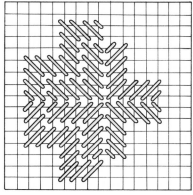	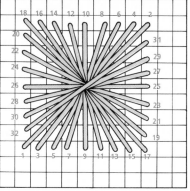	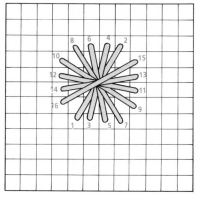

Milanese

This is a diagonal stitch usually worked in two colors, with the arrowheads facing in opposite directions.

Work the first row diagonally from a corner over 1, 2, 3, and 4 threads; repeat this over the length of the diagonal. Start the second row with a stitch over 1 thread joining the stitch over 4 threads previously worked, and fit stitches into the first row, to work the arrowheads in the opposite direction as shown.

Work compensation stitches along the sides of areas worked in this stitch to give a straight edge.

This stitch can easily be rescaled by working more or fewer diagonal stitches in each block, say, over 1, 2, 3, 4, and 5 threads before the repeat.

Border satin stitch cross

Work the inner part of the cross first as shown in the chart, working each stitch over 2 thread intersections, except at the tips of the cross where a stitch over 1 thread is needed to give a straight edge.

Then work the stitches around the cross in contrasting thread as shown, again working small compensation stitches where shown.

This can be used as a single motif, but could be worked to interlock as an all-over design.

Rhodes stitch

This is a dramatic stitch that can easily be worked over 4, 6, 8, and 10 or 12 threads, depending on the scale of stitch required. The diagrams show the stitch worked over 8 threads. Follow the numbers, bringing the needle up at the odd numbers and down at the even ones so you are going around clockwise, which means that there is a long stitch behind the work.

It is important to start each Rhodes stitch with a stitch at the same angle and to travel around the square in the same direction, as then the last stitches will all lie at the same angle.

Each stitch can be worked in a single color or the color and/or thread can be changed halfway around – when the stitches start to descend the other side.

Rhodes stitch variation

This is worked like Rhodes stitch, but the corners are left unworked. Like Rhodes stitch, work clockwise, always in the same order so that the top stitch is always on the same diagonal (follow the order of stitching given in the diagram).

Boxes

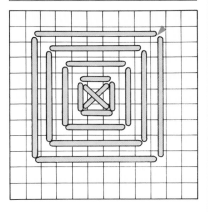

Reversed eyelet

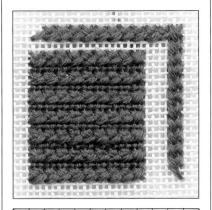

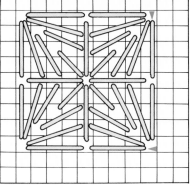

Long-legged cross stitch

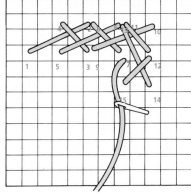

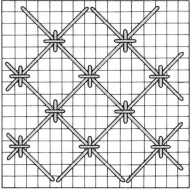

Jacobean couching

Form boxes by working stitches over 8, 6, 4, and 2 threads worked at right angles to each other, then reversing them to "close" the box. When working two subsequent boxes, the stitch indicated in the chart with an arrow is shared; that is, it is not worked twice.

Finish each box by working cross stitches (see page 146) in the center of each box, each one in the same order, so the top stitches all lie on the same diagonal.

Instead of squares being formed by all the stitches going down into the center, squares are formed by stitches radiating out from each corner. A star is then worked in the center of the square, also unlike eyelet stitch (see page 157). Complete each corner in turn, working 4 stitches down into the corner and 2 stitches into the hole, 1 thread intersection short of the corner. Next, form stars by working 8 stitches down into the center hole in each square in a contrasting color and/or thread. Work the vertical and horizontal stitches over 4 threads and the diagonal ones over 2 thread intersections.

After the first square has been worked, the lines of stitches with an arrow by them in the chart do not need to be repeated, but are shared.

When working in horizontal rows, always start and finish the row with a basic cross stitch. The long-legged part of the stitch is over 4 threads instead of 2. Work a shorter stitch over 2 threads back over this long stitch before working another long stitch; continue in this way until the end of the row, and finish it, as described, with a diagonal stitch to the right over 2 threads. Follow the numbers on the diagram to turn a corner. On the back of the work, you will see a series of short, upright stitches. Underneath the row of long-legged cross stitch, work a row of continental tent stitch (see page 144) from right to left to make the return journey.

A comparatively easy and very decorative form of couching when worked in a square area.

Lay the threads to be couched diagonally across the canvas at intervals, laying all the threads for one diagonal first, then laying the threads for the other diagonal, weaving under and over the threads you laid first to help them stay in place. Then couch down the threads with a small upright cross stitch (see page 169) over each intersection as shown in the chart. If a curved area needs to be worked, draw a square, and count the diagonals off the straight edges.

If you need to continue Jacobean couching around an object, count across it carefully to be sure that you keep the diagonal lines in line with each other.

Alisia's lace stitch

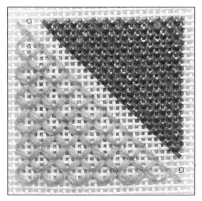

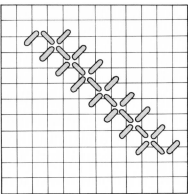

Split stitch

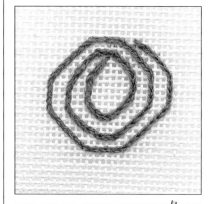

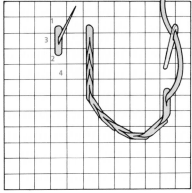

Long and short stitch

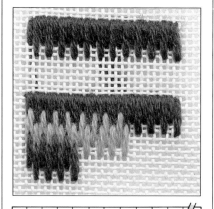

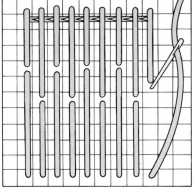

Start this stitch in the lower right-hand corner of the area to be filled, and work a row of basketweave tent stitch (see page 144) diagonally up to the top of the area. Then work backstitch (see page 158) from top left to bottom right below the row of basketweave tent stitch. Repeat this, working basketweave tent stitch up and backstitch down, until the area is filled.

This stitch can also be worked over 2 thread intersections for a very lacy appearance. The backstitches again share holes with the basketweave tent stitches.

This is a stitch that can be used to form curves on canvas.

Bring the needle up at 1, go down at 2, usually 2 canvas threads away. Bring the needle up at 3, the mid-point between 1 and 2, piercing the thread in the middle. Take the needle down at 4 (2 threads from 3, but only 1 from 2) and come up at 2, splitting the second stitch. Continue in this way.

To form a smooth line, it is important always to come up in a hole that has previously been used for going down. On straight lines, the size of the stitch may be increased, but on tight curves, the stitch must be kept short.

This stitch is frequently used for shading. It can be worked straight or curved, to shade areas such as petals (see chapter 6).

Practice the straight version before attempting it in any of the projects in this book.

Work a row of split stitch along the outline of the area; this will be covered by the long and short stitches, but will give a padded edge and a smooth curve on curved edges.

Work the first row of long and short stitches from left to right, with first a long and then a short stitch, over say 6 and 4 threads. Work the second row over 6 threads in another shade, usually slightly lighter or slightly darker than the first. Keeping the second row of stitches the same length will maintain the stepped appearance of the first row. Subsequent rows are worked in the same way as the second row. The best effect is obtained if the rows are shaded from dark to light or vice versa.

When working in a curved area, the principal difference is to work the first stitch on the center of the curve to be worked and work down one side and then down the other, angling the stitches to fit the shape.

Knitting stitch

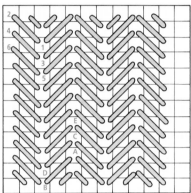

This is a diagonal stitch worked over 2 threads of canvas in vertical rows on alternate diagonals, giving the effect of a piece of knitting (see the numbers in the chart for the order of working the first row and the letters for the order of working the second row).

If a straight edge is needed at either end, work a compensation stitch at the top and bottom of each row as shown in the chart.

Alternate pairs of rows can be worked in contrasting colors and further texture can be added by working a line of backstitch over 2 threads along the center of each pair of rows.

Bargello stitch variations

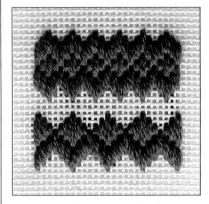

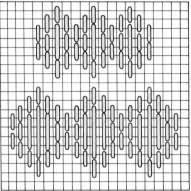

These two Bargello patterns are basically the same shape, but the upper one has small diamonds formed by stitches over 2, 4, and 2 threads, while the lower one has larger diamonds formed by stitches over 2, 4, 6, 4, and 2 threads. The linking stitches in both cases, though, are worked over 2 threads.

Each pattern could be used separately for individual projects, but used together they create an interesting background (suit the scale of the stitches to the other designs around them).

Stepped couching

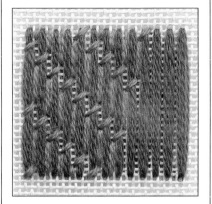

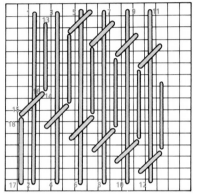

Lay the threads to be couched vertically on the canvas between 2 canvas threads, making a long stitch behind the work to keep the tension, laying a second thread two canvas threads away.

Then work the couching stitches across the threads laid down and along between them, following the numbers for the order in which the stitches are to be worked, using a fine thread.

If a curved area is to be worked, set up the threads to be couched from edge to edge of the design, then work the couching stitches, counting carefully as you go.

Braid stitch

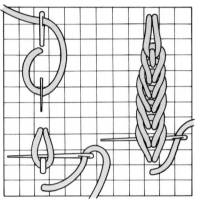

This stitch forms a heavy outline, best for leaves and foliage.

Start by working a single chain stitch, as shown, coming up and going down at 1, forming a loop and coming up at 2 inside the loop and going down again just outside the loop to hold it in place. Now come up 1 thread away from, and in line with, this last little stitch and, not piercing the canvas, slide the needle under the loop of the first chain stitch. Take it down through the same hole you came up through. Come up 1 thread below this last stitch, slide the needle under the loops of the first and second stitch at the 1 thread gap, and return through the canvas where you came up. Continue in this way, each time passing the needle from right to left under the last 2 stitches, and the finished stitching looks like a neat braid.

Raised needleweaving over bars

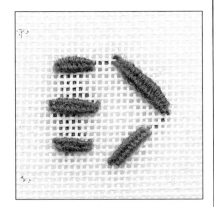

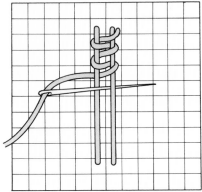

Make 2 long stitches – the bars – side by side in adjacent canvas holes, as shown.

Come up at the starting point once more, then, on the surface of the work, start to weave, first under the right-hand thread and over the left-hand thread, then under the left-hand thread and over the right-hand thread, and so on. Pack the weaving quite tightly, pushing the thread back with the needle as you go. When the bottom of the bars is reached, take the thread down through the canvas.

Raised bars

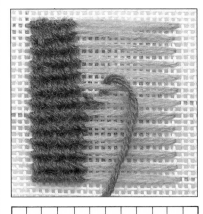

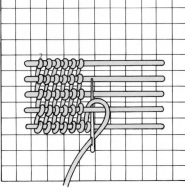

Lay bars across the area to be worked, making a long stitch behind the work to keep the bars at the correct tension (see diagram). (It is not necessary to strip threads for these bars.)

Bring the needle up at 1 (just above the bottom bar), then, without going down through the canvas, weave over the bottom bar, under 2 bars, back over the second one up, under that one and the next, back over the third bar up, back under that one and the top one; back over the top one, then take the needle down through the canvas at 2. Repeat this along the length of the bars, starting the next under and back-over movement just right of 1, packing the rows together tightly for the best effect.

In a shaped area, radiate the bars and make them of different lengths to fit the shapes. They may need to be stitched down in places to produce a curved outline. When working shaped areas, pack the stitches even tighter.

Braided edge stitch

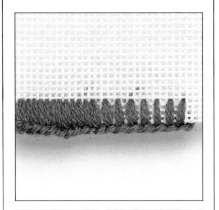

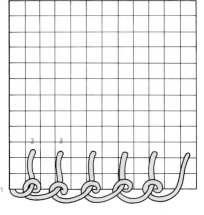

This is a good edging stitch that should be used over two layers of canvas around the edge of a completed design.

When the central design has been completed, remove the canvas from the frame, block it and trim the excess canvas, leaving at least twice the number of threads you plan to work the plaited edge stitch over. Fold the spare canvas to the back, leaving the number of threads you wish to work over visible, and run your thumbnail along the fold to get a crisp edge and keep it in place while you work.

Come out at 1 (see the diagram) through the fold, go down at 2, 1 thread across and 3 threads up from 1 through both layers of canvas, and pull the thread almost through. When the thread is almost snug onto the fold of the canvas, take the needle and thread over and down through the loop, then go down at 3, through both canvas layers as before. Continue the row in this way, and the loops will form a braid lying along the fold.

Work this stitch into every hole for a tight, firm edge, or into alternate holes as shown here for a slightly looser effect. If you need to go around corners, work a number of stitches through the same hole at the corner.

Cushion stitch variation II

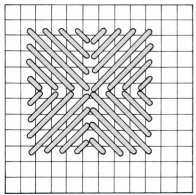

Parisian stitch

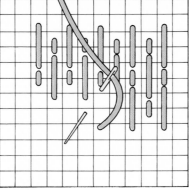

Victorian patterned darning variation III

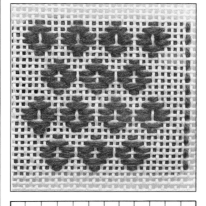

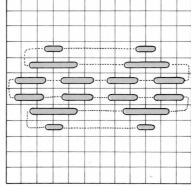

In the Christmas tree for the Christmas Card project in Chapter 7, four cushion stitch boxes have been worked in two colors to form stripes which represent presents very well. The stitches are worked in the same manner as cushion stitch (see page 148), but here different colors are used for each alternate stitch, using two needles, completing each cushion stitch in turn. Note, too, that the diagonal is alternated for each cushion stitch.

This horizontal stitch is worked in rows that fit together. The stitches are worked over 3, 1, 3, 1 threads.

As with all versions of patterned darning, it is important to work each line of stitching straight across each row and anchor it in the border at each end. As the thread lying beneath the unworked areas of canvas shows and contributes to the pattern, it has to be as neat as the stitches on top of the canvas (see the dotted lines in the chart).

The first row of the pattern is worked by passing the needle from left to right under 5 threads, over 1 thread, under 5 threads, and so on, to the end of the row. For the second row, anchor the thread in the bordering stitches and pass from right to left 1 thread up behind 4 threads, over 3 threads, under 3 threads, and so on, to the end of the row. For the third row, anchor the thread as before and run it from left to right 1 thread up behind 3 threads, over 2, behind 1, over 2, behind 1, and so on, until the end of the row. For the fourth row, repeat this last row; for the fifth row, repeat the second row; and for the sixth row, repeat the first row.

These 6 rows form small circles on the surface of the work. For the next row of circles, stagger them with the first row by running the thread up one thread behind 2 threads, over 1 thread, behind 5 threads, and so on, to the end. Work rows 2 to 6 as set, just altering the number of threads you pass under at each end.

Ribbed spider stitch	**Moorish stitch**	**Moorish stitch variation**	**Checkered stitch**
	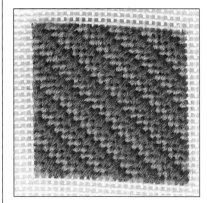		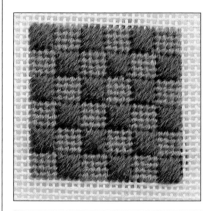
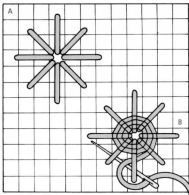	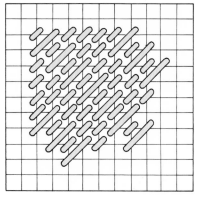	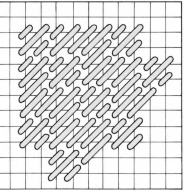	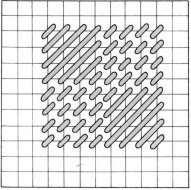

Ribbed spider stitch

Set up spokes of the desired length. Then bring the needle and thread up as close to the center as possible between two of the spokes and, without piercing the canvas, slide the needle under the first bar, back over it, then forward under 2 bars. Bring the needle back over the second spoke, forward under 2, back over the third and so on, spiraling out to the ends of the spokes (see diagram B). Pack the thread tightly into the center as you go. Turning the work as you stitch makes it easier to maintain an even tension around the center.

The threads do not need to be stripped for this stitch. The color or texture of the thread can be changed once or more after a number of circuits. Very large ribbed spider stitch base bars can be worked on top of other stitches, and only the center woven for a different effect.

Moorish stitch

Work stitches diagonally over 1 and 2 thread intersections alternately. Then work 2 rows of basketweave tent stitch (see page 144), using a second needle on each side of this first row. Continue by working the first row (of stitches over 1 and 2 thread intersections) on each side of the tent stitch rows. Continue in this way across the area.

This stitch can also be worked with the first and subsequent fourth rows being worked over 1, 2, 3, 2, and 1 thread intersections, still with every second to fifth rows worked in basketweave tent stitch for a slightly different effect.

Moorish stitch variation

In this variation, small Moorish stitch boxes are worked in the positions shown in the chart, and sloping Gobelin stitch (see page 145) is worked between them. Work the Moorish stitches over 1, 2, and 1 thread intersections first, then work sloping Gobelin stitch over 2 thread intersections, using a second needle on each side of the row of Moorish boxes, before working the second row of Moorish stitch.

Checkered stitch

Work each box by working straight diagonal stitches over 1, 2, 3, 4, 3, 2, and 1 thread intersections, and work these boxes in diagonal rows across the area to be filled from top left to bottom right, staggering the boxes to create the checkered effect. Then, work basketweave tent stitch (see page 144) in each of the squares of unworked canvas, working 16 stitches in each square.

Spaced Cretan stitch

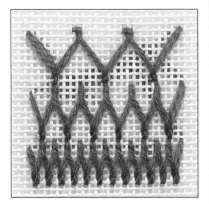

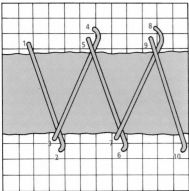

This is worked from left to right over 4 vertical and 8 horizontal threads of canvas. Come up at 1, go down at 2, and come up at 3, one thread inside 2, making sure that the yearn is under the point of the needle before pulling it through. Then go down at 4 and up at 5.

The stitch is usually worked over empty canvas, and it can be worked in exactly the same way to couch down ribbon.

The stitch can be altered by working it over different numbers of vertical and horizontal threads, working it closer together to use as a filling stitch and further apart for dainty couching of ribbon or thread.

Trellis stitch

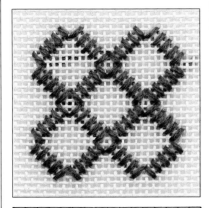

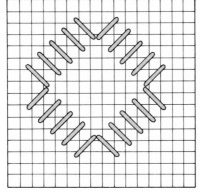

This stitch can be pulled or unpulled, depending on the requirements of the design being worked.

Start at the dot in the chart, and work 5 diagonal stitches over 2 thread intersections from bottom left to top right. Then, sharing the same starting hole of the fifth stitch, work 5 diagonal stitches from top left to bottom right. Repeat these 10 stitches, forming a zigzagging line across the canvas. Work the second row from right to left, but working the stitches in the directions shown by the arrows in the chart.

When the first full trellis is complete, that is, the stitches have been worked once from left to right and once from right to left, finish the thread or run the thread through the backs of the last 5 stitches and then diagonally out to the start of the next row (as indicated by the dotted line in the chart).

Diamond eyelet

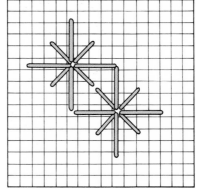

This stitch can either be worked pulled or not as necessary. It is generally worked with either 16 stitches or 8 stitches all going down into the central hole.

If a solid area is to be worked in diamond eyelet stitch, work the stitches counterclockwise in diagonal rows from upper left to lower right, then turn the canvas so the top is at the bottom and work back up again along the diagonal.

If a single horizontal row is required, start each diamond eyelet stitch at the top, and work counterclockwise, leaving 8 threads between the starting points of the stitches.

It is sometimes necessary to work diamond eyelet in a clockwise direction to maintain the central hole.

Trellis stitch and diamond eyelet stitch

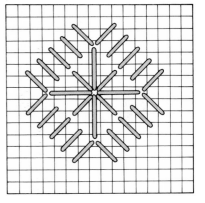

Work trellis stitch, not pulling it, as shown in the chart. Then work a diamond eyelet stitch with 8 stitches down into the central hole. Work these stitches clockwise, pulling them, in the order shown in the chart. Use the backs of the trellis stitches to get from eyelet to eyelet.

Satin-stitch boxes	**Four-sided stitch**	**Satin stitch boxes with four-sided stitch and cross stitch**	**Pulled ringed backstitch**

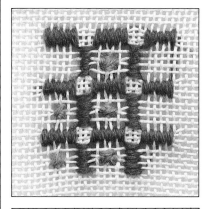
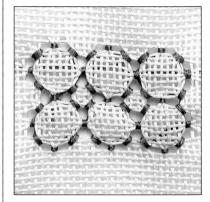

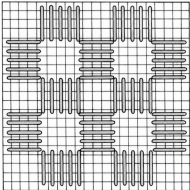
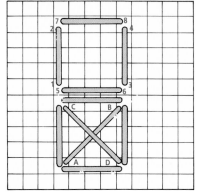
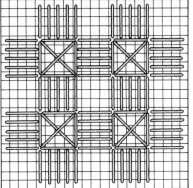
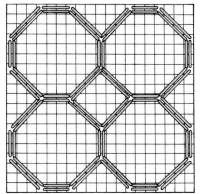

Satin-stitch boxes

These can be pulled or not as needed.

To achieve maximum pull, work the groups of 5 stitches over 4 threads of each box in horizontal rows back and forth across the canvas, leaving 4 threads between rows, *then* work the vertical rows up and down the canvas (as shown by the numbers and arrows in the chart).

The boxes can easily be worked larger or smaller if required and/or a decorative stitch worked in each center area.

Four-sided stitch

This is a pulled stitch.

Work a square, stitching in the order shown, following the numbers for maximum pull.

This stitch can easily be worked larger or smaller if desired. Also a pulled cross stitch can be worked in the center.

Satin stitch boxes with four-sided stitch and cross stitch

Work the satin stitch boxes first, in horizontal then vertical rows, pulling them and taking care not to trail any threads behind the pulled areas. Then work four-sided stitch around the satin stitch boxes, and a cross stitch over the center of each of the boxes, pulling all the stitches extra hard.

Pulled ringed backstitch

Starting at 1 on the right of the chart, work horizontally across the area toward the left, working each backstitch over 3 threads twice, except where only 1 stitch is shown (such as stitch 13/14), pulling each stitch. When a row is complete, return toward the right, completing each ring and adding the second vertical and horizontal stitches where there was only 1 on the first row.

Note that the horizontal stitches at the top and bottom of the area (stitches 5 and 6 in the chart), and the vertical stitches at the sides of the area (stitches 1 and 2 in the chart), will have to be worked twice as you go, since there are no more rows that would otherwise add the second stitches at these points.

| **Upright cross stitch** | **Pulled ringed backstitch with Rhodes stitch variation and upright cross stitch** | **Flower trellis stitch** | **Pulled Smyrna stitch** |

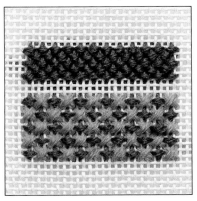 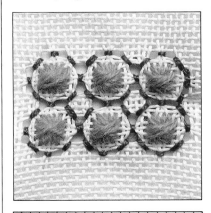 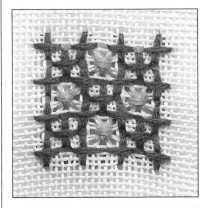 

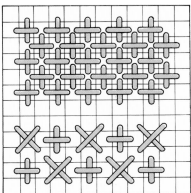  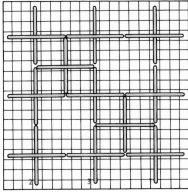 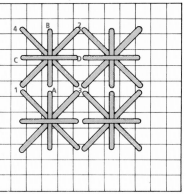

This is a small stitch. Work a vertical stitch over 2 threads and a horizontal stitch crossing it also over 2 threads. Work subsequent rows so they fit in between those of the first as shown.

Upright cross stitches can be worked alternately with basic cross stitches as shown, to become St. George and St. Andrew stitch.

Work the pulled ringed backstitches (see page 168) first, starting with the top horizontal stitch for it to balance in the area shown in the chart.

Next, work the Rhodes stitch variation (see page 160), not pulled, inside each octagon (note the compensation stitches on the right-hand side of the Rhodes variation stitch; the stitches at the left-hand edge will have to be worked in a similar way).

Work an upright cross, not pulled, in the small diamond-shaped areas between the rows of pulled ringed backstitch.

Start at 1 on the chart close to the lower right-hand corner, and stitch diagonally up the area, working vertical stitches over 6 canvas threads; then work back down, crossing these stitches with horizontal stitches over 6 threads as shown. Start the second row in the hole immediately left of the twelfth thread away from the first row at 2. Work only full stitches – do not work any compensation stitches.

When these diagonals have been worked, work these stitches from lower right to upper left, starting at 3; the second cross is worked over a cross of the previous row. On both diagonals, a horizontal stitch is always worked last.

Work a basic cross stitch over 4 threads, then work a vertical, and last a horizontal stitch, pulling each stitch firmly as it is worked.

Work the stages of the stitches in the same order, with the horizontal stitch always last.

Flower trellis stitch with pulled Smyrna stitch	**Star rosette stitch**	**Pulled cushion stitch**
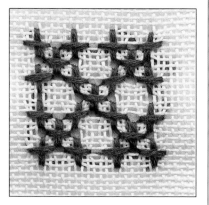		
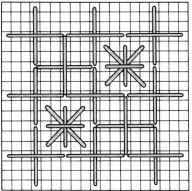	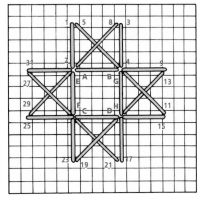	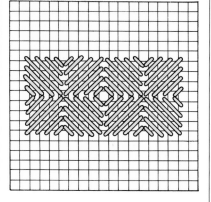

Work the trellis stitches (see page 167), but when this is complete, work a Smyrna stitch (see page 147) over four threads in the center of each large box created by the trellis. Remember that the horizontal stitch is always worked last.

Follow the numbers in the chart carefully for the order of stitches that outline the star, pulling the thread tightly as you go. The order given prevents any threads from showing through the pulled areas (it is particularly important to do the second half of each cross as indicated for this reason).

Work diagonally down across the area, so the starting point for the second rosette shares the hole at steps 11 and 16, and step 27 of the second shares the hole at steps 17 and 21 of the first.

The lettered stitches are worked afterward and can be stitched in a contrasting color if wished.

For the pulled thread version of cushion stitch, it is important to work the "cushions" in two rows, working two cushions in one row, and two cushions in the lower row, working from left to right, filling in the spaces on the return journey from right to left. This is the method that should be followed even if only one color is being used.

INDEX

APPLETON CREWEL – PATERNA YARN SUGGESTED COLOR CONVERSIONS

Note: the lightest color in the Appleton shades is the lowest number, whereas in the case of Paterna, it is the highest number. In many cases, there are no direct alternatives, and one shade of Paterna may be the alternative to two shades of Appleton (i.e., Appleton's Terra Cotta 127 & 128 to Paterna's Wood Rose 920); also color ranges in Appleton may span different ranges in Paterna and vice-versa (for example, Appleton's medium blue range, 151-159, matches shades in Paterna steel gray, old blue, and blue spruce, and Paterna's pine green range, 660-666, are matched in Appleton's Jacobean green, sea green, peacock blue, and bright peacock blue ranges).

APPLETON Shade name	Number	APPLETON Shade name	Number
Purple	101-104	Grape	313-312
Terra Cotta	121-122	Toast brown	474-473
Terra Cotta	123-126	Terra cotta	483-481
Terra Cotta	127-128	Wood rose	920
Dull rose pink	141-143	Wood rose	924-922
Dull rose pink	144-146	Dusty pink	912-910
Dull rose pink	147-149	American beauty	900
Medium blue	151	Steel gray	203
Medium blue	152	Old blue	514
Medium blue	153	—	D389
Medium blue	154-159	Blue spruce	534-530
Chocolate	181 & 186	Toast brown	475 & 471
Chocolate	182	Beige brown	463
Chocolate	183	Khaki brown	453
Chocolate	184-185 & 187	Chocolate brown	432-430
Flame red	201	Beige brown	463
Flame red	202	Fawn brown	406
Flame red	203-204	Terra cotta	486-485
Flame red	205-208	Rust	872-870
Flame red	209	—	D211
Bright Terra Cotta	221	Flesh	490
Bright Terra Cotta	222 & 225	Rusty rose	933 & 931
Bright Terra Cotta	223	—	D275
Bright Terra Cotta	224	—	D234
Bright Terra Cotta	226	—	D211
Bright Terra Cotta	227	American beauty	900
Olive green	241	—	D531
Olive green	242 & 245	Olive green	652 & 650
Olive green	243-244	Khaki green	642-641
Grass green	251 & 255-6	Olive green	653 & 651-0
Grass green	252-254	Loden green	694-692
Jacobean green	291-296	Forest green	603-600
Jacobean green	297-298	Pine green	660

PATERNA Shade name	Number	PATERNA Shade name	Number
Red fawn	301	Chocolate brown	435
Red fawn	302	Earth brown	412
Red fawn	303-305	Fawn brown	402-400
Brown olive	311-312	—	D531
Brown olive	313-314	—	D521
Brown olive	315-316	—	D511
Dull marine blue	321-328	Old blue	513-510
Drab green	331-334	Khaki green	644-642
Drab green	335-336	—	D511
Drab green	337-338	Khaki brown	451-450
Medium olive green	341-348	Khaki green	644-640
Gray green	351-358	Forest green	605-600
Sea green	401-405	Hunter green	613-610
Sea green	406	Loden green	690
Sea green	407	Pine green	660
Leaf green	421	Hunter green	614
Leaf green	422-428	Shamrock	623-620
Leaf green	429	Peacock green	680
Signal green	431-438	Peacock green	687-680
Orange red	441-445	Tangerine	823-820
Orange red	446-448	Salmon	841
Bright mauve	451	Plum	323
Bright mauve	452-456	Violet	302-300
Cornflower	461	Glacier	564
Cornflower	462-465	Cobalt blue	544-540
Autumn yellow	471 & 474-479	Autumn yellow	727 & 725-720
Autumn yellow	472	Butterscotch	703
Autumn yellow	473	Honey gold	732
Kingfisher	481-482 & 486-489	Sky blue	584-583 & 582-580
Kingfisher	483-485	Caribbean blue	592-590
Scarlet	501-502	Salmon	842-841
Scarlet	503-504	Strawberry	951-950

PATERNA		PATERNA	
Shade name	Number	Shade name	Number
Scarlet	505	Cranberry	940
Scarlet	506	—	D211
Turquoise	521-523 & 529	Teal blue	525-523 & 520
Turquoise	524-527	—	D502-D501
Turquoise	eee528	Federal blue	501
Early English green	541	Khaki green	644
Early English green	542	Olive green	653
Early English green	543-547	Loden green	693-691
Early English green	548	Forest green	600
Bright yellow	551 & 553-555	Sunny yellow	773 & 772-770
Bright yellow	552	Mustard	713
Bright yellow	556-557	Sunrise	813-812
Sky blue	561 & 566-568	Federal blue	505 & 501-500
Sky blue	562-563	Ice blue	555
Sky blue	564-565	Sky blue	584-583
Brown groundings	581	Toast brown	470
Brown groundings	582-588	Coffee brown	422-420
Mauve	601-603 & 607	Plum	325-323 & 321
Mauve	604-606	Grape	312-310
Flamingo	621-626	Bittersweet	835-830
Peacock blue	641	Teal blue	523
Peacock blue	642	—	D546
Peacock blue	643	Forest green	602
Peacock blue	644	—	D522
Peacock blue	645-647	Pine green	662-660
Honeysuckle yellow	691	Golden brown	444
Honeysuckle yellow	692	Old gold	754
Honeysuckle yellow	693-695	Honey yellow	734-732
Honeysuckle yellow	696-697	Tobacco	740
Honeysuckle yellow	698	Earth brown	412
Flesh tints	701-716	Flesh	494-490
Wine red	711-716	Dusty pink	914-910
Bright China blue	741-746	Glacier	564-560
Bright China blue	747	Navy blue	571
Bright China blue	748-749	Navy blue	571-570
Rose pink	751-752	Cranberry	946-945
Rose pink	753	—	D281
Rose pink	754	Dusty pink	913
Rose pink	755-756	—	D275
Rose pink	757-759	American beauty	902-900
Biscuit brown	761-762	Golden brown	444-443
Biscuit brown	763	Chocolate brown	434
Biscuit brown	764-765	Earth brown	413-412
Biscuit brown	766	—	D419
Biscuit brown	767	Fawn brown	401
Fuchsia	801 & 803-805	Fuchsia	353 & 351-350
Fuchsia	802	Marigold	802
Royal blue	821-825	Cobalt blue	543-540

APPLETON		PATERNA	
Shade name	Number	Shade name	Number
Bright Peacock blue	831	—	D522
Bright Peacock blue	832-835	Pine green	662-660
Heraldic gold	841	Butterscotch	704
Heraldic gold	842-843	Honey gold	734-733
Heraldic gold	844	Mustard	714
Custard yellow	851	—	D541
Navy blue	852	Navy blue	571-570
Winchester blue	853	—	
Coral	861-862 & 866	Spice	855-854 & 850
Coral	863	Copper	862
Coral	864-865	Bittersweet	832-831
Pastel shades	871-872	Mustard	716-715
Pastel shades	873	Hunter green	615
Pastel shades	874	Shamrock	624
Pastel shades	875	Cool gray	236
Pastel shades	876	Pearl gray	213
Pastel shades	877	Cranberry	948
Pastel shades	881-882	White/cream	263-262
Pastel shades	883	—	D147
Pastel shades	884-885	Grape	314-313
Pastel shades	886	Glacier	564
Golden brown	901-903	Golden brown	443-443
Golden brown	904-905	Earth brown	412-411
Fawn	911 & 916	Khaki brown	453 & 450
Fawn	912	Coffee brown	424
Fawn	913-915	Chocolate brown	433-431
Dull China blue	921	—	D591
Dull China blue	922	Blue spruce	534
Dull China blue	923-929	Old blue	513-510
Dull mauve	931	—	D143
Dull mauve	932	—	D133
Dull mauve	933	—	D123
Dull mauve	934-935	—	D115
Bright rose pink	941-943	Rusty rose	934-932
Bright rose pink	944-948	American beauty	904-901
Drab fawn	951-956	Khaki brown	454-452
Drab fawn	957	Beige brown	460
Iron gray	961-967	Steel gray	204-200
Elephant gray	971-976	Beige brown	463-461
Putty groundings	981-982, 984 & 986	Khaki brown	455-453
Putty groundings	983, 985 & 988	Beige brown	465 & 463
Putty groundings	987	Warm gray	256
Putty groundings	989	Neutral gray	246
White/Off white	991-992	White/cream	263-260
Black	993	Black	220
Rust	994	Spice	852
Cherry red	995	Cranberry	940
Lemon & lime	996-997	Lime green	673-672
Charcoal	998	Charcoal	221

ORDERING KITS

The projects listed below can be ordered as kits. Full instructions are included

as well as canvas, yarns and needles. All canvas is supplied taped.

All yarn is Appleton's crewel except for the Flower and

Trellis Rug, which is stitched in Medici.

Dolls' House Rug *page 35*
Brick Door Stop *page 43*
MacIntyre Pillow (coordinating with doorstop) *page 47*
Kelim Rug *page 51*
Wedding Kneelers *page 52*
Outdoor Sampler *page 60*
Maltese Tile *page 68*
Bokhara *page 72*
Cluny *page 76*
Samarkand *page 77 (left)*
Honeycomb *page 77 (right)*

Mayan Pyramid *page 79*
Suzanne *page 80*
Hearts & Flowers *page 81*
Tulip Pillow *page 85*
Tulip Rug *page 89*
Christmas Card (panel only) *page 97*
Christmas Pincushion (ribbon included) *page 100*
Pill Box (silver-plated box included) *page 107*
Playing Card Box (polished wood box and contents included) *page 111*
Pulled Thread Pincushion (ribbon not included) *page 115*

Mirror (canvas, threads, and instructions only – no mirror or frame) *page 119*
Flower and Trellis Rug *page 129*
Hydrangea Rug *page 131*
Victorian Rose *page 134*

The following accessories can also be ordered:
All sizes of artists' stretcher bars
Palettes, both sizes
Floor frames
Magnification lamps
Laying tools, scissors, etc.

For prices and further information on the above write to
Pearson Design, 25 Kildare Terrace, London W2 5JT, England.

CREDITS

The author would like to thank the following people who helped stitch her designs for this book: Caroline Blois, Jennifer Butler, Kris-Ann Crane, Val Darby, Pat de Winton, Joan Downes, Jacynth Fitzalan Howard, Vivien Frank, Ethne Gittus, Connie Levy, Ruth Levy, Sara Low, Ann Moody, Karen O'Dwyer Russell, Patrick Pearson, Mila Pond, Liz Salmon, Virginia Sidi, Sara Stonor (who also advised on the finishing techniques), Cassandra Taylor, Sara Turnbull and Day Whitelegge.

The following museums and companies for allowing me to illustrate their designs or helped with making up the projects.

Atelier d'Anaïs, Vivien Frank Framing, Gilt Edge Framing Company, MacIntyre Homes, Royal School of Needlework, Victoria and Albert Museum.

And/ in particular members of my Needlepoint Network who teach my designs in various parts of the country, Sandrine Laffargue who helped tremendously in the studio, Caroline Beattie and Chloë Alexander of Quarto, and my husband, Patrick, who thought he had retired to work on his stamp collection . . . !